The Man in the Panther's Skin

A Romantic Epic

By

Shot'ha Rust'haveli

Translated by

Marjory Scott Wardrop

First published in 1912

Published by Left of Brain Books

Copyright © 2023 Left of Brain Books

ISBN 978-1-397-66884-4

First Edition

All rights reserved. No part of this publication may be reproduced, distributed, or transmitted in any form or by any means, including photocopying, recording, or other electronic or mechanical methods, without the prior written permission of the publisher, except in the case of brief quotations permitted by copyright law. Left of Brain Books is a division of Left Of Brain Onboarding Pty Ltd.

PUBLISHER'S PREFACE

About the Book

"Georgia is a central Asian region which is situated in the mountains between the Black and Caspian seas. This, the 'Man in the Panther Skin' (also known as 'the Knight in the Panther Skin') is a 12th century medieval epic poem. It is considered one of the masterpieces of Georgian literature, and has been called the Georgian national epic. The author, Prince Shota Rustaveli, was a noble in the court of Queen Tamar, and served as her treasurer. He was also a painter who created frescoes in the Georgian monastery of the Holy Cross in Jerusalem. We do not know specific birth and death dates for Rustaveli. The poem was first printed in 1712 in Tblisi. This translation is, thankfully, into clearly written prose, unlike some of the awful 19th century attempts to versify translated poetry. Wardrop's translation, which she modestly called an attempt, makes enjoyable reading.

The poem, strangely enough, is not set in Georgia, but in fictionalized versions of Arabia, Persia, India and fairy-tale lands set in the environs of the Indian Ocean. (However the characters are at one point described as speaking fluent Georgian!) There are two chief male protagonists, Avt'handil and Tariel. Tariel, the eponymous 'Knight in the Panther's Skin' is made heir to all India, but tragically falls in love with his adoptive sister, Nestan. Driven mad by this love, he ends up killing the man she is to marry and fleeing India. Nestan is also spirited away to parts unknown. The search for Nestan, described as radiant as the sun, so beautiful that everyone she meets falls in love with her, is the central thread of the story. Avt'handil, the suitor of the Queen of Arabia T'hinat'hin, sees Tariel wandering disconsolate one day and goes in quest of this mysterious knight. Eventually they meet up and after a long quest end up finding Nestan. Nestan and Tariel marry, and Avt'handil marries T'hinat'hin. I have appended a short synopsis of the story to this etext, based on my reading notes.

The narrative and characterizations are remarkable for a work of this period. Rustaveli had great psychological insight, providing backstory and motivations for his cast. The women characters are well written and memorable (particularly the merchant P'hatman). Rustaveli's female characters are not just props as in some of the medieval romances. Emotional relationships between characters of the same sex (both male and female), like the Biblical David and Jonathan, are portrayed as tender and sensual, shedding light on how our conventional sex roles are modern cultural constructs.

For technical reasons, I had to omit most of the footnotes from the body of the text. However, I did type in some of these footnotes by hand where they clear up obscure passages. Since a facsimile of this particular translation is in print and the footnotes are mostly of interest to scholars, this should not present a problem."

(Quote from sacred-texts.com)

CONTENTS

PUBLISHER'S PREFACE
PREFACE 1
   INTRODUCTORY QUATRAINS 14
   STORY OF ROSTEVAN, KING OF THE ARABIANS 20
   HOW THE KING OF THE ARABIANS SAW THE KNIGHT CLAD IN THE PANTHER'S SKIN 29
   AVT'HANDIL'S LETTER TO HIS VASSALS 42
   AVT'HANDIL SETS FORTH IN QUEST OF TARIEL 44
   THE TELLING OF HIS TALE BY TARIEL WHEN HE FIRST TOLD IT TO AVT'HANDIL 66
   TARIEL TELLS THE TALE OF HIS FALLING IN LOVE WHEN HE FIRST FELL IN LOVE 71
   FIRST LETTER WRITTEN BY NESTAN-DAREDJAN TO HER LOVER 77
   FIRST LETTER WRITTEN BY TARIEL TO HIS BELOVED 78
   TARIEL WRITES A LETTER AND SENDS A MAN TO THE KHATAVIANS 80
   THE LETTER WRITTEN BY THE KING OF THE KHATAVIANS IN ANSWER TO TARIEL 83
   LETTER OF TARIEL TO THE KING OF THE INDIANS WHEN HE TRIUMPHED OVER THE KHATAVIANS 93
   LETTER OF NESTAN-DAREDJAN WRITTEN TO HER BELOVED 98
   TARIEL'S LETTER IN ANSWER TO HIS BELOVED 100
   TARIEL HEARS TIDINGS OF THE LOSS OF NESTAN-DAREDJAN . 111
   THE STORY OF NURADIN P'HRIDON WHEN TARIEL MET HIM ON THE SEASHORE 116
   TARIEL'S AID TO P'HRIDON, AND THEIR VICTORY OVER THEIR FOES 120
   P'HRIDON TELLS TARIEL TIDINGS OF NESTAN-DAREDJAN 122
   THE STORY OF AVT'HANDIL'S RETURN TO ARABIA AFTER HE HAD FOUND AND PARTED FROM TARIEL 130
   AVT'HANDIL'S REQUEST TO KING ROSTEVAN, AND THE VIZIER'S DISCOURSE AND ENTREATY 140

AVT'HANDIL'S DISCOURSE WITH SHERMADIN WHEN HE STOLE AWAY 148
THE TESTAMENT OF AVT'HANDIL TO KING ROSTEVAN WHEN HE STOLE AWAY 151
AVT'HANDIL'S PRAYER IN THE MOSQUE, AND HIS FLIGHT 155
KING ROSTEVAN HEARS OF AVT'HANDIL'S SECRET FLIGHT...... 156
AVT'HANDIL'S SECOND DEPARTURE AND MEETING WITH TARIEL 159
HERE IS THE GOING OF TARIEL AND AVT'HANDIL TO THE CAVE, AND THEIR SEEING OF ASMAT'H 174
OF THE GOING OF AVT'HANDIL TO P'HRIDON'S WHEN HE MET HIM AT MULGHAZANZAR 181
OF AVT'HANDIL'S GOING TO P'HRIDON'S WHEN HE PARTED FROM TARIEL 185
AVT'HANDIL'S DEPARTURE FROM P'HRIDON TO SEEK NESTAN-DAREDJAN 195
THE STORY OF AVT'HANDIL'S ARRIVAL IN GULANSHARO 201
AVT'HANDIL'S ARRIVAL AT P'HATMAN'S; HER RECEPTION OF HIM AND HER JOY 204
P'HATMAN BECOMES ENAMOURED OF AVT'HANDIL; WRITES HIM A LETTER AND SENDS IT 205
THE LETTER OF LOVE WRITTEN BY P'HATMAN TO AVT'HANDIL 206
AVT'HANDIL'S LETTER IN ANSWER TO P'HATMAN'S 208
HERE IS THE SLAYING OF THE CHACHNAGIR AND HIS TWO GUARDS BY AVT'HANDIL 212
P'HATMAN TELLS AVT'HANDIL THE STORY OF NESTAN-DAREDJAN 214
THE STORY OF THE CAPTURE OF NESTAN-DAREDJAN BY THE KADJIS, TOLD BY P'HATMAN TO AVT'HANDIL 230
LETTER WRITTEN BY P'HATMAN TO NESTAN-DAREDJAN 240
THE LETTER WRITTEN BY NESTAN-DAREDJAN TO P'HATMAN . 243
THE LETTER WRITTEN BY NESTAN-DAREDJAN TO HER BELOVED 245
AVT'HANDIL'S LETTER TO P'HRIDON 250
AVT'HANDIL'S DEPARTURE FROM GULANSHARO, AND HIS MEETING WITH TARIEL 252
TARIEL AND AVT'HANDIL GO TO P'HRIDON 260
THE COUNCIL OF P'HRIDON, AVT'HANDIL AND TARIEL AS TO THE ASSAULT ON THE CASTLE OF KADJET'HI 264

THE GOING OF TARIEL TO THE KING OF THE SEAS AND TO
P'HRIDON'S 271
THE WEDDING OF TARIEL AND NESTAN BY P'HRIDON 278
TARIEL GOES AGAIN TO THE CAVE AND SEES THE TREASURE . 283
HERE IS THE MARRIAGE OF AVT'HANDIL AND T'HINAT'HIN BY
THE KING OF THE ARABS 293

APPENDICES 302

AN ENGLISH RENDERING OF THE RUSSIAN TRANSLATION BY
PROFESSOR MARR OF THE INTRODUCTORY QUATRAINS OF "THE
MAN IN THE PANTHER'S SKIN" ("TEKSTY," T. XII., PP. 7-9) 303
BIBLIOGRAPHICAL NOTE 309
GROUPS OF REFERENCES 317
ENDNOTES 338

PREFACE

THIS is an attempt to give a faithful rendering, word by word, of a book which is the mirror of the soul of a cultured people with a great past; the mirror is chipped and tarnished by time and mischance, but the loving labour of scholars may soon renew its lustre and repair some of its injuries. Even in the state in which it is here presented the work can hardly fail to provoke interest. The history of the poem makes it worthy of perusal, for it has been in a unique manner the book of a nation for seven hundred years; down to our own days the young people learned it by heart; every woman was expected to know every word of it, and on her marriage to carry a copy of it to her new home. Such veneration shown for so long a period proves that the story of the Panther-clad Knight presents an image of the Georgian outlook on life, and justifies the presumption that merits tested by the experience of a quarter of a million days, most of them troublous, may be apparent to other races, that such a book may be of value to mankind, and chiefly to those peoples which, like the Georgian, came under the influence of Greek and Christian ideals. Here we are dealing with no alien psychology, but with a soul which, though readily responsive to the great cultural movements of nearer Asia, [1] showed in a thousand years of struggle that its natural gravitation was towards Western Europe, whither with pathetic constancy it kept its gaze fixed. [2] Iberia of the East and Iberia of the West, the high-water marks of Arab conquest, were both fertilized by the Semitic flood, and, whether or not they have some ancient ethnic affinity, this has given them not a few common characteristics; Spain had Christendom at her back, Georgia carried on her glorious crusade in isolation till the struggle was hopeless, and a century ago she was forced into an alliance with the Russian Empire. From her situation, geographical and political, Georgia was the country most likely to show that approximation of Eastern and Western thought typical of the epoch of the Crusades, and in these latter days it is largely due to the infusion of Iberian blood that Turkey and Persia have still sufficient vitality to attempt reforms.

It might have been expected that a people whose life was a ceaseless fight to keep for Christendom the bridge between Asia and Europe would have put into its greatest artistic effort an uncompromising confession of faith; but freedom of thought rather than fanaticism is characteristic of Shot'ha, so at various times, down to the eighteenth century, the orthodox clergy destroyed manuscripts of the poem, and the editio princeps of 1712 could only appear because its royal editor appended to it a pious mystical commentary. We find one reference apiece to Mohammed (1010) and Mecca (1144), and three mentions of the Koran (339, 514, 1144); the official representatives of Islam are spoken of with scant sympathy (339). To Christianity as an ecclesiastical system we have, possibly, allusions (Easter Eve, 536; icon, 247; shrine, 1345; halo, aureole, 226, 229, 1110, 1410); there may be a few quotations from the Scriptures ("gall of bitterness," 99; "hart and waterbrooks," 835, 1564; "tinkling cymbals," 772;" charity faileth not," 1520; "through a glass darkly," 110, 656, 707, 1431; "hidden treasure," ?882; "be content," "judge not," 18; "rivers run into the sea," 49); the Biblical personages incidentally mentioned are--Adam, Beelzebub, ?Ezra, Goliath, Levi, and Satan, and the geographical, names Eden, Euphrates, Gihon, Pison, and Gibeon, are used in similes; there seems to be a reference to the doctrine of regeneration (184), and another perhaps to purgatory (785). When he wrote his poem, Rust'haveli had evidently no violent prejudice for one religion more than another, but was of a critical and eclectic turn of mind, and formed for himself a working philosophy of life, showing Persian and Arabian tendencies, but with so much of Christianity and Neo-Platonism as to bring it near to Occidental minds. "The Georgians in the tenth and eleventh centuries interested themselves in the domain of philosophy in those same questions which occupied the leading minds of the Christian world of that period both in the East and the West, with this distinction from the others--e.g., Europeans--that in those days the Georgians responded earlier than others to the newest tendencies of philosophic thought, and worked in a panoply, exemplary for its time, of textual criticism directly on the Greek originals." [3]

There is throughout the poem manifest joy in life and action: God createth not evil (1468, 1485); ill is fleeting (1337); since there is gladness in the world, why should any be sad? (687); it is after all a good world, fair to look upon despite its horrid deserts, a world to sing in either because one is happy or because one wishes to be so (946); there are flowers to gaze on, good wine to drink, fair apparel and rich jewels to wear, beasts worth hunting, games worth playing, foes to be fought, and friends to be loved and helped. There are grievous troubles, but they are to be battled against; it is a law with men that they should struggle and suffer (776); for them is endeavour, and victory lies with God (883); however black the outlook, there must be no shirking, for the one deed especially Satan's is suicide (728, 768, 815, 854, 1169); the game must be played to the end manfully, and God is generous though the world be hard (911, 1338); He will make all right in the end (1365), and sorrow alone shows a man's mettle (945). The keynote is optimism quand même. Life is a passing illusion (1572), brief and untrustworthy (1575), in itself nothing but a silly tale (697); we are gazers through a cloudy, distorting glass (110, 656, 707, 1431); our deeds are mere childish sports making for soul-fitness. The one way of escape from illusion is in the exercise of that essential part of ourselves which unites us with the choir of the heavenly hosts (771); love lifts us out of the mundane marsh (772); brother must act brotherly (914); we must loyally serve our chosen friends, those with whom we have formed a bond stronger than the ties of blood: for such we must die if need be (296). The poem is a glorification of friendship, and the story is of the mutual aid of three starlike heroes wont to serve one another (6); even the gratification of the tenderest love must be postponed to this high duty; the betrothed, the newly-wedded, must part for this (292, 685, 688, 1541); friend makes of himself a road and a bridge (685) by which his friend passes to joy. That women have their share in such friendships is shown by the fraternity between Asmat'h and Tariel, and it is a proof of the deep culture of the people that such bonds still exist; there is probably no country where men have so many pure ties with women, where they are bound by affection to so many with whom the idea of marriage is never permitted to present itself. It is to the influence of such customs that we may partly attribute the high civilization of the race; it is equally true that respect for women is a sign of ancient culture. Rust'haveli is the poet of the whole people, and refinement of manners is not limited to, or absent from, any rank of life; the passage (234, 235) in which Avt'handil forgets for a moment that he is a "gentleman" makes every Georgian blush, and even in these days of comparative degeneracy one never hears of any man behaving with discourtesy in the presence of a woman. Woman is man's equal; the lion's whelps are alike lions (39); the three heroines are queens in their own right, free to dispose of themselves in marriage, fitted to rule kingdoms; Dame P'hatman is Acting Collector of Customs and Master of the Merchant Guild in her husband's absence.

Friendship is thus the main fact of life, the thing that makes it worth living; but its highest form is that noblest love (12) of which some of the introductory quatrains treat. This is the divine frenzy (27, 29), breathed only into the gentle, the fair, the wise, the brave, and the generous (9), unseating the charioteer Reason, antecedent to a nuptial choice, transforming the lover into the divine likeness, and thus preparing him for the creative act by which mankind is renewed from age to age. It is a tender feeling (9), pure in its essence (10), hiding itself from the view of the world (12), needing not love in return, but enduring patiently the wrath of the beloved (10); it is changeless in its object (11), steadfast to the end; when it is reciprocated it sweetens death, for in eternity it finds full fruition (1280-1282). It is in this passion, relentless and beautiful like the panther whose coat he wears, that Tariel is wrapped.

If in his advocacy of reticence in affairs of the heart, and his insistence on "playing the game," Rust'haveli makes a special appeal to British readers, there are at least two points wherein he might seem likely to lack their approval: his hyperbolic descriptions of grief at separation, and his hackneyed astronomic similes for human beauty. But such emotional excesses are by himself disapproved (855, 911), and they find parallels in our own literature as late as the eighteenth century, and with passages like those in 806 and 1423 we have numerous analogies in Western literature; it is to be remembered that every parting is looked upon as possibly, or even probably, the last, and is thus invested with the bitterness of death (994). The radiant loveliness of the heroes and heroines is described in terms of the brightest celestial lights, because the shining forth of the soul through a fair countenance is in sober fact more brilliant, even, than those heavenly bodies which were of old the objects of worship.

Then, again, there are three unpleasant incidents in the story: Avt'handil's murder of the Chachnagir, and his intrigue with P'hatman, and Tariel's assassination of Khvarazmsha. We are not concerned to defend the morality of those transactions, and prefer to suppose that they were as repugnant to Rust'haveli as to ourselves; they are necessary to the working out of the plot, and they were all for the sake of women and directly instigated by women. As for Tariel's ill-treatment of Rostevan's men and the Cathayans, we are to presume that his madness is his excuse; like Hamlet, grief at a father's death, loss of both sovereignty and mistress, combined to produce a mania sometimes murderous in its manifestations; but as soon as he is cured, his natural kindness of heart returns, and his boyish disposition exhibits itself in frolic (1351, 1352).

Enough has been said to show the main idea of the poem, and in the Appendix will be found groups of references to particular points of interest, things abstract and concrete. It now becomes necessary to say something of the poet, though we have much less historical knowledge of him than of Shakespeare. His life seems to have lasted from 1172 to 1216. The personal name Shot'ha is said to be a form of Ashot'ha, an appellation of the idol of Armaz (Ormuzd), and is occasionally met with in the chronicles of the twelfth and thirteenth centuries. Rust'haveli means Rust'havian, man of Rust'havi; one place of that name was an episcopal see, but the other is evidently the poet's birthplace, for he describes himself as a Meskhian (1572); so it is from Rust'havi in the district of Akhaltzikhe (which means Newcastle) that he came; he was thus of the race of Meshech (Gen. x. 2; Ps. cxx. 5; Ezek. xxvii. 13, xxxii. 26). Tradition says he was early left an orphan in the care of an uncle who was a monk, that he was educated at the church school of Rust'havi and the monasteries of Tbeti, Gremi, and Iqalt'ho, and was then, in accordance with the custom of the period, sent to Athens, [4] Olympus, and Jerusalem. On his return he wrote Odes [5] in honour of the sainted Queen T'hamara (A.D. 1184-1212), and as a reward was appointed treasurer at the brilliant court of that great and good sovereign, whose reign saw Georgia's political power and literary culture at their highest point of achievement. We are told that his native place was given to him as an estate in lieu of salary. There is a document preserved in the Tiflis Synodal Archives, dated 1190 (?), signed by him as royal treasurer; he must have been singularly precocious if the date of his birth were really 1172. The popular story tells how, hopelessly in love with his queen, he retired to the monastery of Holy Rood at Jerusalem, where, on a pillar, over a portrait is the inscription: "May God pardon Shot'ha, the painter of this. Amen. Rust'haveli." [6] It seems strange that the word "Rust'haveli" should be added after "Amen"; in any case there is a portrait which readers can accept as not discordant with the character displayed in the epic. Many legends are attached to his name; they represent him as enamoured of T'hamara and married to an unworthy wife.

The oldest manuscript is said to be an undated parchment, which, according to Plato Ioseliani, was the property of a Colonel Gregory Tseret'heli; another copy, on paper, is alleged to be of the year 1443; and a third is dated 1678. These were used by King Vakhtang VI. for his edition of 1712; but they have apparently been lost, and, so far as we know, there is no existing manuscript earlier than the seventeenth century, and none dated before 1646. [7] It is most desirable that attention should be devoted to the purification of the text.

The poem is written in quatrains of rhyming lines of sixteen syllables, with an accentuation dividing the lines into halves . [8] It is meant to be sung to the "Davidic" harp (1574), which may have come to the Caucasus with the Jews of the Babylonish Captivity. In the remoter parts of the country, minstrels may perhaps even now be heard chanting the story of Tariel.

The following transliteration of a quatrain will give an idea of the verse, and may help to remove from the language the reproach cast upon it by some writers who had not even an elementary acquaintance with it:

1281.

Mzé ushénod vér ikmnébis/ rádgan shén khar mísi tsíli
gághanámtza más iákhle/ mísi étli ár t'hu tsbíli
múna gnákho mándve gsákho/ gánminát'hlo gúli chrdíli
t'hú sitzótzkhle mtsáre mkónda/ sícvdilímtza mkóndes tcbíli.

The Europeans who have heard of Georgian think it a cacophonous assemblage of consonants with many gutturals and a sparing use of vowels. It is true, indeed, that groups of consonants repellent to a Western eye and ear are frequently found, and herein lies the vigour of the language. A modern Turkish poet addresses a Georgian lady thus: "O thou whose speech is like a lion's roar!" This, however, is but one phonetic aspect of a tongue which in its love lyrics and lullabies can be as soft and caressing as Italian, ("sweet-sounding Georgian," 692) in its rhetorical and philosophic passages as sonorous and dignified as Castilian. Georgian has been a highly-developed literary language from the dawn of the Christian era, and students of cuneiform are engaged in the task of tracing it back to the earliest periods of history; it has a vocabulary so rich, a flexibility so great, that it renders metaphysical Greek works not only word for word, but sometimes syllable by syllable. In the monastery of Petritzos, now called Bachkovo, in the Rhodope, founded, or renovated, by Georgians in 1083, and still bearing traces of their occupation, was a philosophic seminary where many Neo-Platonist and other translations were made. One of the monks, John Petritzi, in the late eleventh or early twelfth century, wrote thus: "In the translation of difficult speculative and philosophic works I consider myself obliged to apply all possible simplicity, and follow the peculiarities of the language (of the original) to the utmost." In commenting on this passage, Professor Marr [9] writes: "John Petritzi translated not only ideas, but words, even words existing in the Georgian language: terms do not satisfy him unless they cover the original etymologically, or even in some cases by the number of their syllables. . . . To him we owe a ready-made philosophic terminology in the Georgian language, marvellously exact and concisely rendering by Georgian roots all those terms which in European languages are borrowed from Greek and Latin."

It was such a language that Rust'haveli used, with a perfection of art which makes a foreign student at first despair of perceiving even the outline of the story. A quatrain may have four quadrisyllabic endings apparently identical (e.g., asadages, 136), and no little knowledge and thought are needed to arrive at the sense in which each of them is to be taken. The beginner is occasionally tempted to believe that the poem is rather music than narrative, that it aims more at inspiring moods than speaking clearly to the intelligence; it is only after some labour that the logical unity of the fable is grasped.

Some controversy has arisen as to the dramatic story which forms the groundwork of the epic, and not a few inkhorns have been emptied by commentators on the passages, "This Persian tale now done into Georgian" (16) and "I, Rust'haveli, have composed this work by my art" (15). It may here suffice to say that no trace of such a Persian story has yet been discovered; and even if it were found, our author's fame would thereby suffer no more than Shakespeare's does from Luigi da Porto's novel. Perhaps Rust'haveli used a pre-existing fable; this, at least, seems the simplest way of accounting for the episode of Avt'handil's intrigue with P'hatman, which is treated with distaste, though it serves to throw a brighter light on Tariel as the faultless lover compared with his sworn brother the tactful, heroic man of the world, and the poet would hardly have invented it, or even used it, unless it had been indispensable in the working out of the plot. It is true that nearly all the characters have Persian names--perhaps none but Tariel, T'hinat'hin, Davar, and Avt'handil are originally Georgian (and the last is doubtful)--and a large number of Persian words are used [10]; but this seems to be due partly to a desire of avoiding the appearance of hinting at current events, and partly to a fashion of the time, the natural result of literary sympathies between two neighbouring cultured peoples. There is something to be said in favour of Professor Khakhanov's theory, [11] that the folk ballads about Tariel and Avt'handil, of which variants are still sung, especially by the mountaineers, were part of the popular literature before the T'hamaran age; while the historical fact of the great queen's elevation to the throne during her father's lifetime was used as a preface to the story.

There is a point to which attention might be given: In Arabic literature one of the earliest forms is that of the eulogy in brief epigrammatic verse. Now, in The Man in the Panther's Skin we find a remarkably frequent use of the word keba (praise); in a score of quatrains [12] keba occurs; we also meet with the Arabic word khotba (3, 1009, 1025) in approximately the same sense, and there is one reference to a professional eulogist, makebi catzi (1527); finally, one passage (1574) says the poem is made up out of kebani (eulogies). It is for scholars to inquire into the matter, and see whether the numerous kebani may not be more ancient than the poem, and perhaps the determinant factor in the choice of the verse form (called shairi); whether, in fact, Rust'haveli did not take from oral tradition certain short verses uniform in their prosody, and weave his work round them after their pattern. In the Athos manuscript of the Georgian Bible, copied in A.D. 978 for the great warrior-monk T'hornici from an earlier translation, the "Song of Songs" is Keba

Kebat'ha; this seems to show that in ancient Georgia the keba, or eulogy, was the poem par excellence. [13]

The English translation endeavours to present the author's ideas and expressions with such fidelity that it may be of use to those who wish to read the original. This version was begun in Kent in 1891, and the first draft was completed at Kertch on November 1, 1898; but in spite of frequent revision and correction, carried on till December, 1909, it is imperfect, and the translator estimated that ten more years of study at least would be required to bring it to its final shape. Nevertheless, as it stands it is a contribution to Georgian studies in Europe, a stepping-stone to help others in a difficult task. It is believed that several attempted literal translations into Russian (including one by the late M. Poltoratzky), and one into French (by M. Meunargia), exist, but the translator never saw them. Since her death an attempt has been made to publish a Russian version in a Tiflis newspaper, but the public received it so ill that the editor was, unfortunately, compelled to desist. Herr Arthur Leist's metrical paraphrase in German (Der Mann im Tigerfelle, Dresden and Leipzig, no date) gives an excellent summary of the poem, and is recommended to readers. Through the corruption of the text and the lack of critical editions and such aids, lexicographic, grammatical, philological, historical, as readers of other great literatures enjoy, there are many passages which seem incapable of satisfactory interpretation; these are rendered as literally as possible. It is a pleasing duty to set down here an acknowledgment of the generous assistance given in preparing this work for the press; so many have collaborated that it is impossible to mention them individually, but special thanks are due to M. Michel Tseret'heli for reading through the whole manuscript, and to Professor Nicholas Marr, of the University of St. Petersburg, who has supplied additional material, and has permitted the publication, in the Appendix, of an English version of his Russian rendering of the obscure introductory and concluding quatrains, and of other passages. Helpers will find sufficient recompense in the thought that they are co-workers with one who loved Rust'haveli and Georgia.

Last of all, this book, designed to be the translator's chief work, should contain some notice of her life. She was born in London on November 26, 1869; died at Bucharest on December 7, 1909; and was buried at Sevenoaks. She began the study of Georgian, as her learned predecessor, M.-F. Brosset, had done, with an alphabet and a Gospel, and when she had made some progress it was his grammar and dictionary she first used; as a girl of twenty she chose this as the idea of her life. She was already equipped with a sound education, and during her varied, busy career she not only used French, German, Italian, Russian, and Roumanian in the daily concerns of the household and the amenities of social intercourse, but applied herself to those tongues and their literatures. From early womanhood she spent nearly all her time abroad--in Italy, France, and North Africa, comparatively short periods; in Hayti over a year; in Roumania three years; in various parts of the Russian dominions about ten years. Her published works are--Georgian Folk-Tales; London, 1894 (D. Nutt). The Hermit, a legend by Prince Ilia Chavchavadze (in verse); London, 1895 (B. Quaritch). Life of St. Nino; Oxford, 1900 (Clarendon Press). She left The Man in the Panther's Skin and other translations in manuscript.

A letter to Ilia Chavchavadze, asking permission to translate The Hermit, was printed in his newspaper Iveria of September 8 (O.S.), 1894, as a model of style, and led to a revival of interest in their language and literature among the younger generation. On her arrival in Transcaucasia in December, 1894, she was received with enthusiasm, and her travels during a second visit, in 1896, brought her into touch with every class of the people. She formed many lasting friendships, and kept up a large correspondence in the Georgian language. There is hardly a household in the Western Caucasus where her name is unknown. Others, have studied the language, literature, and history, of Georgia; she in addition felt an affection for the nation, [14] kept herself informed of all that concerned its welfare, and was sometimes able unobtrusively to do good work for it. To the less fortunate of her own countrywomen, with whom she had much opportunity of acquaintance abroad, she was a sincere friend and comforter; her loss was deplored even by many who knew her but slightly, for, though fragile and weak of body, she never spared herself in her efforts for others. Her intimates found in her a mastery of the arts that make an English home, subtle humour, strength of mind, and warmth of heart. Her reticence about her own achievements was such that few of those who prized her social charm and domestic virtues were aware that her leisure was devoted to study. She calmly, cheerfully, and helpfully faced pestilence, war, and other dangers; at three successive places of residence--Port-au-Prince (1902), St. Petersburg (1905), Bucharest (1907)--she heard cannon fired in civil strife, and she shared the perils, joys, and sorrows, of the peoples among whom she lived. In accordance with a wish she had frequently expressed, the nucleus of a fund for the encouragement of Georgian studies has been formed at Oxford, and her books and manuscripts are being transferred to the Bodleian Library..

INTRODUCTORY QUATRAINS

1   HE who created the firmament, by that mighty power made beings inspired from on high with souls celestial; to us men He has given the world, infinite in variety we possess it; from Him is every monarch in His likeness.

2   O one God! Thou didst create the face of every form! Shield me, give me mastery to trample on Satan, give me the longing of lovers lasting even unto death, lightening (of the burden) of sins I must bear thither with me.

3   Of that lion whom the use of lance, shield and sword adorns, of the king, the sun T'hamara, the ruby-cheeked, the jet-haired, of her I know not how I shall dare to sing the manifold praise; they who look upon her must offer her the sweets for which she hungers.

4   By shedding tears of blood we praise King T'hamara, whose praises I, not ill-chosen, have told forth. For ink I have used a lake of jet, and for pen a pliant crystal. Whoever hears, a jagged spear will pierce his heart!

5   She bade me indite sweet verses in her praise, laud her eyebrows and lashes, her hair, her lips and teeth, cut! crystal and ruby arrayed in ranks. An anvil of soft lead breaks even hard stone.

6   Now want I tongue, heart and skill for utterance! Grant me strength! And if I have aid from thee I shall have understanding, so may we succour Tariel; tenderly indeed should we

cherish his memory and that of the three starlike heroes wont to serve one another.

7   Come, sit ye down, ye who have been born under the same fate; let us shed a never-drying tear for Tariel's sake. I sat me down, I, Rust'haveli, indited a poem, my heart I pierced with a lance. Hitherto the tale has been told as a tale; now is it a pearl (of) measured (poesy).

8   To a lover, beauty, glorious beauty, wisdom, wealth, generosity, youth and leisure are fitting; he must be eloquent, intelligent, patient, an overcomer of mighty adversaries; who has not all these qualities lacks the character of a lover.

9   Love is tender, a thing hard to be known. True love is something apart from lust, and cannot be likened thereto it is one thing; lust is quite another thing, and between. them lies a broad boundary; in no way do they mingle hear my saying!

10   The lover must be constant, not lewd, impure an faithless; when he is far from his beloved he must heave sigh upon sigh; his heart must be fixed on one from whom he endures wrath or sorrow if need be. I hate heartless love--embracing, kissing, noisy bussing.

11   Lovers, call not this thing love: when any long for one to-day and another to-morrow, (lightly) bearing parting's pain. Such base sport is like mere boyish trifling; the good lover is he who suffers a world's woe.

12   There is a first (? noblest) love; it does not show, but hides its woes; (the lover) thinks of it when lied is alone, and always seeks solitude; his fainting, dying, burning, flaming, all

are from afar; he may face the wrath of kings, yet will he be fearful of her.

13   He must betray his secret to none, he must not basely groan and put his beloved to shame; in nought should he manifest his love, nowhere must he reveal it; for her sake he looks upon sorrow as joy, for her sake he would willingly be burned (or? willingly burns [with love]).

14   How can the sane trust him who noises his love abroad, and what shall it profit to do this? He makes her suffer, and he himself suffers. How should he glorify her if he shame her with words? What a chance if one hurt not his beloved's heart!

15   I, Rust'haveli, have composed this work by my art. For her whom a multitude of hosts obey, I lose my wits, I die! I am sick of love, and for me there is no cure from anywhere, unless she give me healing or the earth a grave.

16   This Persian tale, now done into Georgian, has hitherto been like a pearl of great price cast in play from hand to hand; now I have found it and mounted it in a setting of verse; I have done a praiseworthy deed. The ravisher of my reason, proud and beautiful, willed me to do it.

17   Eyes that have lost their light through her long to look on her anew; lo! my heart is mad with love, and it is my lot to run about the fields. Who will pray for me? The burning of the body sufficeth, let (her) give soul-comfort! In praise of threefold hue, the verse must needs fall short. 18 With what Fate gives to a man, therewithal should he be content, and so (? contentedly) speak of it. The labourer should ever work, the warrior be brave. So, also, should the lover love Love, and recognize it. Who judges not will not be judged by others.

19   Minstrelsy is, first of all, a branch of wisdom; divinely intelligible to the godlike, very wholesome to them that hearken; it is pleasant, too, if the listener be a worthy man; in few words he utters a long discourse: herein lies the excellence of poetry.

20   Like a horse running a great race on a long course, like a ball-player in the lists striking the ball fairly and aiming adroitly at the mark, even so it is with the poet who composes and indites long poems, when utterance is hard for him and verse begins to fail.

21   Then, indeed, behold the poet, and his poesy will be manifest. When he is at a loss for Georgian (words), and verse begins to fail, he will not weaken Georgian, nor will he let it grow poor in words. Let him strike the ball cunningly; he will show great virtue.

22   He who utters, somewhere, one or two verses cannot be called a poet; let him not think himself equal to great singers. Even if they compose a few discrepant verses from time to time, yet if they say, "Mine are of the best!" they are stiff-necked mules.

23   Secondly, lyrics which are but a small part of poetry and cannot command heart-piercing words--I may liken them to the bad bows of young hunters who cannot kill big game; they are able only to slay the small.

24   Thirdly, lyrics are fit for the festive, the joyous, the amorous, the merry, for pleasantries of comrades; they please us when they are rightly sung. Those are not called poets who cannot compose a long work.

25   The poet must not spend his toil in vain. One should seem to him worthy of love; he must be devoted to one, he must employ all his art for her, he must praise her, he must set forth the glory of his beloved; he must wish for nought else, for her alone must his tongue be tuneful.

26   Now let all know that I praise her whom I (erstwhile) praised; in this I have great glory, I feel no shame. She is my life; merciless as a leopard is she. Her name I pronounce hereafter with triumph and praise.

27   I speak of the highest love--divine in its kind. It is difficult to discourse thereon, ill to tell forth with tongues. It is heavenly, upraising the soul on pinions. Whoever strives thereafter must indeed have endurance of many griefs.

28   Sages cannot comprehend that one Love; the tongue will tire, the ears of the listeners will become wearied; I must tell of lower frenzies, which befall human beings; they imitate it when they wanton not, but faint from afar.

29   In the Arabic tongue they call the lover "madman," because by non-fruition he loses his wits. Some have nearness to God, but they weary in the flight; then again, to others it is natural to pursue beauty.

30   I wonder why men show that they love the beloved. Why shame they her whom they love, her who slays herself for them, who is covered with wounds? If they love her not, why do they not manifest to her feelings of hatred? Why do they disgrace what they hate? But an evil man loves an evil word more than his soul or heart.

31   If the lover weep for his beloved, tears are her (? his) due. Wandering and solitude befit him, and must be esteemed as roaming. He will have time for nothing but to think of her. If he be among men, it is better that he manifest not his love.

STORY OF ROSTEVAN, KING OF THE ARABIANS

32   There was in Arabia Rostevan, a king by the grace of God, happy, exalted, generous, modest, lord of many hosts and knights, just and gracious, powerful, far-seeing, himself a peerless warrior, moreover fluent in speech:

33   No other child had the king save one only daughter, the shining light of the world, to be ranked with nought but the sunny group; whoever looked on her, she bereft him of heart, mind and soul. It needs a wise man to praise her, and a very eloquent tongue.

34   Her name is T'hinat'hin; let it be famous! When she had grown up to full womanhood, she contemned even the sun. The king called his viziers, seated himself, proud yet gentle, and, placing them by his side, began to talk graciously to them.

35   He said: "I will declare to you the matter on which we are to take counsel together. When the flower of the rose is dried and withered it falls, and another blooms in the lovely garden. The sun is set for us; we are gazing on a dark, moonless night.

36   "My day is done; old age, most grievous of all ills, weighs on me; if not to-day, then to-morrow I die--this is the way of the world. What light is that on which darkness attends? Let us instate as sovereign my daughter, of whom the sun is not worthy."

37   The viziers said: "O king, why do you speak of your age? Even when the rose fades we must needs give it its due; it still excels all in scent and fair colour. How can a star declare enmity even to the waning moon!

38   "Speak not then thus, O king. Your rose is not yet faded. Even bad counsel from you is better than good counsel from another, It was certainly fitting to speak out what your heart desires. It is better. Give the kingdom to her who prevails against the sun.

39   "Though indeed she be a woman, still as sovereign she is begotten of God. She knows how to rule. We say not this to flatter you; we ourselves, in your absence, often say so. Her deeds, like her radiance, are revealed bright as sunshine. The lion's whelps are equal (alike lions), be they male or female."

40   Avt'handil was general, son of the commander-in-chief. He was more graceful than the cypress; his presence was like sun and moon. Still beardless, he was to be likened to famous crystal and glass. The beauty of T'hinat'hin and of the host of her eyelashes was slaying him.

41   He kept his love hidden in his heart. When he was absent and saw her not, his rose faded; when he saw her, the fires were renewed, his wound smarted more. Love is pitiable; it makes man heart-slain.

42   When the king commanded that his daughter should be enthroned as king, gladness came upon Avt'handil; the extinction (concealment) of that jewel irks him. He said to himself: "Often will it now fall to my lot to gaze upon her crystal face; perchance I may thus find a cure for my pallor."

43   The great sovereign of the Arabs published throughout Arabia an edict: "I, her father, appoint my T'hinat'hin king; she shall illumine all, even as the shining sun. Come and see, all ye who praise and extol!" (or, praise and extol her!).

44   All the Arabians came; the crowd of courtiers increased. The sun-faced Avt'handil, chief of ten thousand times a thousand soldiers, the vizier Sograt, the nearest to the king of all his attendants. When they placed the throne the people said: "Its worth is beyond words!"

45   T'hinat'hin, radiant in countenance, was led in by her sire. He seated her, and with his own hands set the crown on her head; he gave her the sceptre, and clad her in the royal robes. The maiden looks on with understanding, all-seeing, like the sun.

46   The king and his armies retired and did homage. They blessed her and established her as king, many from many places told forth her praises; the trumpets were blown and the cymbals sounded sweetly. The maiden wept, she shed many tears; she drooped her raven eyelashes (the tail feathers of the raven).

47   She deemed herself unworthy to sit on her father's throne; therefore she weeps, filling the rose-garden (of her cheeks) with tears. The king admonishes her: "Every father hath a peer in his child," quoth he. "Until now the raging fire in my bosom has not been extinguished."

48   He said: "Weep not, daughter, but hearken to my counsel: To-day thou art King of Arabia, appointed sovereign by me; henceforth this kingdom is entrusted to thee; mayest thou be discreet in thy doings, be modest and discerning.

49   "Since the sun shines alike on roses and middens, be not thou weary of mercy to great and small. The generous binds the free, and he who is already bound will willingly obey. Scatter liberally, as the seas pour forth again the floods they have received.?

50   "Munificence in kings is like the aloe planted in Eden. All, even the traitor, are obedient to the generous. It is very wholesome to eat and drink, but what profits it to hoard? What thou givest away is thine; what thou keepest is lost."

51   The maiden hearkened discreetly to this her father's advice; she lent ear, she heard, she wearied not of instruction. The king drank and sported; he was exceeding joyful. T'hinat'hin contemned the sun, but the sun aped T'hinat'hin.

52   She sent for her faithful, trusty tutor, and said: "Bring hither all my treasure sealed by thee, all the wealth belonging to me as king's daughter." He brought it; she gave without measure, without count, untiringly.

53   That day she gave away all she had gathered since her childhood; she enriched both small folk and great. Then she said: "I do the deed my father taught me; let none keep back any of my hoarded treasure."

54   She said: "Go, open whatever treasure there is! Master of the Horse, lead in the droves of asses, mules, and horses." He brought them. She gave them away without measure; she wearied not of generosity. The soldiers gathered together stuff like pirates.'

55   They pillaged her treasury as 'twere booty from Turks; they carried off her fine, sleek Arab steeds. Her munificence was like a snowstorm whirling down from the sky; none remained empty, neither youth nor maiden.

56   One day passed; there was a banquet, food and drink--a feast of fruit. A great gathering of warriors sat there to make merry. The king hung his head, and his brow was furrowed with sadness. They began to discuss this one with another: "What weighs upon him, and why grieves he?"

57   At the head sat the sun-faced Avt'handil, desirable to them that look upon him, the agile leader of the hosts; like a panther and a lion is he. The old vizier Sograt sat by his side. They said one to the other: "What ails the king, and why has he grown pale?"

58   They said: "Some unpleasant thought has come into the king's mind, for nothing has happened here to make him sad." Quoth Avt'handil: "Let us inquire, O Sograt, let him tell us why he is displeased with us; let us venture on some pleasantry; why hath he shamed us?"

59   Sograt and the graceful Avt'handil arose; each filled his winecup, and with meek mien drew nigh. Then with smiling faces they cast themselves on their knees before the king. The vizier sportively spoke thus, with eloquent words:

60   "You look sad, O king; there is no longer a smile on your face. Thou art right, for, lo! your daughter with lavish hand has given away all your rich and costly treasure. Make her not king at all; why bring grief on thyself?"

61   When the king heard him he looked up with a smile. He marvelled how he had ventured thus, how he dared to speak

such words! "Well hast thou done!" He thanked his vizier. He confirmed this by what he said: "He who lays avarice to my charge is a lying chatterer.'

62   "That afflicts me not, O vizier. This it is that troubles me: Old age draws nigh; I have spent the days of youth, and nowhere in our dominions is there a man who hath learned from me the knightly arts.

63   "It is true I have a daughter tenderly nurtured, but God has given me no son; I suffer in this fleeting life. There is none to be compared with me in archery or at the game of ball. It is true that Avt'handil resembles me somewhat, thanks to my teaching."

64   The proud youth hearkened modestly to these words of the king; with bent head he smiled. Well did a smile befit him; his shining white teeth gleamed like sunshine on a mead. The king asked: "Why smilest thou? or why wert thou shy of me?"

65   Yet again he said: "Why dost thou smile at me? What is laughable in me?" The youth replied: "I shall tell you if you grant me leave to speak. With what I say be not offended; be not wroth, blame me not, call me not bold, ruin me not for this!"

66   He answered: "How can I take aught thou sayst a displeasing?" He took an oath by the sun (i.e., life) of T'hinat'hin, that contemner of the sun. Avt'handil said "Then will I speak boldly; vaunt not yourself of your archery, it is better to speak modestly.

67   "I, Avt'handil, earth under your feet, am an archer before you; let us lay a wager; let your armies attend as

witnesses. 'Who is like me in the lists?' said you vain indeed is denial!--that is decided by the ball and the field."

68 "I will not let thee thus dispute with me! Say the word, let us draw the bow; do not shirk. Let us make good men witnesses of our rivalry; then in the field it will be manifest whose praises should be sung."

69 Avt'handil obeyed; they ceased their discourse. They laughed, they sported like children, lovingly and becomingly they behaved. They fixed the wager, and laid down this condition: Whoever shall be beaten, let him go bareheaded for three days.

70 (The king) commanded, moreover: "Let twelve slaves be chosen to attend us, twelve to give me arrows and wait upon me; Shermadin alone is for thee; he is equal to them (my retinue). Let them count the shots and the hits, and give a faithful, unerring report."

71 To the huntsmen he said: "Travel over the plain, beat in many droves, go yourselves to do this, invite the soldiers to look on, (bid them) assemble and close round!" The wassail and banquet broke up; there were we pleasantly merry.

72 Early in the morning he (Avt'handil) came forth like a well-grown lily; he was clad in crimson, his face was of crystal and ruby, over his face was a golden veil, he was fair in huntsman's apparel. He rode upon a white steed; he invited the king to come forth.

73 The king was arrayed, he mounted, they set out for the chase. The people surrounded the field, they made a ring round about it; there was much mirth and excitement; the armies kept

the ground. For their wager were they shooting and striving together.

74 The king commanded the twelve slaves: "Come, accompany us, bring us the swift bows, prepare the arrows, compare what is struck and keep count of the shots." Game began to come in from every corner of the plain.

75 Herds of game, innumerable, flocked in: stags, goats, wild-asses, high-leaping chamois. Lord and vassal pursued them; what sight could be fairer! Behold the bow, the arrow, and the untiring arm!

76 The dust from their horses' tracks cut off the sun's rays. They slew, their arrows sped, blood flowed through the field; as the shafts were shot away the slaves brought more of them. The beasts wounded by them could not take another step.

77 They ran through that field; they drove the herd before them. They slew and exterminated, they made wroth the God of the heavens, the fields were dyed crimson with the blood they shed from the beasts. Those who watched Avt'handil said: "He is like an aloe-tree planted, in Eden."

78 They coursed over the whole of that plain only they had travelled over. There on the farther edge of the plain flows a stream; on the bank of the stream are rocks. The game fled into the wood, where horse could not follow. (Rostevan and Avt'handil) were both fatigued, (yet) how spirited they were! (? They were tired in spite of their strength.)

79 Each laughingly said to the other: "'Tis I that have won!" Merry were they; they sported, hither and thither they

frolicked. Then came the slaves who had tarried, and (the king) said: "Tell the truth; we seek not flattery from you."

80   The slaves said: "We shall speak the truth; think not we shall deceive you, O king; we may by no means liken you to him. Slay us at once if you will, it matters not; this cannot help you in any way. We observed the beasts stricken by him; they could not move a forward step.

81   "Together ye have slain in all a hundred score, but Avt'handil killed more by a score; he missed not even one at which he aimed his bow, but of yours we cleaned up many which left blots on the earth."

82   The king heard this with as little concern as (if it had been the result of) a game of backgammon, he rejoiced so at the victory of his foster-son; he loved him as the rose loves the nightingale; smiling he made merry, all grief was gone from his heart.

83   There they both sat to cool themselves at the foot of the trees; the soldiers assembled and stood round them, countless as chaff; near them were the twelve slaves, bravest of the brave. As they sported they gazed at the stream and the edge of the glens.

HOW THE KING OF THE ARABIANS SAW THE KNIGHT CLAD IN THE PANTHER'S SKIN

84   They saw a certain stranger knight; he sat weeping on the bank of the stream, he held his black horse by the rein, he looked like a lion and a hero; his bridle, armour and saddle were thickly bedight with pearls; the rose (of his cheek) was frozen in tears that welled up from his woe-stricken heart.

85   His form was clad in a long coat over which was thrown a panther's skin, his head, too, was covered with a cap of panther's skins; in his hand he held a whip thicker than a man's arm. They looked and liked to look at that wondrous sight.

86   A slave went forth to speak to the knight of the woestricken heart, who, weeping with downcast head, seems not a spectacle for jesting; from a channel of jet (his eyelashes) rains a crystal shower. When (the slave) approached, he could by no means bring himself to speak a word (to Tariel).

87   The slave was much perturbed; he dared not address him. A long time he gazed in wonder till his heart was strengthened; then he said: "(The king) commands thee (to attend him)." He (the slave) came near, (and) greeted him gently; he (Tariel) wept on and heard not, he knew not that (the slave) was there.

88   He heard not a word of the slave, nor what he said; he was wholly unconscious of the shouting of the soldiers, he was sobbing strangely, his heart burnt up with fires; tears were mingled with blood, and flowed forth as from floodgates.

89   Elsewhither his mind was wafted, by the weight of his head! Once again the slave uttered the king's message, but (Tariel) ceased not from weeping and heard him not, nor was the rose-bouquet (of speech) plucked from his lips.

90   Since he answered not, the slave went back and said to Rosten: "I have told him what you said, but he will not listen. Mine eyes were dazzled as by the sun; my heart was sorely troubled. I could not make him hear a word though I have tarried there so long."

91   The king wondered, he was wroth, he was vexed in heart against him. He sent the twelve slaves standing before him; he commanded: "Take weapons of war in your hands; go and bring hither him who sits yonder."

92   The slaves went forth, they drew nigh to him, their armour clanked. Then indeed the knight started up, he wept still more woefully; he raised his eyes and looked round, he saw the band of warriors. But once he said, "Woe is me!" and spoke no word more.

93   He passed his hands over his eyes, he wiped away the hot tears, he made fast his sabre and quiver, and braced his strong arms. He mounted his horse--why should he heed the words of slaves? He wended his way elsewhither, and healed not their troubles.

94   The slaves stretched forth their hands to seize that knight; he fell upon them--alas! even their enemies would have pitied them; he beat one against another, he slew them without raising (on high) his hand, some with his whip he smote, cleaving them down to the breast.

95   Wrathful was the king, and annoyed; he shouted to the slaves. The youth looked not back nor heeded his pursuers till they were upon him; as many as overtook him he made to look like dead men, he threw down man on man; Rosten lamented thereat.

96   The king and Avt'handil mounted to follow the youth. Proud and haughty, his form swayed to and fro, his steed was like Merani, the sun shone brightly on the field; he perceived that the king pursued him.

97   When he saw that the king was come, he struck his horse with his whip; in that very moment he was lost, our eyes see him not; he seemed to have sunk into an abyss or flown to heaven; they sought, but could find no trace of his course.

98   His footprints they sought, and marvelled to find no trace. Thus, leaving no vestige, the man passed away like a Devi. The soldiers mourned for their dead; they hastened to bind up the wounded. The king said: "I have seen cause for loss of joy."

99   He said: "God is weary of the happiness I have had hitherto, therefore He turns my pleasure into the gall of bitterness; He has wounded me unto death, none can cure me. Such, by His grace, is His will and desire."

100   Thus he spoke, and returned; he went frowning away. They summoned not to the lists; groan was mingled with groan. Each ceased from the chase wherever he was following it. Some said: "He is right!" others said: "O God!" (?)

101   The king went into his bedchamber sad and frowning. Avt'handil watched like a son that none save himself should

follow; all went away, the household dispersed; merriment ceased, the castanet and the sweet harp.

102 T'hinat'hin heard of her father's great sadness. She rose and came to the door; she with whom the sun strove asked the chamberlain: "Sleeps he or wakes he?" He answered: "He sits brooding; his colour has suffered a change.

103 "Avt'handil alone is present; he sits in a chair before, him. They have seen a certain stranger knight; this is the cause of his melancholy." T'hinat'hin said: "I will now depart; it is not time for me to go in. When he asks for me, say: 'She was here but now.'"

104 Time passed; he inquired: "What doth the maiden, my solace and jewel, my water of life?" The chamberlain replied: "She came, pale-faced, but now; she learned of your sadness and went away, but she is ready to come to your presence."

105 He said: "Go, call her; how can I bear absence from her! Say unto her: 'Why didst thou turn back, O life of thy father? Come, drive away my grief, heal my wounded heart. I will tell thee wherefore my joy fled.'"

106 T'hinat'hin rose and came; she did as her father wished. The light of her face is like the splendour of the moon. Her father set her by his side, and, kissing her tenderly, gently, said: "Why tamest thou not to me? wert thou waiting till I sent for thee?"

107 The maiden said: "O king, who, however venturesome, would dare to approach you aware that you were frowning? This sadness of yours upsets even the lights of heaven. Let a man seek to solve the difficulty; this, I think, would be better

than grieving."

108   He answered: "O my child, however much this sad affair grieves me, thy sight and life cause me joy. My grief is dissipated as if I had taken an electuary. I believe that when thou knowest thou too wilt justify my sighing and groaning.

109   "I met a certain beautiful, wondrous youth; his ray enlightened the firmament and the bounds of the earth. I could not find out why he was afflicted, nor for whom he wept. He came not to see me; I was irritated and quarrelled with him.

110   "When he saw me, he mounted his horse and wiped the tears from his eyes. I cried out that he must be seized; he utterly destroyed my men; like an evil spirit, he was lost to me, he saluted me not like a man. Even now I know not whether he was real or a vision.

111   "His (God's) tender mercies at length have become thus bitter to me; I have forgotten the past days of my joy. Every one will make me sad and comfort me no more. However long my days may be, I can no more rejoice."

112   The maid replied: "Deign to hearken to my uttered words. O king, why repine at God or fate! Why accuse of bitterness the All-seeing, who is tender to all! And why should the Creator of good make evil:

113   "If this knight was indeed (a man) of flesh wandering over the earth, others must have seen him; they will appear to instruct you. If not, it is a devil who has appeared to you to disturb your joys. Refrain from sadness. Why art thou become

cheerless?

114 "This is my advice: Thou art king, ruler over kings; wide is your boundary, boundless is your power; send everywhere men with news of this story; soon shall you know whether this youth be a mortal or not."

115 He commanded men and sent them forth even to the four corners of the heavens, saying: "Go, spare yourselves no pains; search, hunt for that youth, let nothing hinder you; send a letter whither ye cannot go nor attain."

116 The men went, they wandered about for a year; they looked, they sought that youth, they inquired again and again. They could find none of God's creatures who had seen him. Wearied in vain, they returned, dissatisfied with themselves.

117 The slaves said: "O king, we have wandered over the lands, yet could we not find that youth, so we could not rejoice; we could meet no living man who had seen him; we have not been able to serve you, now devise some other plan."

118 The king replied: "My daughter, my child, spoke truth. I have seen a hideous, unclean spirit; he has been sent as my foe, flying down from heaven. Grief is fled from. me; I care nothing for all that."

119 Thus he spoke, and sporting was increased with, rejoicing; they called the minstrel and the acrobat! wherever they were found, many gifts were distributed, he summoned all to the throne-room. What other did God create with generosity like unto his!

120   Avt'handil sat alone in his chamber, clad only in an under-garment; he was singing and making merry, before him stood a harp. To him came T'hinat'hin's black slave, and said: "She of the aloe form, the moonfaced one, sends for thee."

121   Avt'handil was glad to hear this joyful news. He rose and donned his best and brightest coat. He rejoiced to meet the rose; they had never yet met alone. Pleasant is it to gaze on beauty, and be near one beloved.

122   Proudly and boldly Avt'handil came to her; he was ashamed of none. He will see her for whom the tear of woe full oft had flowed. The peerless one sat mournful, she shone like lightning, her rays eclipsed the moon.

123   Her fair form was clad in unlined ermine, she wore negligently veils whose price it were hard to tell; but her black, heart-piercing eyelashes and the thick, long tresses which embraced her white throat were her real adornments.

124   Pensive she sat in her red veil; she quietly greeted Avt'handil, and gently bade him be seated. The slave placed a seat; he sat down modestly and respectfully. Face to face he gazed on her, full of great joy.

125   The knight said: "How indeed can I speak to one so dread! If the moon meet the sun it is consumed, it fades away. I am no longer at leisure to think; I fear for myself. Tell me, then, why you are sad and what will relieve you."

126   The maiden replied with elegant words, not ill-chosen, saying: "Although thou hast hitherto remained far from me, yet I wonder thou shouldst be timid even for a moment. But first I must tell thee of the malady which afflicts me, as a plague.

127 "Dost thou remember, when thou and Rostan killed game in the plain, how ye saw a certain stranger youth who wiped his tears away? Since then I have been a prey to thoughts of him. I beg thee to search for him, to seek him even to the bounds of the earth (within the bounds of the sky).

128 "Although I have been unable to hold converse with thee hitherto, yet from afar have I perceived thy love for me; I know that without pause the hail has fallen from thine eyes upon thy cheek. Thou art made prisoner by love; thy heart is taken captive.

129 "This service of mine which I bid thee do befits thee for these two reasons: First, thou art a knight, among all flesh there is none like unto thee; secondly, thou art in love with me, this is true and no slander. Go, seek that brother-in-arms, be he near or far.

130 "Thereby shalt thou strengthen my love for thee; by delivering me from my sadness, thou shalt cripple the foul demon; plant the violet of hope in my heart, strew roses; then come, O lion, I shall meet thee like a sun; meet thou me.

131 "Seek three years him whom thou hast to seek; if thou find him, come gaily telling thy victory. If thou find him not, I shall believe he was a vision. Thou shalt meet the rosebud unwithered, unfaded.

132 "I swear if I wed any husband but thee, even should the sun become man, incarnate for my sake, may I be cut off for ever from Paradise, may I be swallowed up in Hell; love for thee would slay me, piercing my heart with a knife!"

133 The knight replied: "O sun, who causest the jet [15] to blink, what have I said to thee, and what have I done to make thee suspect me? I awaited death; thou hast renewed my will to live. I shall certainly obey thee like a slave in service."

134 Again he spoke: "O sun, since God has created thee a sun, so that the heavenly planets obey thee wherever they may be, I have heard from you than which has overwhelmed me with grace; my rose shall not wither, thy ray shines generously upon it."

135 Once more they made an oath together, they promised each other, they confirmed it and discoursed much, with many a word; what grief they had borne until now became easy. Their white teeth flashed white lightning as if transparent.

136 They sat together, they made merry, they talked simply of a hundred things, they spoke with their crystal and ruby (faces) and jet (eyes). The knight said: "Those who gaze upon thee become mad; my heart is burned to ashes by the fire that comes from thee."

137 The youth went away, but he could not bear parting from her; he looked back, his eyes were dazed, crystal hails down and freezes the rose, his graceful form was trembling; he had heart for heart, he had lent (his) to love.

138 He said to himself: "O sun, separation from thee is thus early manifested on the rose; my crystal and ruby have faded, I am become yellower than amber. What shall I do, then, when I cannot see thee for a long time? This shall be my law: death for the beloved is fitting.

139   He lay down on his bed, he weeps, it is difficult for him to wipe away the tears, he shivered and swayed, like an aspen in the wind; when he fell into a slumber he dreamed his beloved was near, he starts, he cries out loud, his suffering increases twentyfold.

140   Separation from his beloved made him jealous. Tears like pearls were shed upon the rose, making it tender. When day dawned he apparelled himself, fair to look upon; he mounted his horse, set out, and came to court for an audience.

141   He sent a chamberlain into the hall of audience with a message from him to the king, saying: "O king, I venture to tell you what I have thought: all the face of the earth is subjected to you by your sword; now, if it be better, I shall make known these tidings to all the vicinage.

142   "I will go, I shall travel, I shall wage war, I shall go the rounds of the marches, I shall, by piercing the heart of your enemies, announce T'hinat'hin's accession; I shall cause the obedient to rejoice, the disobedient will I make to weep, I shall send you gifts incessantly, I shall not be sparing of greeting."

143   The king expressed his great gratitude; he said: "O lion, stretching thine arm in battle irks thee not. Behold, this thy counsel is matched by thy valour. Thou mayst go, but what shall I do if it happen that thou tarry long?"

144   The knight came in; he did homage, and spoke some words of thanks: "O monarch, I wonder that you should deign to praise me. Now God will perchance lighten for me the darkness of separation, and let me see again in joy your joyful face."

145   The king hung upon his neck and kissed him like a son; like unto them have none been, neither upbringer nor up-

brought. The knight rose and went away, to him their day seemed separated; Rostan, wise and soft-hearted, wept for him.

146   Avt'handil set out, a brave knight marching boldly; twenty days he journeyed, many a day he made one with the night. She is the joy of the world, she is treasure and due; he puts not away the thought of T'hinat'hin, of her for whom the flame burns.

147   Whenever he came there was rejoicing in the kingdom, nobles met him, they gave generous gifts; the sun-faced had not wasted time in his rapid journey. A dawning joy met them that came into his presence.

148   He had a strong city to strike terror in the marches; outside was a rock, I tell thee, with an unmortared wall. The knight spent there three days in the pleasant chase; he appointed his pupil, Shermadin, as vizier.

149   This is the slave Shermadin mentioned above, brought up with (Avt'handil), faithful and self-sacrificing to him. He knew not hitherto of the fire which burned the knight; now he (Avt'handil) revealed the hopeful words of the sun (T'hinat'hin).

150   He said: "Lo, Shermadin, for this I am ashamed before thee; thou knowest all my affairs and hast given heed to them; but hitherto thou hast not known what tears I have shed; in her from whom I had suffering I now find joy.

151   "I am slain by love and longing for T'hinat'hin; from the narcissus (eyes) hot tears moistened the frosted rose; I could not till now show my hidden woe, now has she bidden me hope, therefore thou seest me joyful.

152   "She said to me: 'Learn news of that lost knight, then come, I shall fulfil thy heart's desire; I want no husband save thee, a planted tree falls to my lot.' She gave me the balm of my heart, until that moment bound captive.

153   "First, I am a knight; I wish to go forth to serve my lady. Faithfulness to kings is fitting, vassal must act as vassal; then, she has extinguished the fire, my heart is no longer consumed to soot; a man must not bend before misfortune, but meet it like a man.

154   "Of all lords and vassals thou and I are most friendly; therefore I entreat thee to hear this from mine own mouth; in my stead I appoint thee lord and chief over mine armies, I could not entrust this matter to others.

155   "Lead forth the soldiers to battle, rule the nobles, send messengers to court telling the state of affairs, write letters in my stead, present priceless gifts; why should it be known that I am not here? (thou must not let my absence be perceived).

156   "Represent me in military duties and in the hunting-field, wait here for me three years, keep my secret; perchance indeed I shall return, my aloe-tree shall not fade; but if I come not back, mourn me, weep for me, utter sighs.

157   "Tell the king forthwith--it is not a desirable deed--announce my death to him, be as if thou art drunk; say to him: 'For him is come to pass the thing which none escape.' Give to the poor my treasure--gold, silver and copper.

158   "Thus shalt thou help me after the best fashion, by this thou shalt aid me most; do not forget me soon, think of me often, take good thought of provision for me, pray for my soul.

Remember my childhood; let thy heart be motherly towards me."

159   When the slave heard this he wondered, he was alarmed, from his eyes the hot tears poured like pearls. He said: "How can the heart deprived of thee rejoice? I know thou wilt not stay; so I cannot hinder thee in this matter.

160   "Why didst thou say thou wouldst appoint me in thy stead? How can I undertake the lordship, how can I imitate thee or resemble thee? It were better that the earth cradled me too than that I should have to think that thou art alone; rather let us both steal forth, I will accompany thee, take me with thee."

161   The knight replied: "Hearken unto me, I tell thee truth without beating about the bush: when a lover would roam the fields, alone he must wander; a pearl falls to the lot of none without buying and bargaining. An evil and treacherous man should be pierced with a lance.

162   "To whom could I tell my secret? save thee, none is worthy. To whom can I entrust the lordship save thee, who else can do it well? Fortify the marches that the enemy may not encamp near! Perchance I shall return, if God make me not to be wholly lost.

163   "Hazard kills equally be it one or a hundred. Loneliness can matter naught if the group (? grouping) of the heavenly powers (? planets) protect me. If I come not hither in three years, then will it beseem thee to mourn and wear funeral garb. I will give thee a letter, whoever is my courtier must obey thee."

AVT'HANDIL'S LETTER TO HIS VASSALS

164   He wrote as follows: "My vassals, my instructors and some my pupils, faithful, trusty and tried, attentive to my behests like shadows, hearken to my letter all assembled!

165   "Give ear! I, Avt'handil, earth beneath your feet, write this unto you; with mine own hand have I written this epistle. For a little while I have preferred roaming to drink and song; for bread and meat I shall trust to my bow and thumb.

166   "I have in hand a certain matter which makes me journey to a far country; I depart alone, and this year shall I travel. I ask you only this: I beseech you let me find the realm unshaken by the foe.

167   "I have appointed Shermadin to be lord in my stead; until he learn of my life or death he will shine upon you all like the sun; he will make the rose to be frosted and not fade, he will cause all misdoers to melt away like wax.

168   You know, too, how he has grown up with me like a brother and like a son; you must obey him as if he were Avt'handil; let him make to sound the trumpet, do everything as I have hitherto done; if I come not at the time appointed, mourning and not laughter will be seemly, to you."

169   The eloquent and nice-worded one ended this letter, he tied gold round his waist, habited himself to travel alone; he said: "I shall mount in the plain." The soldiers formed in line, then they came forth; he tarried no time indoors.

170 He said: "Let all go hence; herein I need none as a partisan." He sent the slaves away also, he remained by himself, alone he withdrew himself, he hastened through the rushes. His slayer, T'hinat'hin, is always in his thoughts.

171 He galloped over that plain; he was lost to the soldiers' sight. Whatever human being might have seen him and pursued him, his sword could not harm him; his arm was hampered. He was heavy laden with a burden of grief for her sake.

172 When the soldiers hunted and sought their lord, and could no longer find the sun-faced, their countenances paled, their great joy turned into heaviness, they ran everywhere to seek him, whoever had a swift horse,

173 O lion, whom can God put in thy place! They ran and brought out other messengers from elsewhere; they could learn nothing of him; he passed from that place. His disheartened hosts shed hot tears.

174 Shermadin assembled together the courtiers and nobles; he showed them the letter in which he (Avt'handil) had told them his tidings. When they heard it, all remained heart-pierced, they beat themselves, there was not a tearless heart, not an unbruised breast.

175 All said: "Though our state without him is irksome to us, to whom save thee could he give his seat and throne? Of a truth we shall obey thee, whatever thou commandest any of us." They made that vassal lord; all did him homage.

AVT'HANDIL SETS FORTH IN QUEST OF TARIEL

176   Dionosi the wise, Ezros bear me witness in this: It is pitiable when the rose wherewith the ruby of Badakhshan is not to be compared and whereto a reedstem serves as form, becomes covered with rime and frost-bitten; wherever he wanders abroad he is wearied of abodes.

177   Avt'handil travelled over that plain at a flying pace, he left the bounds of the Arabs, he journeyed in foreign lands; but separation from his sun had taken away part of his life; he said: "If I were near her now I should not shed hot tears."

178   Fresh snow had fallen, and, freezing on the rose, blasted it. He wished to strike his heart; sometimes he uplifted his knife. He said: "Fate (the world) has increased my grief ninety, an hundred fold. I have gone away from all rejoicing, from harp, lyre and pipe."

179   The rose separated from its sun faded more and more. He said to his heart: "Be patient!" Thus he fainted not wholly. He journeyed through passing strange I places on his quest, he asked tidings of wayfarers, he was friendly with them.

180   There seeks he the shedder of tears which flowed to increase the sea. The land seems to him a couch, his arm his pillow. He says to himself: "O beloved, I am far from thee, my heart stays with thee; I lament. for thy sake death would be joy to me."

181   He journeyed over all the face of the earth, he went thoroughly over it, so that beneath heaven was no place left where he had not been; but he met none who had heard tidings of him he sought; meanwhile three years save three months had passed.

182   He arrived in a certain dreadful country, exceeding rough; for a month he saw no man, no son of Adam. Neither Vis nor Ramin saw such woe like unto his. By day and by night he thought of her, his beloved.

183   He reached as a resting-place the slope of a great high mountain; thence appeared a plain which it would take seven days to cross. At the foot of the mountain flowed a river that could not be bridged; both sides were covered down to the water's edge with forests.

184   He goes up, turns round (?) and counts the time, the remaining days--he has two months left. He sighs at this, he rejoices not. "Alas! if the thing were revealed!" Again he is timid in heart by reason of this. No man can turn evil to good; none can be born again of himself.

185   He became thoughtful; he stood to consider the matter. He said to himself: "If I return thus, why have I spent so much time in the field? What can I dare say to my star, how I have spent the days? I have learned not even gossip regarding him I seek.

186   "If I return not, I must spend yet more time in the quest, if I can learn no tidings of him I seek; when the time agreed upon with Shermadin is past, his cheeks will be bathed (in tears), he will go and tell the king what soever things are fitting.

187 "He will tell him of my death, as I myself bade him. Then would there be mourning, weeping; bitter would the matter be for them. Thereafter should I return after travelling everywhere." On this he thinks, weeping, distressed in mind.

188 He said: "O God, why make Thy judgments crooked because of me? why, alas! should I have made such a journey in vain? Thou hast rooted up joys from my heart; Thou hast given griefs a nest there. All my days my tears will never cease."

189 Then he said, "Patience is better," and communed thus with himself: "Let me not die a day too soon, cast not down my heart; without God I can do nothing, my tears flow in vain. No one can change that which is decreed; that which is not to be will not be."

189a He said to himself: "Die, for thee it is better than shameful life. Thou wilt go back; T'hinat'hin, who brightens the sunny day, will meet thee; she will ask thee for tidings of that sun; what does groaning avail?" Thus thinking, he forthwith sets out for the reedy, watery edge of the wood.

190 "All beings under the heavens have surely passed me by in turn, but regarding that man nought can I learn anywhere. Doubtless they who called him a Kadj spoke truth. Now tears avail me not; why should I weep in vain?"

190a Avt'handil descended the mountain, he crossed river and woods, he put his steed to a gallop towards the plain; the murmur of the water and trees annoys him; his power (arms) and pride were spent; the crystal field with the jetty growth was beautiful (i.e., his face was beautified by the growth of his beard).

191   He resolved to return, he sighed and groaned; he turned towards the plain; he traced out the road with his eyes; for a month he has seen no human being anywhere; there were terrible wild beasts, but he hunted them not.

192   Though Avt'handil was become wild with heart groaning and sighing, yet he wished to eat, after the wont of Adam's race; he killed game with his arrow, with arm longer than Rostom's; he alighted on the edge of the reedy ground and kindled a fire with a steel.

193   He let his horse pasture while he roasted the meat. He saw six horsemen coming towards him. He said: They look like brigands; else what good is to be found? No other human being has ever been here."

194   He took his bow and arrow in his hand, and went gaily towards them. Two bearded men were leading their beardless brother, his head was wounded, his heart had swooned from loss of blood; they wept and grieved, his poor spirit was almost fled.

195   He called out: "Brothers, who are ye? I took you for brigands." They replied: "Be calm, help us and put out the fire; if thou canst not help us, add grief to our grief, and make it complete; weep with us who need pity, scratch thy cheeks too."

196   Avt'handil approached; he spoke to the men with the grieved hearts. They told him their story, speaking with tears: "We are three brothers, for this we shed bitter tears; we have a large fortified town in the region of Khataet'hi.

197   "We heard of good hunting ground, we went forth to the chase, countless soldiers accompanied us, we dismounted

on the bank of a stream; the hunting pleased us, for a month we went not away; we killed wild beasts without measure in the plain, on the mountain and on the ridge.'

198   "We three brothers shamed the archers with us, so we three vied still one with another: 'I kill best, I am better than thou,' thus each pushed his claim with words; we could not manifest the truth, we wrangled, we strove with one another (none wanted to be last).

199   "To-day we sent away the soldiers loaded with stags' hides. We said among ourselves: 'Let us judge truly who of us is mightier with his arm.' We remained alone, we were private, we killed in our own sight, we shot not before onlookers.

200   "We had three armour-bearers (squires) with us; we ordered the soldiers to go away, mistrusting nought; we hunted over plain, through wood and den, we slaughtered the wild beast, and not even a bird flew up.

201   "Suddenly there appeared a knight, morose and gloomy of visage, seated on a black horse, black as Pegasus; his head and form were clad in a panther's skin with the fur outside, and beauty such as his has ne'er been seen by man before.

202   "We gazed upon his rays, we scarce could support the brightness, we said: 'He is a sun on the earth; we cannot say (there is a sun) in heaven.' We wished to seize him, we were venturesome and tried; this is the cause of our sighs, moans, weeping.

203   "I, the eldest, earnestly begged the man from the younger, my next brother asked for his horse as a keepsake, this one only asked leave to conquer him. We granted him this as his

due. As we went towards him he came forward unchanged, calmly and in beauty.

204   "Ruby mingled with crystal beautified the pale roses (of his cheeks). He withered up tender thoughts towards us, he explained nothing, neither did he let us go, he showed not any consideration for us at all, with his whip he ripened us who had spoken tartly to him.

205   "We gave him over to our youngest brother, we elders kept back, he seized upon him (and said): 'Stand!' Thus he spake to him with his tongue. He (Tariel) held no sword in his hand, so we moved away; he struck him on the head with his whip, we saw the blood flow indeed.

206   "With a stroke of his whip he cleft his head thus, like a corpse he became lifeless, like earth he was brought to earth; thus he humbled, levelled with the ground, him who had been audacious to him. Before our eyes he went away, bold, severe and haughty.

207   "He turned not back again; he went away quietly and without haste. Lo! there he rides--look! like the sun and moon." The weeping ones joylessly showed him far off to Avt'handil; there only appeared his black steed carrying along that sun.

208   Behold, it befell Avt'handil that his cheeks need no longer be covered with snow from tears, since he had not passed so much time abroad in vain; when a man attains the thing wished for, when he must find what he sought, then need he no longer remember past woes.

209   He said: "Brothers, I am a wanderer without a place. To seek that knight I have gone far from the home of my upbring-

ing. Now from you I have learned what it was by no means easy to discover. May God never again give you cause to grieve.

210   "As I meet my wish, my heart's desire, so even may God not let your brother suffer." He showed them his resting-place. "Go at your ease," said he, "give him repose in the shade, rest your weary selves."

211   Thus he spoke and went his way, he spurred on his horse, he flew like a hawks not hindered by the string, or like the moon meeting the sun, the sun of heavenly light, for this cause he has extinguished his burning fires.

212   He drew nearer, he bethought himself how he might contrive the meeting: "Senseless converse yet more enrages a madman. If a wise man would compass a difficult deed, he must not lose his presence of mind and tranquillity.

213   "Since yon man is so unreasoning and dazed that he suffers not any to speak with him or look on him, if I go up we shall meet only to slaughter each other, either he will kill me or I shall kill him; he will be still more hidden."

214   Avt'handil said: "Why should I suffer so many woes in vain? Whatever he is, it cannot be that he has no nests; let him go whithersoever he will, whatever walls encompass him there shall I seek him if my powers fail not."

215   Two days and nights they fared, one behind, one before, wearied by day and by night, eating no food; nowhere they paused, not one moment of time, from their eyes tears flowed, moistening the plains.

216   One day they travelled, and at eventide high rocks appeared. In the rocks were caves, in front a stream flowed

down, it was not possible to say how many rushes were at the water's edge, tall trees whose tops eye could not reach rose high against the rock.

217   The knight made for the cave; he passed the streams and rocks. Avt'handil alighted from his horse, he betook himself to the great trees, he climbed up to look, at the foot he tethered his horse, thence he watched; that knight went shedding tears.

218   When the knight, the panther-skin-clad, passed the woods, a maiden dressed in a black mantle came forth to the door of the cave, she wept aloud, her tears uniting with the sea; the knight dismounted, with his arms he embraced her neck.

218a   The knight said: "Sister Asmat'h, our bridges are fallen into the sea (i.e., we are lost); we shall never, timely, come upon the track of her for whom fires burn us." Thus he spoke and beat his hands upon his breast; the tears rained down. The maiden swooned, he embraced her; they wiped each other's tears of blood.

219   The forest became thicker from the tearing of their hair; each embraced the other, the youth the maid, and the maid the youth; they wailed, they lamented, the rocks re-echoed their voices; Avt'handil gazed in wonder on their behaviour.

220   That maid composed her soul, she endured the wound of her heart, she led the steed into the cave, she took off its trappings, she unbuckled the knight, she ungirded his armour. They went in. That day passed to its close.

221   Avt'handil was surprised. "How am I to know this story?" said he. Day dawned. The maiden came forth clad in the

same colour; she put the bridle on the black (horse), she furbished it (the bridle) with the end of her veil; she saddled it, she carries the armour quietly, with no clattering.

222   It was the custom, it seems, with that knight never to tarry longer. The maiden wept and beat her breast, she tore her thick hair; they embraced each other, he kissed her and mounted his horse. Asmat'h, already gloomy, became still more gloomy.

223   Avt'handil once more saw near him the face of that man, his moustaches had hardly grown, he was without a beard. "Is it not the sun of heaven?" said he. He smelt the smell of the aloe wafted on the wind. For him the killing of a lion was just as easy as for a lion to kill a goat.

224   He rode out the same road he had come in by the day before, he passed the rushes, he went beyond, far into the plain. Avt'handil gazed in wonder; secretly he was hidden in the tree. He said: "God has managed this matter exceeding well for me.

225   "How could God have done better for me than this? I will seize the maid, I will make her tell me the story of that knight; I shall also tell her all mine, I shall make her know the truth. I shall not smite the knight with the sword, nor shall I have to be pierced by him."

226   He came down and loosed his horse, which he had tied to the tree, he mounted and rode up; the door of the cave was open, the heart-shaken, tear-flooded maiden ran out thence; she thought the rose-faced, crystal-haloed one was come back.

227   She knew not the face, it was not like the face of that knight; swiftly she turned, with a cry she made for rock and

tree; the knight leaped from his horse, seized her like a partridge in a net; the rocks resounded with the maid's monotonous cry.

228   She yielded not to that knight; even the sight of him was hateful. Like a partridge under an eagle she fluttered hither and thither; she called on a certain Tariel for help, but he succoured her not. Avt'handil threw himself on his knees; he entreated her with his fingers.

229   He said: "Hush! what (ill) can I do thee? I am a man of Adam's race. I have seen those roses and violets grown pale. Tell me something of him. Who is the cypress-formed, the halo-faced? I shall do nought else to thee, be comforted, cry not thus loudly."

230   The weeping girl, like a suppliant for justice, said: "If thou be not mad, let me go; if thou art mad, return to reason. Now thou lightly askest me to tell thee a very hard matter; try not in vain, look not to me to tell his story."

231   Again she said: "O knight, what wilt thou, or what dost thou request of me? This thing cannot be even written with the pen. Once thou shalt say 'Tell me!' a hundred times I shall tell thee 'No!' As smiling is better than weeping, so I prefer mourning to song."

232   "Maiden, thou knowest not whence I come, what woes I have endured! For as long as I have sought tidings, from none have I heard them. I have found thee; however much my words may annoy thee, I cannot let thee go till thou tell me. Be not bashful with me."

233   The maiden said: "Why have I fallen in with thee? Who am I? or who art thou? The sun is not near me, this thou knewest, O hoarfrost, therefore thou thus annoyest me; long discourse is tedious, so I shall speak shortly to thee; on no account shall I tell thee aught, do whatsoever thou wilt."

234   Yet again he adjured her, he threw himself on his knees before her, but nought could he win from her; he wearied of entreaty, his indignation mounted to his face, blood flowed to his eyes, he arose, he drew her by the hair, he put a knife to her throat.

235   Thus he spoke: "How can I forgive thee so much ill-will? If I weep, shall the tear be in vain? It is better for thee to tell me, I shall trouble thee no more; if not, may God slay mine enemy as I slay thee!"

236   The maid replied: "Thou hast done exceeding ill to think of using force. If thou kill me not I shall not die; I am hale and alive. Why shall I tell thee anything until the time when I shall no longer see woes, and if thou kill me I shall have no head to converse with thee."

237   Again she said: "Oh, why didst thou find me! Who art thou that speakest with me? Who? I cannot be made to tell this story with living tongue. I will make thee kill me at mine own wish; like a despised letter, easily shalt thou tear me.

238   "Think not that death would be suffering to me, for it would free me from weeping; it is the drier-up of the ford of tears; the whole world seems to me as straw, even so do I weigh it; I know not who thou art, that I should tell thee trusty words?"

239 The knight said (to himself): "Thus shall I not make her speak, I must think of some other way; it is better to ponder the matter." He let her go, and sat down apart; he wept, he began to shed tears. He said to the maiden: "I have angered thee; now I know not, alas! how I shall survive."

240 The maiden sat morose, she is sulky, she is not yet sweetened. Avt'handil sits below weeping; no longer does he speak. In the rose-garden the pool of tears is dammed up. The maiden, too, weeps over yonder, her heart! softening towards him.

241 She pitied the weeping knight, therefore her hot tears flowed, but she sat, strange to the stranger, she spoke not. The knight perceived that her hasty thoughts towards him were calmed; with flowing tears he entreated her; he arose and bent his knee before her.

242 He said: "I know that now I am by no means worthy to hope from thee; I have angered thee; I remain a stranger to thee and thus lonely; yet even now I have hope for myself from thee, for it is said that sin shall be forgiven unto seven times.

243 "Though my beginning in service has pleased thee ill, it is fitting to pity the lover; understand thou this: from any other, whomsoever, I can have no aid, none is my strength. I yield thee my life for my heart's sake. What more can I do?"

244 When the maid heard from the knight of his love, with heart sobs she began to shed tears a hundredfold snore; again she raised her voice in wailing, she smiled not. God gave Avt'handil his wish, his heart's comfort.

245 He said (to himself): "These words have changed her colour; doubtless her tears flow faster (for that) she is mad for someone." He spoke once more: "O sister, a lover is pitied even by his foes; thou, too, knowest that he himself seeks death, he shuns it not.

246 "I am a lover, a madman to whom life is unbearable. My sun sent me to seek that knight. Even a cloud could not reach me where I have been on that quest. I have found thy heart; his to thee, thine to him.

247 "His face I have imprinted on my heart like a (holy) picture. For him mad, cut off, have I given up all my joy. One of two things do thou to me: make me a prisoner or set me free, give me life or slay me, adding grief to grief."

248 The maiden spoke to the knight a word more pleasant than her first: "What thou hast now thought of is much better; just now thou didst sow enmity in my heart, now thou hast found in me a friend more sisterly than a sister.

248a "Then, since thou hast thought of love as thine aid, henceforth it will not be that I shall not be thy servant; if I devote not myself to thee, I shall make thee mad, I shall make thee sad; I shall die for thy sake if I find not some means to help thee.

249 "Now, whatever I tell thee, if thou wilt be obedient to me therein thou shalt meet whatever thou seekest, thou shalt certainly not fail; if thou hearkenest not to me thou shalt not find, let thy tears flow as they will; discontent with the world shall come upon thee, thou shalt die, thou shalt be put to shame."

250 The knight replied: "This only resembles one thing (This is like a certain story): Two men were journeying somewhere along some road; the one who was behind saw the one in front fall into a well. He came up, called. down, weeps and cries 'Woe!'

251 "Thus he spoke: 'Comrade, stay there, wait for me; I go to bring ropes, I want to pull thee out.' The man who was beneath laughed, he marvelled greatly, he shouted up: 'Unless I wait, whither can I flee from thee, whither can I go?'

252 "Now, sister, thou holdest the rope about my neck; without thee I can undertake nothing; whatever thou doest to me rests with thee, thou art balm to the mad. Otherwise who would bind his sound head with hay-ropes? (? like a madman)."

253 The maid replied: "Thy discourse, O knight, pleases me. Doubtless thou art some good knight, worthy of the praise of the wise. Since thou hast heretofor suffered such griefs, hearken to what I tell thee, and thou I shalt find what thou seekest.

253a "Nowhere can news of that knight be found. If he himself tell thee not it will not be told; none other shouldst thou believe. If thou canst wait so long, wait until he come. Be calm; freeze not the rose, let it not be snowed up in tears.

254 "I will tell thee our names if thou wishest to know them: Tariel is the name of that distracted knight; I am called Asmat'h, whom the hot fire burns, sigh upon sigh, not once alone, but many times.

255 "More words about him than these I cannot tell thee. The elegant, slender-formed roams the plain. I eat, alas! alone

of the meat brought by him from the chase. He may come anon, I know not, or he may tarry a long time.

256   "I entreat thee to wait; go not elsewhere. When; he comes I shall plead with him; it may be I shall be able to do something. I shall make you known to each other I shall make him love thee. He himself will tell thee his story; thou shalt make thy beloved to rejoice."

257   The knight listened to the maid, he was obedient, be submitted. Thereupon they looked round, they heard a splash from the glen, they saw the moon (i.e., Tariel) come forth from the water, its rays beaming. They hastened back; they made no long tarrying there.

258   The maid said: "O knight, God give thee soon what thou desirest; but make thyself unseen, hide thyself inside. No human being is disobedient to that knight; perchance I may so contrive that the sight of thee anger him not."

259   The maiden hastily hid Avt'handil secretly in the cave. That knight alighted from his horse; his quiver and sword adorn him. They wept aloud, their tears flowing even to the sea. Avt'handil gazed from the window, himself hidden from view.

260   The bath of tears turned the crystal to the colour of jasper. A long time the knight and that black-robed maiden wept. She unbuckled his armour and took it in; she also led in the horse. They were silent; the black knife of jet (of their eyelashes) cut off the (flow of) tears.

261   Avt'handil watched from the window, a prisoner but now freed from his dungeon. The maid laid down the panther's skin, the knight sat upon it, he sighs with added grief; the jetty eyelashes are plaited by tears of blood.

262   That maiden betook herself to the lighting of a gentle fire with a steel; she thought he would eat meat roasted, (a bird cooked) whole; she gave it to him, he bit off a piece, it was difficult for him to eat, he had no appetite; he began to spit it out unchewed.

263   He lay down a little, he fell asleep, but only for a short time; he was afraid, he screamed aloud, he leaped up as if dazed, he cried and incessantly beat his breast with a stone and his head with a stick; the maiden sits apart looking at him, ands scratches her face.

264   "Why hast thou returned?" she asked. "Tell me what has happened to thee." He answered: "I came upon a certain king hunting; he had countless soldiers, heavy weighed their baggage, he hunted in that plain where beaters were scattered.

265   "It was melancholy for me to see men, the fire flamed up still more; I came not near to meet him; I pitied myself. I returned pale from them. I hid in the wood. I thought: 'If he pursues me no more, I shall go away at daybreak to-morrow.'"

266   The maiden's tears sprang forth an hundredfold, ten thousandfold more. She said: "Thou roamest alone with wild beasts in the deep forest, thou approachest no man for converse and entertainment; thou canst not help her thus; why dost thou waste thy days in vain?

267   "Thou hast fared over the whole face of the earth; how couldst thou not find one man in whom to take pleasure, and who could be with thee without making thee mad, though it would not lessen thy grief? If thou diest and she perishes, what doth this profit thee?"

268 He said: "O sister, this is like thy heart, but for this wound there is no balm upon earth. Who can find such a man as hath not yet come into the world? My joy is death, the severance of flesh and soul.

269 "Where, why should God cause a man to be born under the same planet as I, even if I desired his companionship and converse! Who could bear my woes, or even attempt it? Save thee, sister, I have no human being anywhere."

270 The maid said: "Be not angry with me, I fear and entreat thee; since God has appointed me thy vizier, I cannot conceal the best that I know in the matter: to go to extremes is of no use; thou hast overstepped the bounds."

271 The knight replied: "I know not what thou askest of me; tell me clearly. How can I create a man for my service without God? God needs me to be unhappy; what can I do? Of a truth I am become as a wild beast, to this pass have I brought myself."

272 The maid again spoke: "I have harassed thee with overmuch advice, but if I could find a man who would come to thee of his own freewill, who would stay near thee, who would rejoice thee by his acquaintance, wilt thou swear not to kill him nor do him any hurt?"

273 He answered: "If thou wilt show him to me, greatly shall I rejoice at sight of him. (I swear) by the love of her for whose sake I wander mad in the fields, I shall do nought unpleasing, I shall never cause any bitterness to him; I shall be pleasant and love him, and do all I can to be amiable."

274 The maid rose and went to bring that knight. "He is not angry," quoth she, to encourage him. She took him by the hand

and led him forth, like the full moon. When Tariel saw him he thought him like the sun.

275   Tariel met him. They were both fit to be ranked as suns, or as the moon in heaven, cloudless, spreading her rays on the plain beneath. Compared with them the aloe-tree was of no worth; they were like the seven planets; to what else shall I liken them?

276   They kissed each other, they were not bashful at being strangers; they opened the rose, from their lips their white teeth shone transparent. They embraced each other's neck, together they wept; their jacinth, which was worth rubies, they turned into amber.

277   The knight turned, he grasped Avt'handil's hand in his hand; they sat down together, and wept long with hot tears. Asmat'h calmed them with wonderful words: "Slay not yourselves; darken not the sun with your eclipse."

278   Tariel's rose was only covered with a light frost, not frozen. He said to (Avt'handil): "Haste, tell me thy secret. Who art thou? Whence art thou come? Where is thy home? As for me, death has forgotten me; even by it am I abandoned."

279   Avt'handil gave answer; beautiful are his words: "O lion and hero Tariel, thou who behavest gently, I am an Arabian, from the court of Arabia; I am consumed by love, unquenchable fire burns me.

280   "I love the daughter of my lord; her lusty-armed servants now view her as their king. Though thou knowest me

not, I have seen thee, if thou wilt call it to mind. Dost thou remember when thou slewest the strong-armed slaves?

281 "We saw thee roaming in the plain, and we came upon thee. My lord was angry with thee, and we quarrelled fiercely with thee. We called thee, thou earnest not, we pursued thee with soldiers; thou didst dye the fields crimson with the blood thou madest to flow.

282 "Thou didst cut the heads of all with a whip, without a sword. The king mounted, thou wert lost to us, we could . not cut off thy track; like a Kadj thou wert hidden, the slaves were terrified. This enraged us still more; we were completely stunned.

283 "The king became gloomy; you know that a monarch also has humours. They looked for thee, they sought thee everywhere, they wrote a letter of command. They could find none who had seen thee, neither young nor old. Now she has sent me, she to whom neither sun nor ether is to be compared.

284 "She said to me: 'Learn for me news of that vanished sun; then will I do that which thou desirest.' She told me that for three years the stream of tears was to flow without her; dost thou not marvel that I could bear the lack of the sight of her smile?

285 "Until now I have seen no man who saw thee. I saw robbers who spoke rudely with you; thou didst strike them with thy whip; one thou madest like a corpse; they whose brother was dying told me."

286 Tariel recalled their bygone fight. He said: "I remember the affair, though it happened long ago. I saw thee and thy

master together at the chase. I was weeping because I was thinking, alas! of my destroyer.

287   "What did you want with me? What did you desire? What had we in common? You, mighty, were sporting; we bathed our cheeks in tears. When you set the slaves upon me you dared to take me; now, methinks, instead of capturing me you bare away corpses.

288   "I looked round when I saw thy lord approach me, I had pity on his kingship; therefore I laid not my hands upon him, I fled before your eyes, I said nothing. My horse looks invisible: in what other way shall I describe him?

289   "Before a man can blink or wink the eye, I can flee that which I know to be unpleasant. Those Turks, on the other hand, I did not consider myself unjust to them; their overbearance and my prowess ill became them.

290   "Now thou art come with good intent, the sight of thy face rejoices me, O cypress-formed, sunlike-faced, brave as a hero; but thou hast toiled, thou art not untried by trouble; hard is it to find a man (like me) abandoned by God in heaven."

291   Avt'handil said: "How dost thou praise me, thou worthy of the praise of the tongue of the wise? What am I to deserve such praise from thee? Thou art the image of the one sun, the light of heaven above, for the misery of the flowing of so many tears cannot change thee.

292   "This day has made me forget her who darkened (by eclipse) my heart. I renounce her service; as for that, it shall be as thou wishest. Thus, though a jacinth is better, still a thousand

times more do I desire glass. I shall stay near thee till death; more than this I desire not."

293   Tariel said: "Thy heart now is warm to me. I am amazed. What service worthy of thine attachment have I done for thee? But such is the law: lover pities lover. Thou art parted from thy beloved; what can recompense thee for this

294   "Thou art come forth to seek me in thy lady's service. God has made thee find me. Thou also hast endeavoured manfully. But how shall I tell thee why I am thus wandering? If I speak of it, hot fire will burn me; I shall become a flame, a smoke."

295   Upon this Tariel was silent, burned and enflamed. He said to Asmat'h: "Since thou hast been near me all the time, how dost thou not know that this bruised bruise is incurable? Anew this weeping knight burns me; I am his debtor for tears."

296   He said to the knight: "Whatever man takes to himself a brother--ay, or a sister--must have no care of death and trouble for their sake. How should God save the one if He cause not the other to perish? Listen, and I shall tell thee (my story) whatever befall me."

297   He said to Asmat'h: "Come, sit down here, bring water with thee, sprinkle me when fainting, bathe my breast. If thou seest me a corpse, weep for me, sob ceaselessly, dig a grave for me, here let the earth cradle me."

298   He sat down unbuttoned to tell his tale; he laid bare his shoulders. Like the sun clad in clouds he sat; a long time he shed no ray. He could not open his lips to speak; he clenched them. Then he drew his breath, cried out, hot tears gushed forth.

299   He sobbed: "O beloved, mine own, lost to me! My hope and life, my thought, my soul, my heart! Who cut thee off I know not, O tree planted in Eden! How can the hot fire not consume thee, O heart a hundred times kindled!

THE TELLING OF HIS TALE BY TARIEL WHEN HE FIRST TOLD IT TO AVT'HANDIL

300   "Hearken, give heed to the hearing of my tidings, discourses and deeds such that I can scarce utter them! She who maddens me, for whom I am overpowered by melancholy, for whom flow streams of blood, from her I never expect comfort.

301   "Thou knowest, as every man knows, of India's seven kings. P'harsadan possessed six kingdoms; he was sovereign, generous, rich, bold, ruler over kings, in form a lion, in face a sun, a conqueror in battle, a leader of squadrons.

302   "My father sat on the seventh throne, king, terror of adversaries; Saridan was his name; not underhanded in the destruction of enemies, none dared offend him either openly or secretly; he hunted and made merry, careless of Fate.

303   "He hated solitude; it created hosts of cares in his heart. He said to himself: 'By conquest I have taken from foes the vicinage of the marches, I have chased them forth everywhere, I am seated in power, I have pomp and might; he said: 'I will go and enjoy the favour of King P'harsadan.'

304   "He resolved to despatch an envoy to P'harsadan; he sent a message saying: 'Thou hast the rule of all India; now I also wish to exhibit before you the power of my heart; may the glory of my faithful service remain!'

305 "P'harsadan, on hearing those tidings, made great jubilation. He sent a message: 'I, ruler of the lands, give thanks to God, because thou, a king like me enthroned in India, hast done this; now come, I shall honour thee like a brother and parent.'

306 "He bestowed on him one kingdom well worthy of a good knight (or vassal), also the dignity of Amirbar (Grand Marshal)--the Amirbar in India is also Amirspasalar (Commander-in-Chief); when he sat as king, he was not absolute: he only lacked the overlordship, in all else he was sovereign lord.

307 "The king considered my father equal with himself; he said: 'I wager that no man has an Amirbar like mine.' They waged war and they hunted; they forced their enemies to make peace. I am not like him, as no other man is like me.

308 "The king and the sunlike queen had no child, for this they were sad; a time came when the armies were seized with alarm thereat. Woe befall that cursed day when I was given (born) to the Amirbar! The king said: 'I shall rear him as my son; he is even of mine own race.'

309 "The king and queen took me as their child, they brought me up as lord of all the soldiers and countries, they gave me wise men to instruct me in the behaviour and deportment of kings. I grew up, I became like the sun to look upon, like a lion in mien.

310 "Asmat'h, tell me whatever thou knowest to be false in my story! When I was five years old I was like an opened rosebud; to me it appeared no labour to slay a lion--it was like a sparrow. P'harsadan cared not that he had no son.

311   "Asmat'h, thou art witness of my pallor! I was fairer in beauty than the sun, as the hour of dawn than darkness. Those who saw me said: 'He is like a nursling of Eden.' My person now is but a shadow of what it was then.

312   "I was five years old when the queen became with child." When he had said this the youth sighed, and weeping said: "She bare a daughter." He was like to faint; Asmat'h sprinkled water on his breast. He said: "She for whom these flames now burn me was like the sun even then.

313   "The tongue with which I now speak cannot utter the praise of her. P'harsadan sat down to announce the good news with jubilation and pomp. From everywhere came kings bringing many kinds of gifts. They gave away treasure; they filled the soldiers with presents.

314   "The guests at the birth festivities separated. They began to rear me and the maiden; even then she was like the sun's rays augmented threefold; the king and queen loved us and looked on us alike. Now shall I utter the name of her for whom my heart is consumed by flame."

315   The knight swooned when he sought to mention her name. Avt'handil also wept; his fire made his heart like soot. The maiden revived (Tariel); she sprinkled water on his breast. He said: "Hearken! but this truly is the day of my death.

316   "That maiden was called by the name Nestan-Daredjan. When she was seven years old she was a gentle and wise maid, moonlike, not equalled by the sun in beauty; from her how can the heart bear separation (even if it were) adamant or forged (steel)?

317 "So she grew up, (and) I was able to go to battle. Since the king looked upon the maid as the heir to the kingship, he gave me back into the hands of my father. When I was of that age I played at ball, I sported in the lists, I killed a lion like a cat.

318 "The king built a house, and in it a dwelling for the maid; for stone he used bezoar, cut jacinths and rubies; in front was a little garden and a fountain of rose-water for bathing; there abode she for whose sake a furnace of flame consumes me.

319 "Day and night cut aloes poured forth their incense from censers. Sometimes she sits in the tower; sometimes she descends to the garden when it is shaded. Davar was the king's sister, a widow who had been wedded in Kadjet'hi; to her the king gave his child to be taught wisdom.

320 "The palace was curtained with cloth of gold and costly brocades; none of us saw her (how) she became crystal and rose of face; Asmat'h and two slaves she had, they played backgammon. There her shape was formed; she grew up like (? a tree) in Gabaon.

321 "I was fifteen years old. The king brought me up as a son; by day I was before him, (and) he did not even give me leave to sleep (at home). In power a lion, to the eye a sun, in form I was like one reared in Eden; they lauded the feats done by me in archery and in the lists.

322 "The arrow I shot slew beasts and game; returned from the plain, I played at ball in the square; then I went home, I used to make a feast, accustomed continually to rejoice. Now Fate has sundered me from the crystal-ruby-faced!

323 "My father died; the day of his death was come. This event brought to nought all sign of merriment for P'harsadan; it rejoiced those whom terror of fear of him as a foe exhausted; the loyal began to mourn and recall the reproaches of their enemies.

324 "I sat in the dark (mourning) for a year, annihilated by Fate; by day and by night I groaned, calmed by none; then courtiers came to conduct me, they told me the king's command; he said: 'Son Tariel, wear mourning no longer!

325 "'We are even more grieved (than thou) at the loss of our peer.' He gave a hundred treasures, and commanded that I should put off my black (raiment). He gave me all the lordship that had belonged to (my father). 'Thou shalt be Amirbar; fulfil the duties of thy father.'

326 "I was inflamed; inextinguishable furnaces burned me for my father's sake. The courtiers standing before me led me out from the dark; the monarchs of India made jubilation at my coming forth; they met me afar off, they kissed me with regard like parents.

327 "They seated me near their thrones, they honoured me like their son, they both told me gently of my obligation of duty; I was recalcitrant, and to behave as he (my father) had done seemed a horror to me. They would take no denial; I submitted, and bent to them (did homage) as Amirbar."

TARIEL TELLS THE TALE OF HIS FALLING IN LOVE WHEN HE FIRST FELL IN LOVE

328   When he had wept for some time he again began to tell his tale: "One day the king and I had come home from the chase, and he said: 'Let us see my daughter!' He took me by the hand. . . . Does it not surprise thee that I live when I remember that time?

329   "I saw the garden fairer indeed than all places of delight: the voice of birds was heard, sweeter than a siren's, there were many fountains of rose-water for baths, over the door were hung curtains of cloth of gold.

330   "The king ordered me to take some wood-partridges and carry them to the maiden. I took them and went to burn myself at a flame. Then I began to pay the debt of Fate. It needs a lance of adamant to pierce a heart of rock.

331   "I knew he wished none to see his sunlike one; I stood outside, and the king went in through the curtain of the door; I could see nothing, I only heard the sound of talk; he commanded Asmat'h to take the partridges from the Amirbar.

332   "Asmat'h drew aside the curtain; I stood outside the curtain. I saw the maiden (Nestan); a lance pierced my mind and heart. (Asmat'h) came, I gave her the partridges, she took them from me who was burned with fire. Ah me! since then in eternal furnace I burn!"

333   Now failed that light which despised even the sun; he could tell no more, he fainted, groaning bitterly. The knight (Avt'handil) and Asmat'h wept; the vicinage reechoed their voices. They said gloomily: "The arms that brought to nought heroes are become useless, alas!"

334   Asmat'h sprinkled water (upon him), Taria came back to consciousness; for a long time he could not speak, melancholy bound and overcame his heart; he sat down and moaned bitterly, his tears were mingled with the earth; he said: "Woe is me! what a great agitation is her memory to me!

335   "Trusters in Fortune have their pick of her gifts, they are lucky, but at last are not spared her treachery; I praise the prudence of those sages who oppose her. Hearken to my tidings if life remain in me!

336   "They took in the partridges; I could make no way for myself. I fell, I fainted, force was fled from mine arms and shoulder. When I came back to life I heard the voice of weeping and woe; the household surrounded me like one who is embarking on a ship.

337   "I lay in a fair bed in a great chamber; the king and queen wept over me with undrying tears, they scratched their faces with their hands, tearing their cheeks; mullahs sat round, they called my sickness bewitchment of Beelzebub.

338   "When the king saw mine eyes open he embraced my neck; he said to me with tears: 'My son, my son, dost thou indeed live? Speak one word!' I could give no answer; like a madman I was greatly affrighted. Again I fell into a faint; blood rushed into my heart.

339   "All the muqris and mullahs watched round me, in their hands they held the Koran, all of them read; they thought I was struck by the Adversary of mankind, I know not of what they raved. For three days I was lifeless; inextinguishable fires burned me.

340   "The doctors also marvelled, saying: 'What manner of sickness is this? Nothing medicable afflicts him; some melancholy has laid hold of him.' Sometimes I leaped up like a madman, I uttered idle words. The queen poured forth tears enough to make a sea.

341   "For three days was I in the palace neither alive nor dead; then understanding came back to me, I remembered what had befallen me; I said: 'Alas! in what a plight am I, despairing of life!' I prayed the Creator for patience; I ventured to make a discourse of entreaty.

342   "I said: 'O God! abandon me not, hearken to my supplication, give me strength to endure that I may rise a little; to stay here will reveal my secret; let me reach home!' He did so and I mended; I steeled my wounded heart.

343   "I sat up. . . . Many men were come from the king, they carried back the good news: 'He sits up!' The queen ran in, the king came running bareheaded, he knew not what he did, he glorified God (while) all others were silent.

344   "They sat down on either side of me; I sipped some soup. I said: 'My lord, now my heart is stronger. I long to mount a horse, to see river and field.' They brought me a horse, I mounted, the king went with me.

345 "We went forth; we passed by the moedan (public square) and the river-bank. I went home, I sent back the king, who accompanied me to the threshold of the house. I went in; I felt worse, woe was added to woe; I said to myself: 'I would die! what more can Fate do to me!' (or, what more than this can my ill luck merit!)

346 "The bath of tears changed the crystal (of my face) to saffron colour; ten thousand knives cut my heart still more. The doorkeeper of the bedchamber entered, he called out the steward; I said to myself: 'What news does he know, either this one or that one?'

347 "'It is Asmat'h's slave.' 'What knows she (? he)?' I called, 'Ask!' (? invite him in). He came in. He gave me a love-letter. I read it. I was surprised how I had made another's heart burn with heat; I had no suspicion of her, my heart burned with melancholy for this.

348 "I was surprised wherefore I was loved, or how she (Asmat'h) dared to declare it to me. (But, thought I) disobedience avails not, she will denounce me for silence, she will lose hope of me, then will she reproach me. I wrote what answer was fitting to enamourment.

349 "Days passed, and heart burned me still more with flame. I no longer watched the soldiers going to the plain to sport. I could not go to court. Many physicians began to come. Then I began to pay the joys and debts of the world.

350 "They (the physicians) could do nothing for me; the twilight of darkness fell upon my heart. No one else discovered the burning of the hot fire (of love). They blamed my blood. The king ordered them to bleed my arm; I let it be done, so as to hide my sufferings, to let none suspect.

351   "After my arm was bled I lay melancholy alone in my bed. My slave came in; I glanced at him to ask what he wanted. 'It is Asmat'h's slave,' said he. I told him to bring him in. I thought in my heart: 'What has she found in me, or who is she?'

352   "The slave gave me a letter; I read it slowly.' I learned from the letter that she wished to come quickly to me. I wrote in reply: 'It is time. Thou art right to be surprised. Thou shalt come if thou wantest me; suspect me not of tardiness in coming.'

353   "I said to my heart: 'Why do such lances make thee thus melancholy? I am Amirbar, king; all the Indians are subject to me. If it come to their knowledge they will make the deed a thousand times more weighty; if they find it out they will not let me travel in their regions.'

354   "A man came from the king saying he wished to hear the news. I ordered him in; (the king) commanded me to be bled. I said: 'My arm has been bled; I have begun to mend. I come to your presence; it is fitting for me to rejoice the more for this again.'

355   "I went to court. The king said: 'Now, do this no more!' He seated me quiverless on a horse; he girded not my loins (with weapons). He mounted, he let fly the falcons, the partridges shrank with fear, the archers formed in ranks said: 'Bravo! Bravo!'

356   "We made a feast at home that day for those who had been in the plain; the singers and minstrels were not dumb; the king gave away many precious stones praised as unique; none of those present were left dissatisfied that day.

357   "I strove, (but) could not keep myself from melancholy; I thought on her, the fire burned into a larger flame in my heart. I took my comrades with me, I sat down; they called me an aloe-tree; I drank and feasted to hide my misery and grief.

358   "My treasurer of the household whispered in mine ear: 'A certain woman asks if she can see the Amirbar; veils cover her face, (which is) worthy of the praise of the wise.' I replied: 'Take her to my chamber; she is invited by me.'

359   "I rose up; those sitting at the banquet prepared to depart. 'By your leave!' said I, 'do not rise; I shall not tarry long.' I went forth and entered the chamber, a slave stood on guard at the door, I nerved my heart to suffer shame.

360   "I halted at the door; the woman came forward to meet me and did me homage. She said to me: 'Blessed is he whoever is worthy to come before thee!' I marvelled; whoever saluted a lover? I thought: 'She knows not how to make love; even if she knew she sits quiet.'

361   "She said to me: 'This day makes my heart to burn with a flame of shame. Thou thinkest I came hither to thee for that (purpose), but I find cause for hope in the fact that I have not waited long for thee; since I am worthy of this (attention) I cannot say that God's mercy has failed me.'

362   "She rose; she said to me: 'I am commanded to inquire after thee by one who is bashful of thee. Suspect me not of what has been said by command of my mistress; such great boldness is in order to please her heart. This letter will tell thee for whom I speak.'

FIRST LETTER WRITTEN BY NESTAN-DAREDJAN TO HER LOVER

363 '"I saw the letter; it was from her for whom fire consumes my heart. The sunbeam wrote: 'O lion! let not thy wound appear. I am thine. Die not, but I hate vain fainting. Now Asmat'h tells thee all that is spoken by me.

364 "'Pitiful fainting and dying, what love dost thou think this! It is better to exhibit to the beloved deeds of heroism. All dwellers in Khatavet'hi are our tributaries; now their ill-will towards us cannot be borne by us.

365 "'I was desirous to wed thee even before, but hitherto I have not found opportunity to speak. The other day I saw thee deprived of reason sitting in the litter; then I heard all that had befallen thee.

366 "'I will tell thee truth; hearken to this that I say to thee: Go, do battle with the Khatavians, exhibit thyself to me in a goodly manner, this is better for thee. Weep idly no more; why moisten more the rose! What more can the sun do to thee! Behold, I have turned thy darkness to dawn.'

FIRST LETTER WRITTEN BY TARIEL TO HIS BELOVED

367 '"With mine eyes I gazed upon the letter written by her. I wrote in answer: 'O moon, how indeed can the sun surpass thee! May God not give me that which is not like thee! I feel as in a dream; I cannot believe in my survival.'

368 "I said to Asmat'h: 'I cannot devise more answer than this. Say thus to her: O sun! since thou art arisen as a light for me, behold thou hast quickened me (who was) dead; I shall faint no more henceforth, whatever be the service I am a liar if I shun it.'

369 "Asmat'h said to me: 'She told me: Let us do thus, thus were it better: Whoever sees thee will discover nothing of my discourse with him; he will come to see me as if he were making love to thee. She entreated me to tell the Amirbar so to behave.'

370 "This counsel pleased me, the wisdom of the heart of her whom even the sun took care not to gaze on; she had given to me to hear the refined d conversation of her in whose rays daylight was like darkness.

371 "I gave Asmat'h choice jewels with a golden cup. She said to me: 'No. I do not want them; I have these to satiety.' She took one ring weighing a drachmas; 'this is enough for a token; I am full of other bracelets.'

372 "The maid arose and went forth. The spears spared my heart, joy lightened my darkness, the fire which had burned me was extinguished. I went in and sat down at the banquet where my comrades were drinking; joyful, I distributed gifts, the jubilation increased.

TARIEL WRITES A LETTER AND SENDS A MAN TO THE KHATAVIANS

373 "'I sent a man to Khatavet'hi and a letter from me; I wrote: 'The king of the Indians is of a truth powerful from God; every hungry soul of those faithful to him is sated; whosoever is disobedient will have himself to blame (for any ill that may befall him).

374 "'Brother and lord, by you we will not be embittered. When you see this command wend hither; if you come not we shall come; we will not steal upon you. It is better you should come to us, spill not your own blood.'

375 "I sent the man, I gave my heart up yet more to rejoicing, I made merry at court; the fire unbearable in its burning was extinguished. Then the world, Fate, gave me lavishly what I desired; now I am mad, so that I annoy even the wild beats if I approach them.

376 "At first the plan of roaming, then reason soothed me. I feasted with my comrades, but the greatness of desires hindered me from joy; sometimes they filled me with melancholy, I uttered curses against Fate.

377 "One day, on my return from the king's palace, I came to my chamber. I sat down and thought of her, slumber fell not upon mine eyes, I had the letter of hope, therefore was I merry. The doorkeeper called the slave; he said it was a secret matter.

378 "'It is Asmat'h's slave,' quoth he. I ordered him to be brought into the chamber. She wrote to me that she whose knife had pierced my heart commanded me to come. Joy lightened my darkness; she loosened my chains. I went, I took the slave, I spoke not at all with him.

379 "I entered the garden; I met none to speak to me (?). The maid met me merry, smiling; she said: 'I have bravely extracted the thorn from thy heart, it is no longer therein; come and see thy rose unfaded, unwithered.'

380 "The maid with an effort raised the heavy curtain, there stood a canopy adorned with choice rubies where sat she whose face was like the sun flashing, her eyes, like inky lakes, looked beautifully at me.

381 "A long time I stood, and she spoke no word to me whom she yearned for; she only looked at me sweetly as at an intimate. She called Asmat'h, they spoke together; the maid came and whispered in my ear: 'Now go; she cannot say anything to thee.' Again the flame reduced me to soot.

382 "Asmat'h led me forth, I went out, I passed the curtain. I said: 'O Fate, who not long ago didst heal my heart, thou gayest me hope then; why hast thou scattered my joy? My heart is still more devastated again by the pain of parting.'

383 "Asmat'h promised me comfort. We walked through the garden; she said to me: 'Let not the brand be thus seen upon thy heart because of thy going; shut the terrace of sorrows, open the door of joy. She is ashamed to speak; therefore she behaves with dignity.

384 "I said: 'O sister, I think this heart-balm is from thee. I adjure thee, part me not from life, extinguish this flame with tidings, cut me not off from letters, send them ceaselessly; if thou learnest something for me I think thou wilt not keep it hidden from me.'

385 "I mounted (my horse), I went thence, a stream flowed from the channel of tears. I went to bed; maddened, I had no power to sleep. I, the crystal and ruby, became bluest indigo. I preferred night; I wished not for the dawn of day.

386 "Denizens of Khatavet'hi came--it was time for them to come--they brought a proud and insolent message: 'We are no cowards, neither are our keeps unfortified. Who is your monarch? What lord is he over me?'

THE LETTER WRITTEN BY THE KING OF THE KHATAVIANS IN ANSWER TO TARIEL

387   "He wrote: 'I, Ramaz the king, write a letter to thee Tariel. I marvelled at what was written in the letter penned by thee. How dost thou summon thither me who am lord over many peoples! I will look at no other letter which comes from thee.'

388   "I commanded the soldiers to be summoned; I sent forth the Lord of the Marches. They gathered together the armies of India more numerous than the stars, from near and far all hastened towards me, plain, rock and waste were altogether filled with soldiers.

389   "They came swiftly; they made no tarrying at home. I held a review; the good order of the troops pleased me--their alertness and valour, beautifully drawn up in squadrons, the speed of their steeds, their Khvarazmian armour.

390   "I raised the royal standard with flag of red and black. I commanded the countless troops to set out in the morning. I myself wept, I mourned exceedingly my evil fate: 'If I see not the sun I know not how I can ever depart.'

391   "I went in. The sadness of my pensive heart was increased unto me; burning tears welled forth from mine eyes like a pool. 'My luckless fate,' said I, 'has never yet ruled. Why did my hand lay hold of the rose since thus it could not cull it!'

392   A slave entered; a wondrous thing befell me. He gave to me in my exceeding grief a letter from Asmat'h; she wrote: 'Thy sun for whom thou longest calls thee. Come! 'Tis better than to weep there and moan at the deed of Fate.'

393   "So much did I rejoice as was fitting. It was twilight, I went forth, I entered the garden gate; where Asmat'h had first met me, there she appeared standing; she said with a smile: 'Enter; the moon awaits thee, the lion.'

394   "I entered the house reared beautiful with terrace upon terrace, the moon shone forth surrounded with rays of light at the full; within the curtain she sat clad in green raiment, majestic and rare, wondrous of face and form.

395   "I went in and stood on the edge of the carpet; the fire in me began to be quenched, the darkness of my heart was lightened, joy rose up like a column. She rested upon a cushion--she was far fairer than the sun's rays--she hid her face from me, she looked up a moment to see me.

396   "She commanded: 'Asmat'h, beg the Amirbar to be seated!' She placed a cushion opposite her to be praised as the sun; I sat down, I gave up to joy my heart abused by Fate. I marvel that my life stays in me (while) I speak the words she said.

397   "She said to me: 'Last time thou wert ill pleased that thou wert sent away without being spoken to. I, at parting, as the sun withered thee up like a flower of the field. Thou wert doomed to shed tears from the narcissus-pool; but for me, bashfulness and reserve are necessary towards the Amirbar.

398   "'Though great modesty befits a woman towards a man, yet is it much worse not to speak and to hide woes; if I smile

outwardly I felt inwardly secret grief; last time I sent the maid I gave her a true message.

399   "'What we two have hitherto known of each other, even now know me thine by these firm promises; I assure thee of this by great vows and oaths; if I deceive thee may God make me earth, may I not sit in the nine heavens!

400   "'Go, attack the Khatavians, fight and make raids; may God grant that thou be victorious, come (back) to me of good cheer. But what shall I do until it falls to my lot to look upon thee again! Give me thy heart undivided; take mine for thyself.'

401   "'Now, that of which thou hast deemed me worthy no human being deserves; this grace is unexpected, from God this does not surprise me; thy rays have flooded my dark heart and made it translucent; thine shall I be till the earth cover my face.'

402   "Upon the book of oaths I swore and she swore to me; thus she confirmed her love to me: 'If any save thee give pleasure to my heart may God slay me, henceforth thus will I speak to myself, thus will I train myself.'

403   "I stayed some time before her, we spoke sweet words, we ate some pleasant fruit, talking one to the other; then weeping and shedding tears I rose to depart, the beauties of her rays were spread like light in my heart.

404   "It irked me to go far from her crystal and ruby and glass. The world was renewed to me, I had an abundance of joy; that light appearing in ether as sun seemed to be mine; now I am surprised that being separated from her I have (still) a heart like a steep rock.

405 "In the morning I mounted, I commanded the trumpet and bugle to be sounded; I cannot tell thee of all the armies nor of their readiness to mount; I, a lion, set forth for Khataet'hi, none can accuse me of cowardice; the soldiers marched without a road, they followed no track (?).

406 "I crossed the boundaries of India, I went on a considerable time; a man met me from Ramaz, the khan over Khataet'hi; he repeated to me a message conciliatory to the heart: 'Your Indian goats are able to eat even our wolves.'

407 "He presented me with astounding treasures as a gift from Ramaz; he said: 'He entreats thee, destroy us; not, it is not a thing thou shouldst do; put us on our oath, thereby are our necks bound with twigs, without devastation we shall deliver over to thee ourselves, our children and possessions.

408 "'Forgive us in that we have sinned against thee, we ourselves repent; by God, if thou wouldst have mercy on us, bring not thine armies hither, destroy not our land, let not the heavens fall upon us in wrath; we give thee our castles and cities, let a few knights come with thee.'

409 "I placed my viziers at my side, we discussed and counselled; they said: 'Thou art young, therefore we sages venture to say to thee, alas! they are exceeding treacherous; we have seen it indeed once already; may they not slay thee treacherously, may they not bring on us, woe?

410 "'We counsel thus: Let us go forth with brave heroes only, let the soldiers follow close behind us, let them be apprised of the tidings by a man; if they be true-hearted, trust them, make them swear by God and heaven; if they submit not to thee, pour forth thy wrath and moreover the wrath of heaven upon them.'

411   "This advice counselled by the viziers pleased me: I returned a message: 'O king Ramaz, I know thy decision; life is better than death to thee. We put not our trust in stone walls. I will leave the soldiers, I will come with a few, towards thee will I march.'

412   "I took with me three hundred of the soldiers, good brave knights, I went forth and left all the army; I said: Wherever I shall go, march over the same fields, follow me closely, help me, I shall call you if I need help.'

413   "I travelled three days; another man of the same khan met me, again he presented me with many beautiful robes; he (on behalf of the khan) said: 'I wish thee to be near me, proud and mighty one; when I meet thee then shalt thou know (many) such gifts.'

414   "Yet more he said: 'What I have told thee is true. I myself come forward to meet thee, I haste to see thee.' (I said, says Tariel): 'Tell (the Khan): Certainly, by God, I shall do your commandment, tenderly shall we meet each other, we shall be like father and son.'

415   "Departed thence I alighted on the bounds of a certain deep forest; again messengers came, they were not shy to salute me, they brought fair steeds as a present to me, they said: 'Of a truth kings would desire to see thee.'

416   "They said to me: 'The king informs thee: I myself also come towards thee; having left my house, early to-morrow I shall meet thee.' I kept the messengers, I put up a felt tent, with no patrols; I received them very amiably, they lay down together like groomsmen.

417 "No good deed done to a man can pass away thus (i.e., unrewarded). A certain man (one of the messengers of the khan) returned; he came to me and said secretly: I owe you a great debt hard for me to pay; I cannot for sake and forget thee.

418 "'I was to some extent (or, for a short time) brought up by your father. I heard the treachery planned for you; I ran to let you know of it. It would grieve me to see thy; elegant-formed, the rose-faced, a corpse. I will tell thee all; hearken to me, be calm.

419 "'That thou be not vainly deceived, these men are traitors to thee; in one place are hidden for thee one hundred thousand troops, then in another place are thirty thousand; that is why they call upon thee to hasten; if thou take not measures at once mischance will come upon thee.

420 "'The king will come a little way to meet thee whose admirers can never cease; secretly they will be clad in armour; thou trusting them while they cajole thee the soldiers will make smoke, on all sides they will surround, as it is when ten thousands strike one so must they overwhelm thee.'

421 "I spoke pleasantly to the man and gave him thanks: 'If I am not slain I shall repay thee for this according to thy desires. Now let not thy comrades suspect; go, be with them. If I forget thee may I be surely lost.'

422 "I told no human being; I kept it secret like gossip. What is to be will be; all advice is equal. But I sent men towards the armies though the way was long; I gave the message: 'Come quickly, hasten over mountain and hill.'

423 "In the morning I gave a sweet message to the messengers. They were to tell King Ramaz: 'I am coming to meet thee; come, I also come soon.' Another half-day I journeyed on; I took no heed of trouble; there is a providence, if I am to be killed to-day where below can I hide myself!

424 "I mounted a certain peak; I saw dust in the plain. I said to myself: 'King Ramaz is coming; though he has spread a net for me, my sharp sword, my straight lance, will pierce their flesh.' Then I spoke to my troops; I set forth a great plan.

425 "I said: 'Brothers, these men are traitors to us; why should the power of your arms be weakened on that account? Those who die for their kings, upwards their spirits fly! Now let us engage the Khatavians. Why should we gird on the sword in vain!'

426 "Proudly, with fierce words, I commanded them to don armour; we clad ourselves for fight in chain coats of mail with shoulder-pieces; I formed squadrons, I set out, I went in great haste; that day my sword cut in pieces mine adversary.

427 "We approached. They perceived that our forms were clad in armour. A man came with a message from the king; he said: 'We look upon your treachery as untimely, now we see your armour, this causes us displeasure.'

428 "I sent back a message: 'I too know what thou hast contrived for me; you have made certain plans, but they will not come to pass; give orders, come and fight me as is the law and custom, I have taken my sword in my hand to slay you.'

429 "When the messenger came, why did they send yet another? They made smoke for the soldiers, they made plain

what was hid, they came forth from ambush, they advanced from both sides, they formed into many ranks, though, thank God, they could not harm me.

430 "I took a lance, I applied my hand to helming myself, I was eager for the fray to break them, I extended a stadium's length, I made ranks and advanced in a long line. They drew up innumerable cohorts, they stood calm and undisturbed.

431 "When I came near they looked at me: 'He is a madman,' said they. I, strong-armed, made my way thither where the main body of the army stood; I pierced a man with my lance, his horse I overturned, they both departed from the sun (i.e., life), the lance broke, my hand seized (the sword); I praise, O sword, him who whetted thee.

432 "I swooped in like a falcon among a covey of grey partridges, I threw man upon man, I made a hill of men and horses; the man thrown down by me spins like a dragon-fly; I completely destroyed at one onslaught the two front squadrons.

433 "Crowding they surrounded me, about me was a great fight; when once I struck none could stand, I made blood spurt forth as from a fountain, he whom I clove-hung on his horse like a saddle-bag, wherever I was they fled from me, they were wary of me.

434 "At the evening hour their watchman cried forth from the summit: 'Stand no longer, let us go, heaven looks again on us in wrath, a terrible dust is coming, wee should beware of this, let not their countless tens of thousands of soldiers completely destroy us.'

435 "My soldiers whom I had not brought with me, when they heard of it, set out, they travelled day and night without stopping, neither plain nor mountain could contain them; they appeared, they beat the kettledrum, the trumpet sounded aloud.

436 "(The enemy) saw them, they started to flee, we raised a shout, we pursued over the fields in which we had fought our battle. I unhorsed King Ramaz; we found each other with swords. We captured all his armies; we slew them not.

437 "Those who fled were overtaken by the rearguard, they began to seize them, to throw down the terrified, the vanquished; they (Tariel's troops) had a reward for their sleeplessness and night-watching; the prisoners, even those that were unwounded, ceased not to wail like sick men.

438 "We dismounted to rest on the battle-field. I had wounded my arm with the sword; it seemed to me a mere scratch. My armies came to see me and praise me, they could not speak, they knew not how to express their admiration.

439 "The glories which they thrust upon me were sufficient for one man; some blessed me from afar, some tried to kiss me; those nobles who had trained me wept over me, they saw that which had been cut by my sword, they marvelled exceedingly.

440 "I sent soldiers everywhere to bring in booty; they came together loaded. I was proud of myself; I had dyed the plain with the blood of those who had sought to slay me. I did not fight at the gate of the cities; I seized them without a battle.

441 "I said to Ramaz: 'I have learned of thy treacherous deed; now that thou art captured justify thyself; fortify not

strongholds, count them all into thy hand; else, why should I overlook thy guilt towards me?'

442 "Ramaz said to me: 'I have no more power left; give me one of my magnates over whom I may have lordship; I will send him to the guardians of the castles; let me speak with them; I will give all into thine hands, since I make it thy property.'

443 "I gave him a magnate, I sent knights with him, I caused all the governors of fortresses to be brought before me, they gave the strongholds into my hands; thus I made them repent the war. With what can I compare the abundance of treasure!

444 "Then I went in to travel through and inspect Khataet'hi; publicly they presented me with the keys of the treasuries; I settled the country, I commanded: 'Be ye without fear, the sun shall not burn you, be assured you will be left unburned.'

445 "I examined the treasuries one by one from end to end; I should be weary if I mentioned all the wondrous kinds of treasures. I saw together a marvellous mantle and veil; if thou didst see it thou wouldst desire to know its name.

446 "I could not learn what (stuff) it was nor what kind of work; everyone to whom. I showed it marvelled. (and) said it was a divine miracle; neither was the basis of the tissue like that of brocade nor carpet, its strength was as if it had been wrought like iron--I might say tempered in, fire.

447 "I put them aside as a present for her whose ray enlightened me; I chose as a gift for the king whatever was best: a thousand mules and camels, all strong-limbed, I sent them loaded; he also learned the good news.

LETTER OF TARIEL TO THE KING OF THE INDIANS WHEN HE TRIUMPHED OVER THE KHATAVIANS

448 "I wrote a letter: 'O king, great is your good fortune! The Khatavians plotted treachery to me, though it fell on them to their hurt; therefore am I tardy in telling you my true tidings. I have captured the king; I come to thee with spoil and prisoners.'

449 "When I had put everything in order I set out from Khataet'hi. I took the treasures, I despoiled the kingdom, I could not get enough camels, I loaded bullocks with the burdens; I had found glory and honour, for what I had desired that had I obtained.

450 "I led away captive the King of Khataet'hi. I came to India, sweet was the meeting with my foster-father; what eulogy he uttered to me cannot be repeated, for me to tell it were unseemly; he undid mine arm, he bound it with a soft bandage.

451 "Fair tents stood pitched in the public square (maidan) for him who desired to speak with and gaze upon me. That day he (the king) who rested there spread a banquet, he caressed me, sitting near me he gazed at me.

452 "That night we spent in feasting; pleasantly we made merry there. In the morning we left the maidan; we entered the city. The king commanded: 'Call the soldiers, assemble them, show me this day the Khatavians, lead in the prisoners.'

453 "I led in King Ramaz captive before him. The king looked sweetly on him as on a son whom he had cradled. I made the deceitful and treacherous one seem deserving, and this is the excess of heroism in a brave man.

454 "He entertained the King of the Khatavians, he caressed him, he conversed with him for a long time in a fitting manner; at dawn I was called, he spoke to me a compassionate word: 'Shall I pardon the Khatavian, my former enemy?'

455 "I ventured to reply: 'Since God forgives the sinner, be you also merciful to him whose might is brought to nought.' He said to Ramaz: 'Know that I send thee hence forgiven, but show not thyself before me again disgraced.'

456 "He levied a tribute of a hundred times a hundred drachmas, also a thousand khatauris, also brocades and satins; then he clad him and all his courtiers, and sent them away with pardon in place of wrath.

457 "The Khatavian thanked him, bent, paid lowly homage; he said: 'By God, I repent my treachery towards you; if ever I sin against you again then kill me.' He departed and took all his (folk) with him.

458 "A man of the king's came; it was dawn, and the morning grey was past; he brought a message: 'For three months have I been separated from thee, I have eaten no game killed by arrow in the field; if thou be not tired come forth, though it be time to be tired.'

459 "I apparelled myself, I went into the hall of audience; a pack of harriers met me, all the space round the hall was full of

falcons. The king sat decked in beauty like the sun; he rejoiced at the coming of me, the lovely and fair.

460 "He said secretly to his wife, but unknown to me To gaze on Tariel returned from war is desirable, he brings light to the onlooker's heart, however dark it may be; whatever I ask thee to do, do it without delay.

461 "'Now, without (consulting) thee I have thought of a plan; but thou too must know it: Since the maid is to be king, and has been so nominated by us ourselves, whoever shall see her, now let him who is like a tree in Eden see her--lo! even to-day; seat her by thy side, both of you meet us in the palace, I shall come joyful.'

462 "We hunted over plain, mountain-foot and hill; there was a multitude of hounds, falcons and hawks. We returned early without having gone a stage from the long road. They did not play at ball; they broke up two games.

463 "Folk eager to gaze on me filled the city, the bazaar and the roofs; tasselled robes adorned me who had finished the war; I was fair as a pale-hued rose bathed in tears, he who looked on me fainted; true is this, and no falsehood.

464 "The veils I had found in the city of the Khatavians I bound round me, they became me, I maddened (still more) the heart of the mad. The king dismounted; we entered the apartments of my foster-parents. I saw the flash of her cheeks like sunlight, I trembled.

465 "The form of that sun (Nestan) was clad in robes of orange; behind her was a host of eunuchs in cohorts and lines; with light she quite filled house, street and quarter; there, amid

the roses (of her cheeks), shone in beauty coral-pearl twins (lips and rows of teeth).

466   "I who had fought and been wounded had mine arm hung from my neck in a sling. The queen rose from her throne (and came) forward to meet me. She kissed me hard like a son, she made my rose cheek blue; she said to me: Henceforth expect not the foe to engage thee.'

467   "Near at hand they made place for me, there where it pleased me; opposite sat the sun for whom my heart was dying. Stealthily I looked at her, she looked at me; no other converse was there; (when) I tore away mine eyes from her, thereby was life made hateful to me.

468   "There was drinking and feasting on a scale fitting to their might, such another rejoicing eye has not seen, goblet and cup were all of turquoise and ruby; the king gave order that no drunk man be suffered to depart.

469   "Being there I gave myself up to the excess of joy; when she gazed at me and I at her, my fire began to be extinguished. I called upon my wild, mad heart to have a care of men (that they observe not). How exceedingly pleasant it is to look face to face on the beloved!

470   "The minstrels ceased to sing. 'Be silent!' They bent their heads. He (the king) said to me: 'Son Tariel, how can we tell thee how we rejoice! We are in bliss, therefore (? because) our adversaries are woeful; right are thine admirers, not idly do they vaunt.

471   "Now, though it is fitting that we should clothe thee who art mighty in glory, we clothe thee not, we doff not those robes beauteously adorning thee. Now thou whose rays are

spread abroad hast a hundred treasures from us, thou thyself canst have sewn what thou desirest, be not bashful before us.'

472 "He sat down again joyful, drinking and singing increased, again the feast went on, the lyres and tinkling of harps. The queens retired when day met twilight and until evenings joy was not joy.

473 "We broke up; we could no more endure the drinking of great goblets. I went into my chamber, my perception became like that of one dazed; I had no power in me, made prisoner as I was, to extinguish that fire (of love). I remembered, and the memory of being gazed on by her rejoiced me.

474 "A slave came; he told me true tidings: 'A veiled woman asks tidings of you.' Then I knew at once, I leaped up in all haste, with trembling heart; she came in, I saw Asmat'h, who was coming towards me.

475 "For the sake of her for whom I am dying I was pleased to see Asmat'h, as if I saw herself (Nestan). I hindered her from doing me homage, I kissed her, I took her hand and seated her near me on my couch, and greeted her: 'Blessed art thou, come as a shoot from the aloe-tree!

476 "'Tell me news of her; speak to me of nought else.' She said to me: 'I will tell thee truth; now from me (thou shalt) not (hear words uttered merely) to give pleasure. To-day ye saw each other, and tenderly were pleased; now again she commands to make known news of her through me.'

LETTER OF NESTAN-DAREDJAN WRITTEN TO HER BELOVED

477   "She gave me a letter, I gazed on it; it was from the light of the face of the lands. She wrote: 'I have seen the loveliness of thy gemlike brilliancy; fair wert thou returned from battle, after urging on thy horse; not ill seems to me the cause of the flow of my tears.

478   "If God hath given me my tongue it befits me to use it for thy praise; dead for thy sake I can by no means speak, for lacking thee I die. The sun (i.e., Nestan) made a little garden of rose and jet, as a garden for the lion; by thy sun, my self pertains to none save thee.

479   "'Though thou hast shed a stream of tears yet have they not flowed in vain; henceforth weep no more, put away grief from thee. Those who look upon thee curse unrestrained those who look upon thee. Veil me with that which but now was bound round thee.

480   "'Give me the veils that sometime adorned thee; when thou seest me, thou also shalt be pleased that that which is thine adorns me. Bind on thine arm this bracelet if thou honourest what is mine, and such another night thou shalt not pass as long as thou livest.'"

481   Here Tariel, become like a wild beast, weeps, his grief increases a thousandfold; he said: "I have the armlet which she formerly bound on her arm!" He undid it, took it off, man

cannot estimate its worth, he pressed it to his lips, he fainted and fell like a corpse.

482   He lay more lifeless than a corpse at the door of the tomb. On both sides are seen bruises from his fist which he had struck on his breast. A stream of blood flows from Asmat'h's scratched cheeks; she poured water on him again, she succoured him, the sound of gurgling water is heard there.

483   Avt'handil, too, sighed bitterly; he gazed on the unconscious form. Asmat'h multiplied her groans; her tears hollowed out the stones. Then she restored him to consciousness, his fires she quenched with water; he said: "I live; Fate even now is drinking my blood."

484   Pale he sat up, he stared with his eyes like one dazed; the rose was become quite saffron and wan; a long time he neither spoke nor looked at them; he was mightily oppressed that he remained (alive) and died not.

485   He said to Avt'handil: "Hearken! Though I have the mind of a madman, I will tell thee my tale and that of her who has buried me. It seems to me a joy to meet the friend thou hast not met. It surprises me that I am alive, that I survive hale.

486   "The sight of Asmat'h, in whom I trusted as in a sister, pleased me. When I had seen the letter, she gave me this armlet, I bound it on mine arm at once, I doffed from my head that strange and rare thing of some strong, black (stuff), the veil.

TARIEL'S LETTER IN ANSWER TO HIS BELOVED

487 "'I wrote: 'O sun! thy ray beaming forth from thee struck my heart; my alertness and boldness are brought to nought; mad for thee, I have perceived thy beauty and loveliness; with what service can I pay thee in exchange for life?'

488 "'Then when thou didst make me to survive (and) sufferedst me not to be wholly sundered from life, now this time I compare with that time. I have received thine armlet; I have bound it round mine arm. How can I show my joy as much as is fitting?

489 "'Of a truth I offer thee, lo! the veil which thou demandest; also a cloak, of the same (stuff), the like of which thou wilt not find. Leave me not to faint, help me, succour me, come!' Whom can I entreat in this world save thee?'

490 "The maid arose and forsook me. I lay down and fell pleasantly asleep, but I shivered, I saw my beloved in my sleep; I awoke, I had her no more, life was a burden to me; thus I passed the night, I heard not her voice.

491 "Early in the morning they summoned me to the palace, when day was yet at the dawn. I rose; I learned their tidings and went at the same moment. I saw them both sitting with pleased faces. When I entered they bade me be seated; I sat down before them on a chair.

492 "They said to me: 'God has brought old age upon us so that we are exhausted, the time of age approaches us, youth has passed from us. We have no son, but we have a daughter whose rays fail us not; we care not for the lack of a son, we are reconciled to that.

493 "'Now we want a husband for our daughter. Where shall we find him to whom we may give our throne, whom we may form in our image, make him ruler of the kingdom, guardian of the realm, that we be not destroyed, that we may not let our enemies whet their swords for us?'

494 "I said: 'How can your heart not feel the want of a son! But she who is like the sun suffices for our hope. Whomsoever you choose as son-in-law, he will rejoice greatly. What more can I say? You yourselves know what will be fitting.'

495 "We began to take counsel on the matter. I tried to keep my heart firm though it was weakened; I said to myself: 'I shall say nothing and can do nothing to hinder this.' The king said: "There is Khvarazmsha, King of the Khvarazmians, if he would give us his child for ours there is none like him.'

496 "It was clear that they had settled it beforehand; they glanced at each other, their words also were guarded; it was not for me to venture to say anything to hinder them, only I became as earth and cinders; my heart quivered to and fro.

497 "The queen said: 'Khvarazmsha is a king reigning with power. Who could be better than his son for our son-in-law!' How could I dare to dispute since they themselves desired it! I added assent. The day of the overthrow of my soul was fixed.

498   "They sent a man to Khvarazmsha asking for his son. Their message was: 'Our whole realm is without an heir, there is one daughter fit for childbearing, not to be wedded abroad; if thou wilt give us thy son for her, wait not for aught further.'

499   "The man arrived loaded with mantles and veils. Khvarazmsha rejoiced with great joy; he said: From God has befallen us that which we desired; what other child like unto her could we take to our arms?'

500   "Again they sent other men to bring the bridegroom; they entreated him: 'Tarry not, come at our demand.' I was wearied after exercise at ball-playing, and went to my chamber to rest; sadness entered into my heart, I began to endure woes.

501   "Excessive melancholy approached my heart as if to strike with a knife, (but when) Asmat'h's slave entered I sat proud and strong. He gave me a letter; in it was written: She who is like an aloe-tree in form commands thee to come hither soon without putting off time.'

502   "I mounted, went forth, entered the little garden, as thou canst imagine, with a full measure of joy; I passed through the little garden and arrived at the tower; I saw Asmat'h standing at the foot; I looked and saw that she had been weeping, tear stains could be seen on her cheeks; I was sad, and did not ask; she was troubled by desire for my coming.

503   "I saw her frowning; this oppressed me exceedingly. She no longer smiled on me as she had formerly smiled; she said no word to me, only her tears showered down; thereby she wounded me the more, she healed not my wounds.

504   "She carried my thoughts very far away. She led me into the tower and raised the curtain. I went in, I saw that moon,

every woe forsook me, the ray fell on my heart, but my heart was not melted.

505 "The light falling upon the curtain was not light; her golden face was carelessly covered by the veil I had given her; the peerless one, apparelled in that same green garment, was seated in a reclining position on the couch; a shower of tears fell on her face flashing with radiance.

506 "She crouched, like a panther on the edge of a rock, her face flashing fury; no longer was she like the sun, the moon, an aloe-tree planted in Eden. Asmat'h seated me far off; my heart was struck as by a lance. Then she sat erect with frowning brows, angry, enraged.

507 "She said to me: 'I marvel why thou art come, thou breaker of thy binding oath, fickle and faithless, thou forsworn; but high Heaven will give thee guerdon and answer for this!' I said: 'How can I reply to what I know not?'

508 "I said: 'I cannot answer thee if I know not the truth. Wherein have I sinned, what have I done, (I) senseless and pale?' Again she said to me: 'What shall I say to thee, false and treacherous one! Why did I let myself be deceived, woman-like! For this I burn with flame.

509 "'Knowest thou not of the bringing of Khvarazmsha to wed me? Thou wert sitting as counsellor, thy consent to this was given, thou hast broken thine oath to me, the firmness and bindingness thereof. Would to God I might bring thy cunning to nought!

510 "'Rememberest thou when thou didst sigh "Ah! Ah!" when thy tears bathed the fields, and the physicians and

surgeons brought thee medicines? What else is there that resembles a man's falsehood? Since thou hast denied me, I, too, will renounce thee. Let us see who will be the more hurt?

511   "'I tell thee this: Whosoever shall rule India I have the rule also, whether they go trackless or by the road! It may not be thus! Now thou hast fallen into error. Thine opinions and like thee--even so untrue!

512   "'While I live, by God, thou shalt no more dwell in India. If thou seekest to tarry, the soul shall be parted from thy body! None other shalt thou find like me, even though thou stretch thy hand unto heaven!'" When the knight had ended these words he wept, moaned, and said: "Ah me!"

513   He said: "When I heard this from her, hope revived in me exceedingly; once more mine eyes had power to look upon her light; now I have lost it, why art thou not surprised that dazed I live? Woe to thee fleeting world! why seekest thou to drain my blood?

514   "I looked, and saw on the lectern the Koran lying open; I raised it, I stood up, and, praising God and afterwards her, said: 'O sun, thou burnedst me, and in truth my sun is set; since thou slayest me not, I will venture to make thee some answer:

515   "'If what I tell thee, these words, be falsely cunning, may Heaven itself be wrathful with me, may all the sun's rays be turned against me! If thou considerest me worthy to be judged, I have done no ill.' She said: 'What thou knowest, speak!' She nodded to me.

516   "Then again I ventured to say: 'If I, O sun, have broken my vow to thee, may God now forthwith show His anger by hurling a thunderbolt from heaven upon me! Who save thee

has for me a face like a sun, a form like a tree? so how can I remain alive if a lance strike my heart!

517   "'The sovereigns summoned me to court, they held a solemn council, beforehand they had appointed that youth as thy husband; (even if) I had opposed it I could not prevent it, I should have been a fool for my pains; I said to myself: "Agree with them for the nonce; it is better for thee to fortify thy heart."

518   "'How could I dare to forbid it, since he (P'harsadan) understands not, knows not that India shall not remain masterless! It is I alone who am her (India's) owner; none other has any right. I know not him whom he (P'harsadan) will bring hither, nor who is mistaken (in this matter).

519   "'I said: "I can do nothing in this; I shall contrive some other means." I said: "Be not assailed by a multitude of thoughts." My heart was like a wild beast; a thousand times I was ready to fly to the fields. To whom can I give thee? Why shouldst thou not take me?'

520   "I sold soul for heart's sake; thus the tower became for me a market. That rain which at first had frozen the rose became milder; I saw pearl in the coral, round about (the pearl) (the coral) was tenderly enfolded; she said: Why do I, too, judge this to be right?

521   "'I do not believe thee to be treacherous and faithless, a denier of God, not thankful to him; entreat of him myself and lordship in gladness over India; I and thou I shall be sovereigns-- that is the best of all matches!'

522 "The wrathful, enraged one became tender to me; either the sun was on earth or the full-faced moon; she set me near her, she caressed me, hitherto unworthy of this, she conversed with me; thus she extinguished the fire kindled in me.

523 "She said to me: 'The prudent should never hasten, he will contrive whatever is best, he will be calm under Fate. If thou suffer not the suitor to come in (to India), woe if the king be wroth with thee, thou and he will quarrel, India will be laid waste.

524 "On the other hand, if thou allow the bridegroom to come in, (if) he wed me, (if) it so fall out, we shall be sundered each from other, our gay garb will be turned to mourning, they will be happy and glorious, our sufferings will be magnified an hundredfold. This shall not be said, that the Persians hold sway in our court.'

525 "I said: 'May God avert the wedding of thee by that youth! When they come into India (and) I discover their quality, I shall show forth to them my strong-heartedness and prowess; I shall so slay them that they become of no account!'

526 "She spoke to me saying: 'A woman should act in a womanly way as befits her sex; I cannot have thee shed much blood, I cannot become a wall of division. When they come, slay the bridegroom without killing his armies. To do true justice makes even a dry tree green.

527 "'Thus do, my lion, most excellent of all heroes; slay the bridegroom stealthily, take not soldiers, slaughter not his armies like cattle or asses; how can a man bear the burden of much innocent blood!

528   "'When thou hast killed him, tell thy lord, my father, say to him: "I could never let India be food for the Persians; it is mine own heritage, never will I give up even an ounce of it; if thou wilt not leave me in peace I will make a wilderness of thy city!"

529   "'Say not that thou wantest my love or desirest me, so will the righteousness of thy deed seem the greater; the king will then entreat thee in the most desperate and abject manner; I shall give myself into thy hands, reigning together will suit us."'

530   "This counsel and advice pleased me exceedingly; I boasted that I would wield my sword for the slaying of my foes. Then I rose to depart. She began to entreat me to sit down; I longed to do so, but could not bring myself to clasp and embrace her.

531   "I tarried some time, (then) I left her; but I became like one mad; Asmat'h went in front of me; I shed hot tears; my grief increased a thousandfold, my joy was reduced to one; then I went unwillingly away, and so I went slowly.

532   "A man came. 'The bridegroom cometh,' announced he but, wretched man! he knew not what God was preparing for him. The king looked pleased, he spoke no woeful words; he bade me sit near him; 'Come,' said he, and inclined his head.

533   "He said to me: 'For me this is a day of joy and merriment. Let us celebrate the wedding, since it is necessary that the matter he concluded; let us send a man, let us have all the treasures brought from every part, generously let us distribute, let us fill them (with treasure); avarice is clownishness.'

534 "I sent in all directions men carrying treasure. The bridegroom also came, they were no laggards; our men met them from inside, from outside came the Khvarazmians; the sum of their soldiers could not be contained even by the fields.

535 "The king commanded: 'Prepare the maidan with tents, let the bridegroom rest, let him tarry there a little while; the other armies can go thither without thee to see him, thou shalt see him here, go not, this will suffice for thee.'

536 "I raised on the maidan tents of red satin. The bridegroom arrived and entered (the tent), he dismounted; it seemed not like Easter Eve; those inside began to go out, there was a host of courtiers there, the soldiers began to form in ranks according to their clans.

537 "I was wearied, as is the wont of one who has done duty; tired, I turned homeward, and wished to sleep. A slave came and gave me a letter from Asmat'h the sweet: 'Come quickly! She who is like a full-grown aloe commands thee.'

538 "I dismounted not; I went quickly obedient. The maiden (Asmat'h) had been weeping; I asked her: 'Why flow thy tears?' She said to me: 'Being engaged in thy defence, how can I avoid weeping? How can I justify thee unceasingly, whatever kind of advocate I may have become!'

539 "We went in, we saw her seated on a cushion, her brows puckered; the sun could not more illume the vicinage than she. I stood before her. She said to me: 'Why standest thou there? The day of battle comes--or, wert thou forsaking me, wert thou false to me and deceiving me again?'

540 "I was angered, I said nothing, hastily I went out: again; I called back: 'Now shall it be seen if I did not wish it! Am I

become so cowardly that a woman urges me to fight?' I went home, I concerted his slaughter, I was not idle.

541 "I commanded a hundred servants: 'Prepare for battle!' We mounted, we passed through the city without, letting anyone perceive us. I went into the tent. It is a horror to tell with the tongue how the bridegroom was lying; I killed that youth without shedding of blood (? on our side), though his blood cried out as it flowed.'

542 "I cut the tangled edge of the tent, I tore it, I seized the youth by his legs and struck his head on the tent-pole. Those lying at the door cried; their lamentation was marvellous. I mounted my horse, departed, my coat of chain mail protected me.

543 "An alarm was raised against me; there was a cry to pursue me. I went on, they began to follow, I slew my pursuers. I had a strong city, impregnable to the foe; I reached it in safety, pleasantly, unhurt.

544 "I sent a man, I made known to all the soldiers: 'Let all who will aid me come hither!' My pursuers did not weary of coming in the depth of dark night; when they recognized me they kept their heads whole.

545 "I arose at daybreak; I apparelled myself when night dawned into morn. I saw three lords sent by the king; he sent a message, saying: 'God knows I have fostered thee like my son; why hast thou thus changed my rejoicing into heaviness?

546 "'Why didst thou make Khvarazmsha's innocent blood to fall on our house! If thou didst desire my daughter, why didst thou not tell me so? Thou hast made life distasteful to me, thine

aged foster-father; thou thyself hast brought it about that thou remainest not with me till the day of my death.'

547   "In answer I sent a message: 'O king, I am stronger than bronze, and this alone hinders me from being destroyed by the fire and flame of death; but, as you know, a king should be a doer of justice; by your sun! I am far from desiring your daughter.

548   "'Thou knowest how many palaces and thrones are in India; I am the sole heir left, all has fallen into your hands, all their heirs have died out, their heritage remains to you; by right the throne belongs to none but me.

549   "'I swear by your virtue, I cannot flatter you, now this is not just: God gave thee no son; thou hast an only daughter. If thou appointedst Khvarazmsha king, what would have been left for me in exchange? Can another king be seated on the throne of India while I wear my sword?

550   "'I want not thy daughter, marry her, rid her of me. India is mine, to no man else will I give it; whoever contests my right, him will I cause to be uprooted from the earth; kill me! if I need any foreign helpers.'

TARIEL HEARS TIDINGS OF THE LOSS OF NESTAN-DAREDJAN

551 "I sent those men. I was mad in mind; since I could learn nought of her I grew more inflamed with grief. I went to look from a wall I had built overlooking the plain. I learned a dreadful thing, though I lost not my head.

552 "Two pedestrians appeared, I went to meet them; it was a woman with a slave; I recognized who was coming, it was Asmat'h, with dishevelled head, blood flowing from her face; no more did she call to me smiling, nor did she greet me with a smile.

553 "When I saw her I became perturbed; my mind was maddened. I cried from afar: 'What has befallen us, why does the fire consume us?' She wept pitifully, she could hardly utter words, she said to me: 'God has engirt the sphere of the heavens in wrath for us!'

554 "I came near, I inquired again: 'What has happened to us? Tell me the truth.' Again she wept aloud piteously, again the flame burned her; for a long time she could speak no word to me, not the tenth part of her griefs, her breast was dyed crimson with the blood trickling from her cheeks.

555 "Then she said to me: 'I will tell thee, why should I hide it from thee? but inasmuch as I shall make thee to rejoice, so have mercy upon me, suffer me not to live, let me not survive, I entreat thee, have pity on me, save me from my fate, fulfil thy duty to thy God.'

556 "She said to me: "When thou slewest the bridegroom and the alarm was raised, the king heard it, he leaped up, he was sore stricken thereat; he called for thee, he ordered thee to be summoned, in a loud voice he cried; they sought thee, they could not find thee at home, and thereat the king complained.

557 "'They told him: "He is not here; he has somewhere passed the gates." The king said: "I know, I know, too well I understand; he loved my daughter, he shed blood in the fields, and when they saw each other they could not refrain from gazing.

558 ""'Now, by my head! I will slay her who is called my sister; I told her God's, she has caught her in the devil's net; what have those wicked lovers given or promised her? If I allow her to remain (alive) I renounce God; this is ready for her punishment."

559 "Seldom was it the king's wont to swear by his head, and when he thus swore he brake not his oath, forthwith he fulfilled it. Someone--who knows who?--who heard this wrath of the king told it to Davar the Kadj, who knows even heaven by her sorcery.

560 "'Some enemy of God told Davar, the king's sister: "Thy brother hath sworn by his head, he will not leave thee alive, the people know it." She spoke thus: "The good God knows that I am innocent, and let that same people know who it is that slays me and for whose sake I am slain."

561 "'My mistress was the same as when thou didst leave her, her head was still wrapped in thy veils, beautifully they became her. Davar spoke words such as I had never heard:

"Harlot, thou harlot, why didst thou slay me? I think thou too shalt not rejoice.

562 "'"Wanton, harlot woman, why didst thou cause thy bridegroom to be slain, or why dost thou make me pay for his blood with mine? My brother shall not slay me in vain for what I have done, what I have made thee do! Now God grant thou mayst never meet him whom thou didst incite to hinder this!"

563 "'She seized her, dragged her along, tore her long hair, wounded her, bruised her, fiercely she frowned; (Nestan) could make no answer, but only sighed and moaned, a black woman was of no avail, she could not heal her wounds.

564 "'When Davar was sated with beating and bruising, two slaves with Kadj-like faces came forth; they brought a litter, they spoke rudely to her, they put that sun inside, thus was she made prisoner.

565 "'They passed the windows towards the sea; immediately she was out of sight. Davar said: "Who would not stone me for doing this? Who? Before he (P'harsadan) slay me, I shall die. Life is wearisome to me!" She struck herself with a knife, died, fell in a stream of blood.

566 "Why marvel'st thou not to see me alive, unpierced by a lance! Now do to me what befits a bringer of such tidings; by the Most High, deliver from this unbearable life me who have not yet ceased to breathe." Her tears fell piteously, undiminished, unceasing.

567 "'I said: Sister, why should I kill thee, or what is thy fault? What shall I do in return for the debt I owe her? Now I

devote myself to seek her wherever rock and water are found.' I became quite petrified; my heart grew like hard rock.

568   "Excessive horror maddened me; fever and trembling came upon me. I said to myself: 'Die not! To lie idle (in the grave) is of no avail; better is it to roam forth to seek her, to run and wander in the fields. Behold the time for thee, who wishest to go with me!'

569   "I went in, I arrayed myself quickly, accoutred I mounted my horse. A hundred and sixty good knights of long service joined me, we passed forth from the gates in order of battle. I went to the seashore, I saw a ship, the skipper saw me apparelled.

570   "I entered the ship, I went out to sea, I cruised amidst the sea. I let no ship from any quarter pass unseen. I waited, but I heard nothing. Mad (as I was) I became still more maddened; God hated me so that He forsook me wholly.

571   "Thus I spent a year--twelve months which were to me like twenty--but I found no man, even in a dream, who had seen her. All those who were attendant upon me were dead and perished. I said: 'I cannot defy God; what He wills even that will I do.'

572   "I was weary of tossing on the seas, so I came ashore. My heart had become altogether like a beast's, I hearkened to no counsel; all those who were left to me in my misfortune have been scattered from me, (but) God abandons not a man thus forsaken by (Fortune).

573   "Only this Asmat'h and two slaves remained with me as my comforters and counsellors. I could learn no news of her

(Nestan), not even a grain's weight. Weeping seemed to me as joy, and streams of tears flowed down.

THE STORY OF NURADIN P'HRIDON WHEN TARIEL MET HIM ON THE SEASHORE

574   "I landed by night; I came ashore where gardens were seen. It seemed as if there were a city; we came near, on one side the rocks were hollowed out. The sight of men gave me no pleasure; brands were imprinted on my heart. I dismounted to rest at a spot where there were lofty trees.

575   "I fell asleep at the foot of the trees; the slaves brake bread. Then I woke sad, the soot (of sorrow) made night in my heart; in so long a time I had learned nought, neither gossip nor sooth; my tears pressed from mine eyes wet the fields.

576   "I heard a shout. I looked round, a knight cried out haughtily, he was galloping along the seashore, he was hurt by a wound, his sword was broken and soiled, blood flowed down; he threatened his foes, was wrathful, cursed, complained.

577   "He sat upon a black steed, the same which I now possess; like the wind he swept along, enraged, wrathful. I sent a slave (to tell him) I was desirous to meet him; I bade him say: 'Stand! declare unto me who angers thee, O lion!'

578   "He spoke not to the slave, nor did he hear a word. Hastily I mounted, I went along to meet him; I overtook him, I came before him, I said: 'Stay, hearken to me! I too wish to know thine affair.' He looked at me, I pleased him, he checked his course.

579   "He looked me over, and said to God: 'How hast Thou made such a tree!' Then he said to me: 'Now will I tell thee what thou askest me: Those enemies whom I had hitherto esteemed as goats have proved lions to me; they fell upon me traitorously when I was unready, I could not don mine armour.'

580   "I said: 'Stand, be calm, let us dismount at the foot of the trees! A goodly knight withdraws not when cuts are given with the sword.' I led him with me; we went away fonder than father and son. I marvelled at the tender beauty of the knight.

581   "One of my slaves was a surgeon, he bound up the wounds, he drew out the arrowheads so that the wounds hurt not. Then I asked: 'Who art thou, and by whom was thine arm hurt?' He set himself to tell me his story; he bewailed himself.

582   "First he said to me: 'I know not what thou art, nor to what I can liken thee. What has thus consumed thee, or who first made thee full? What has turned thee sallow who wert planted rose and jet? Why has God put out the candle lighted by Himself?

583   "'Near by is the city of Mulghazanzari, which belongs to me. My name is Nuradin P'hridon, I am the king ruling there; here where ye are stationed is my boundary. I have little, but in all its parts it is of excellent quality.'

584   "'My grandfather shared his territory between my father and uncle. In the sea is an island, this he said was my share, it had fallen into the hands of that uncle whose sons have now wounded me; the hunting remained to them, I did not give it up to them, they quarrelled with me.

585   "'To-day I went forth to the chase, I hunted on the seashore, I wished to cross over there, so I took not many beaters; I told the troops: "Wait for me till I return." I kept no more than five falconers.

586   "'I went by ship; from the sea came forth a creek. I gathered not those divided from me; I said to myself: "Why should I take precautions against mine own folk?" They seemed timid to me; their multitude appeared not. I hunted and hallooed; I withheld not my voice.

587   "'Of a truth, they were wroth to think I scorned them thus; they secretly surrounded me with soldiers, they blocked the roads to the ship; mine own uncle's sons rode at their head, (waving) their arms they rushed on my soldiers to fight.

588   "'I heard them; I perceived the outcry and the flashing of swords. I begged a boat of the boatmen; but once I called out "Woe is me!" I went into the sea, warriors met me like waves, they would have overwhelmed me, but could not compass it.

589   "'Yet more great hosts approached me from behind, from this side and that they came upon me, from one side they could not overpower me. When those in front could not come near me, from the back they shot at me; I trusted in my sword-- it broke, my arrows were exhausted.

590   "'They engirt me; I could do no more. I made my horse leap over from the boat, I crossed the sea by swimming, those who beheld me were amazed; they slew all who were with me, I left them there; whoever pursued me could not affront me, (when) I turned I made them turn.

591   "'Now that will be whatever is God's will. I think my blood will not be unavenged. May I have the power to bring my

boast to fulfilment! I will make their existence a lamentation evening and morning. I will call the crows and ravens and make a banquet of them!'

592   "That youth won me to like him; my heart went out toward him. I said to him: 'There is no need at all for thee to hasten; I too will go with thee, there will they be slain; we two warriors shall surely not be afraid of them!'

593   "This also I said: 'Thou hast not heard my tale; I shall tell it to thee more fully when we have time.' He said to me: 'What joy can weigh against this to me! To the day of my death my life will be devoted to thy service!'

594   "We went to his fair, though small, city. The troops met him; they poured forth lamentations for him, they scratched their faces and threw away the fragments like splinters; they embraced him, they kissed his sword, its hilt and ring.'

595   "Again I pleased; I his new friend seemed fair to him. They spoke my praises: 'O sun, thou art a bringer of fine weather to us!' We went and saw his fair, rich city. Every form was clad in broad brocade.

TARIEL'S AID TO P'HRIDON, AND THEIR VICTORY OVER THEIR FOES

596 "He was healed, and able to fight and use horse and armour. We prepared galleys and the number of a host of troops; it needed a man to pray (to God) for some aid for those who gazed upon them.--Now will I tell thee of that knight's battle, the punisher of his adversaries.

597 "I perceived their design, and saw them donning their headgear. Ships met me, I know not if there were eight (in all); swiftly I threw myself upon then; they began to row; I struck (one of the ships) with my heel and upset it; like women they bewailed themselves.

598 "I betook myself to yet another, and seized the lip (prow) of the ship with my hand; I drowned them in the sea, I slew them; they had no opportunity for battle. The rest fled from me, they made for their harbour; all who saw me marvelled, they praised me, they hated me not.

599 "We crossed the sea, we landed. Mounted they threw themselves on us. Again we engaged; there began the vicissitudes of battle. P'hridon's bravery and agility pleased me then; in warfare a lion, in face a sun, that aloe-tree fought.

600 "With his sword he cast down both his cousins, he cut their hands clean off; thus he crippled them; he led them away bound by the arms; the one did not abandon the two. He made their knights to weep, his knights to vaunt themselves.

601   "Their soldiers fled from us, we threw ourselves upon them, we scattered them; swiftly we seized the city, we wasted no time; we broke their legs with stones, we tanned their skin into leather. Kill me, if it was possible to empty the treasure both by lading and stowing!

602   "P'hridon inspected the treasures and put his seals upon them; he himself led away his two vanquished cousins; he shed their blood in exchange for his, and poured it out on the fields. Of me they said: 'Thanks God who has planted aloe-trees!'

603   "We went back (to P'hridon's). The triumph exhibited by the citizens was heard; suppliants there laid hold on the heart of beholders. All uttered praise to me and Nuradin, in a panegyric; they said to us: 'Through the strength of your (right) arms their blood still flows!'

604   "The soldiers acclaimed P'hridon as king and me as king of kings, themselves as subjects and me as sovereign of them all. I was gloomy, they could never find me culling roses; they knew not my story, there it was not lightly spoken of.

P'HRIDON TELLS TARIEL TIDINGS OF NES-TAN-DAREDJAN

605   "One day the king and I went forth to the chase; we climbed upon a cape jutting out into the sea. P'hridon said to me: 'I will tell thee how, when we were out riding for sport, I once saw a wonderful thing from this cape.'

606   "I bade him speak, and P'hridon told me even this tale: 'One day I wished to hunt, I mounted this steed of mine. It seemed as if there were a duck in the sea, a falcon on the land; I stood here and watched the flight of the hawk thitherward.

607   "'Now and then as I climbed uphill I gazed out to sea. I perceived a small thing far away on the sea, going so swiftly that nothing of its kind could equal it; I could not make it out; in my mind I marvelled at these two things.

608   "'I said to myself: "What is it? To what can I liken it? Is it bird or beast?" It was a boat tented over with many-folded stuff; a steersman guided it. I fixed mine eyes upon it, and there in a litter sat the moon; I would have given her the seventh heaven (as habitation).

609   "'Two slaves as black as pitch crept out, they put ashore a maiden, I saw her thick-tressed hair, the lightning that flashed from her--to what colours can it be likened?--would illumine the earth (and) make the sunbeams of no account.

610   "'Joy made me hasten, quiver, stagger. I loved that rose who appeared torn to mine eyes. I resolved to engage them, I

said: "Let me go towards them; what creature can fly away from my black (steed)."

611   "'I pressed my horse with my heel. There was a noise and rustling among the rushes. I could not reach her, however much I used the spur; they were gone. I came to the seashore and looked round, she appeared only as a last ray of the setting sun, she went farther away, she was gone from me, therefore was I consumed by flame.'

612   "This I heard from P'hridon; heat was added to my fire. I threw myself down from my horse, I wholly abased myself; with mine own blood shed from my cheeks I anointed myself. Kill me! That anyone but I should have seen that tree!

613   "This behaviour of mine astonished P'hridon, it seemed passing strange to him; but he was exceedingly pitiful to me, by weeping he placated me, like a son he soothed me, he pled with me, treated me with deference, and, pearl-like, hot tears sprang from his eyes.

614   "'Alas! what have I, misguided, madly told thee?' I said: 'It matters not, grieve not for that! She was my moon; for her the fire consumes me hotly. Now will I tell thee my tale, since thou thyself wishest to have me as comrade.'

615   "I told P'hridon all that had befallen me. He said to me: 'What have I, mistaken, shamed, said to thee? Thou mighty king of the Indians, wherefore art thou come to me? A royal seat and throne become thee, a whole palace.'

616   "Again he said to me: 'To whom God gives for form a young cypress, from him He withdraws the spear, though at first He lacerate his heart therewith. He will grant us His mercy, He

will thunder it from heaven, He will turn our sorrow to joy, He will never grieve us.'

617   "We went back tearful; we sat down alone together in the palace. I said to P'hridon: 'Save thee, none is mine aid. God has not sent thy like to earth, and since I know thee what more do I want?

618   "'Thou hadst no friend until the time when thou didst meet me; use now thy tongue and mind to counsel me in this: What can I do? What is the best thing to bring joy to her and me? If I can do nought I shall not tarry (i.e., survive) a moment.'

619   "He said to me: 'What better fate could I have from God than this? Thou art come to be gracious to me, king, sovereign of India. Needs it that after this I should desire any gratitude? I stand before thee as a slave to obey thee slavishly.

620   "'This city is the highway for ships coming from all parts, an emporium of much foreign news of all kinds. Here shall we hear of .the balm to assuage the fire which burns thee. God grant that these woes and pains pass away!

621   "'We will send out sailors who have fared on the sea before; let them find for us that moon for whose sake grief is not lacking to us; until then be patient, so that thy mind torture thee not; grief will not last for aye, shall not joy overcome it!'

622   "That very instant we called men, we settled the business; we commanded them: 'Go with ships, sail over the sea, seek her out for us, fulfil the desire of her lover; undergo a thousand hardships for this, not merely seven or eight.'

623   "He appointed men wherever there were havens for ships; he gave orders: 'Seek out everywhere, wheresoever you

hear of her.' Waiting seemed to me a consolation, my pains became lightened; absent from her I felt joy, and for the sake of that day I am ashamed.

624 "P'hridon set up a throne for me in the place for the overlord. He said to me: 'Hitherto have I erred, I could not comprehend what I should have understood; thou art the great king of the Indians; who can please thee? Wherewithal? How? Who is the man who would not be thy subject!'

625 "Why should I lengthen (the story)? From all sides came the seekers of news, empty, and wearied of empty places; they had learned nothing at all, they knew not any news. As for me, afresh the undrying tear flowed still more from mine eyes.

626 "I said to P'hridon: 'How this day seems horrible to me, I have God for my witness thereto; to speak thereof is hard for me; without thee night and day alike seem eventide to me; I am loosed from all joy, my heart is bound with grief.

627 "'Now since I may no longer expect any news of her, I can no longer stay; give me leave, I seek thy permission.' When P'hridon heard this he wept, he watered the field with blood, and said: 'Brother, from this day vain is all my joy!'

628 "Though they tried very hard, they could not hold me back; his armies came before me on bended knees, they embraced me, kissed me, wept and made me weep 'Go not away; let us suffer for thee as long as life is ours.'

629 "I spoke thus: 'Parting from you is very hard for me also, but it is hardly possible for me to have joy without her. I cannot forsake my captive (Nestan), whom you yourselves pity greatly;

let none of you hinder me, I will not stay nor be held back by any.'

630   "Then P'hridon brought (and) gave me this horse of mine; he said: 'Behold! this steed is (given) to you, the sun-faced, the cypress; more I know thou desirest not, why should I despise thy gift? This will please thee by its breaking-in and its swiftness.'

631   "P'hridon escorted me; as we went we both shed tears; there we kissed each other, with cries we parted, all the host lamented for me, truly, in their hearts, not with the tongue; our severing was like that of foster-parent and child.

632   "Departed from P'hridon, I went on the quest, again I fared so that I missed nought on land or out at sea; but I met no man who had seen her, and my heart became wholly maddened, I was like a wild beast.

633   "I said to myself: 'No longer shall I rove and sail in vain; perchance the company of beasts may make my heart forget grief.' I said seven or eight words to my slaves and to this Asmat'h: 'I know I have brought grief upon you; you have good reason to murmur against me.

634   "'Now go and leave me, provide for yourselves, look no longer on the hot tears flowing from mine eyes.' When they heard such discourse they said to me: 'Alas! alas! let not our ears hear what thou sayest!

635   "'Let us not see any master or lord apart from thee, may God not sunder us from your horse's footprints! We would gaze upon you, a fair and adorable spectacle.' Fate, forsooth, makes a man listless, however valiant he may be.

636 "I could not send them away; I hearkened to the words of my slaves, but I forsook the haunts of human tribes, the retreats of goats and stags seemed a fitting abode for me; I roamed, I trod every plain below and hill above.

637 "I found these manless caves, hollowed out by Devis. I combated them, I destroyed them, they could by no means prevail against me; they killed my slaves, ill had they buckled on their coats of mail. Fate made me gloomy; her showers again bespattered me.

638 "Behold, brother! since that day am I here, and here I die. Mad I roam the fields; sometimes I weep and sometimes I faint. This maid will not abandon me; she too is burned by fire for her (Nestan's) sake. I have no other resource to try but death.

639 "Since a beautiful panther is portrayed to me as her image, for this I love its skin, I keep it as a coat for myself; this woman sews it, sometimes she sighs, sometimes she groans. Since I cannot kill myself, in vain is my sword whetted.

640 "The tongues of all the sages could not forth-tell her praise. Enduring life, I think upon my lost one. Since then I have consorted with the beasts, calling myself one of them; I am suitor for death, nought else I entreat of God."

641 He beat his face, he rent it, he tore his cheeks of rose; the ruby turned to amber, the crystal was shattered. Avt'handil's tears flowed too; one by one they dripped from his lashes. Then the maid soothed him (Tariel); on bended knee she besought him.

642   Tariel, calmed by Asmat'h, said to Avt'handil: "I have made everything pleasant for thee, I who never found pleasure for myself. I have told thee the tale of mine irksome life; now go and see thy sun (T'hinat'hin), thou whose time for meeting is nigh."

643   Avt'handil said: "I cannot bear to part from thee; if I separate from thee tears indeed will flow from mine eyes. Verily I tell thee--be not wroth at this boldness--she for whose sake thou diest will not be comforted thereby.

644   "When a physician--however praiseworthy he be--falls sick, he calls in another leech, another skilled in the pulse; him he tells what illness inflaming him with fire afflicts him. Another knows better what is useful; advice for one.

645   "Listen to what I say to thee; I speak to thee as a sage and not as a madman; a hundred times must thou give heed, once sufficeth not. A man so furious of heart can do nought well. Now I desire to see her for whose sake hot fire consumes me.

646   "I shall see her, I shall confirm her love for me, I shall tell her what I have learned; nought else have I to do. I beseech thee to assure me, for God and Heaven's sake, let us not abandon one another, make me swear and make thou an oath to me.

647   "If thou promise me that thou wilt not go hence, I shall assure thee by an oath that for nought shall I forsake thee; I shall come again to see thee, I shall die for thee, for thee shall I rove. If God will, I shall make thee cease to weep thus for her for whom thou diest!"

648 He answered: "How is it that thou, a stranger, so lovest me, a stranger? It is as hard for thee to part from me as for the nightingale from the rose. How can I forget thee, how can I cease to remember thee! God grant that I may again see thee, full-grown young aloe-tree.

649 "If thy form remain a tree (for me), and thy face turn round to see me, (my) heart will not flee into the fields, it will become neither a deer's nor a goat's. If I lie to thee or cheat thee, may God judge me in wrath! Thy presence will charm away my sadness (and) dissolve it!"

650 Hereupon they swore, the frank friends, those jacinths of amber hue, wise-worded (but) mad-minded. They loved each other; for ever would affection's flame burn their hearts. That night the fair comrades spent together.

651 Avt'handil wept with him; fast fell the tears. When day dawned he went forth, kissed him and parted from him. Tariel was so grieved that he knew not what to do. Avt'handil wept, too, as he rode through the rushes.

652 Asmat'h went down with Avt'handil, she conjured him with an oath, she kneeled, she wept, she raised her fingers in entreaty, she besought him to come back soon; as a violet, so she faded. He replied: "O sister, of what can I think save you!

653 "Soon shall I come; I shall not forsake thee nor waste time at home. But let him not go elsewhere; let not that fair form wander. If I come not hither in two months I shall be doing a shameful thing; be assured that I am fallen into unceasing grief."

THE STORY OF AVT'HANDIL'S RETURN TO ARABIA AFTER HE HAD FOUND AND PARTED FROM TARIEL

654 When he was gone thence sadness was surely slaying him; he scratched his face, he rent the rose (of his cheeks), his hand he shortened; all the beasts licked up the blood that flowed from him. His swift pace shortened the long course.

655 He came there where he had parted from his armies. They saw him, they knew him, they rejoiced in such manner as was fitting. They told the good tidings to Shermadin too; .men quickly ran to him: "He is come for whose sake hitherto joy has been embittered to us."

656 He went to meet him, he embraced him, he put his mouth on his (Avt'handil's) hand, pouring forth tears he joyfully kissed the destroyer in the field. Thus he spoke: "O God, do I see really or darkly? How am I worthy of this, that mine eyes should gaze upon thee (safe and) sound!"

657 The knight saluted him low, he put face upon face; he said: "I thank God that no grief afflicts thee!" The magnates did homage, whoever was worthy kissed him; there was great jubilation, great and small alike rejoiced.

658 They came where a dwelling-house had been built; all the city was assembled to see him; forthwith he sat down to feast, gay, proud, merry; an assemblage of tongues could not fully describe the joy of that day.

659   He told Shermadin, he narrated to him all he had seen--how he had found that knight whom he likened to the sun. Avt'handil was hampered by tears; he said with half-closed eyes: "Without him it seems to me alike to dwell in palace or hut."

660   (Shermadin) told him all the home news: "None knows of thy departure; whatever thou toldst me so have I done." He went not thence that day, he feasted and rested; at dawn he mounted, he set out when the sun enlightened the day.

661   He sat no more at feasting, nor stayed he again private; Shermadin, the bearer of good tidings, went to announce (Avt'handil's) arrival; swiftly he fared, in three days he made a ten days' journey. That lion (Avt'handil) rejoiced that he was to see the sun's rival.

662   He sent a message: "O king, proud art thou in might and majesty! I venture to tell thee this thing with fear, respect and precaution: I esteemed myself worthless in that I had learned nought of that knight; now I know and will tell thee all; I come in joy and safety."

663   Rostevan is a king, proud, puissant, imperious, (so) Shermadin delivered all his message in person: "Avt'handil comes to the royal presence having found that knight." The king said: "(Now) I know that which I entreated and prayed for from God."

664   Shermadin made report to T'hinat'hin, that night-less light: "Avt'handil comes to thy presence; he brings thee pleasing news." Thereat, light flashed forth from her, even braver than the sun's. She gave him a gift, and robes to all his people.

665	The king mounted and went to meet the knight who was coming thither, for this (honour) the sun-faced one incurred a great debt (of gratitude); joyous and warm-hearted they met, and some of the multitude of magnates seemed as if drunken.

666	When he approached, the knight alighted and did homage to the king. Rosten, possessed by excess of joy, kissed him. Glad-hearted and merry they entered the royal hall; all there assembled rejoice at the arrival of the knight.

667	Avt'handil, the lion of lions, did homage to her, the sun of suns; there the crystal, rose and jet were beautified by tenderness; her face was brighter than heaven's light; a dwelling-house was no fit abode for them, the sky itself was their (proper) palace.

668	That day they made a feast; drinking and eating they made abundant. The king gazes on the knight, as a tender father on a son. They were both beautified by a snowfall on fresh snow, a dew on the rose; generously they gave gifts, pearls like small coin.

669	The drinking was done, the drinkers separated each to his own home; they suffered not the magnates to go, they set the knight near before them. The king inquires, and he relates what trials he had undergone, and then what he had seen and heard concerning the stranger.

670	"When I speak of him, be not astonished if I ceaselessly lament, saying: 'Ah me!' To the sun alone can I liken him, or the face of him, the extinguisher of the mind of all who see him; a wilted rose among thorns, alas! he is far away!

671   "When unendurable Fate makes a man suffer grief, the reed becomes like a thorn, the crystal turns to saffron colour." While Avt'handil was telling this his cheeks were bedewed with tears. He told in detail the story he had heard from (Tariel).

672   "Having captured the caves in battle, he has for his house the abode of the Devis. He has the damsel of his beloved as his attendant. He is clad in panther's skin; he despises brocade and cloth of gold. No more sees he the world; an ever-new fire consumes him."

673   When he had finished the story--the matter of his grief--the sight of the light of that sun, not ugly to look upon, gladdened him. They praised his rose-like hand which had been firmly held. "This prowess is sufficient for thee since thou art the undoer of grief."

674   T'hinat'hin rejoiced at the hearing of this news. That day she was merry at the drinking, and eating was not wearisome to her. That sun met in his bedchamber a slave with a courteous word. She ordered him to come to her. Tongue cannot tell how pleased he was.

675   The knight went joyful, tender, not ill content, the lion who had roamed the fields with the lions of the field and had lost his colour, a knight of the world, in quality a gem and a faultless ruby, but for heart's sake he had exchanged heart for heart.

676   Bold sits the sun upon her throne, majestic, unconstrained, a fair aloe planted in Eden, generously watered by Euphrates' stream; the jetty hair and the eyebrow thickets adorned the crystal and ruby (of her countenance). Who am I

that I should praise her? It needs the myriad tongues of Athenian sages to praise her fitly.

677 She set the joyful knight before her with his chair, they both sat full of gladness to converse as befitted them; they spoke with dignity and fluency, not with unpolished words. She said: "Thou hast found him in whose quest thou hast seen misfortunes?"

678 He answered: "When the world gives a man his heart's desire, it befits not to recall grief (which is) as a day that is past. I found the tree, an aloe in form, watered by the stream of the world; there (I found) the face (which was) like the rose, but now is wan.

679 "There saw I the cypress, the rose-like, whose power was spent; he (Tariel) says: 'I have lost the crystal, and that where the crystal unites with glass (?).' I burn (for him) because, like me, unendurable fire consumes him." Then again he told the story he had heard from (Tariel).

680 He recounted all his misfortunes and sorrows by the road during the quest. Then he told her how God had thought him worthy to find what he desired. "World, life, man, (all) seems to him as to a beast; alone he roams mad with the brutes, he weeps in the field.

681 "Ask me not, what praise can I speak, how couldst thou understand from me! nothing can please one who has seen him; the eyes of the beholders are weakened as by the brilliance of the sun; the rose is not become saffron, now the violet is gathered in nosegays."

682   He told her in detail what he knew, what he had seen, heard: "Like a panther he has a trail, and for house and abode a cave; a damsel is there ready to cherish him, to maintain his life and bear his sorrows. Alas! Fate makes all dwellers in the world to shed tears!"

683   When the maiden heard this story she had attained the fulfilment of her will; her moon-like face shone as 'twere with radiance at the full. She said: "What answer can I make to give comfort to him, and pleasure, and what is the balm for the healing of his wound?"

684   The knight replied: "Who has confidence in a rash man? He for my sake sacrifices himself to be burned, he who must not be burned. I have appointed the time of my return; I have promised him to sacrifice myself for him. I swear it by my sun whom I contemplate as a sun!

685   "A friend should spare himself no trouble for his friend's sake, he should give heart for heart, love as a road and a bridge. Then, again, the grief of his beloved should be a great grief to a lover. Lo! without him joy is nought to me, and myself I hold of none account."

686   The sun-like one said: "All my heart's desire is fulfilled: first thou art come in safety having found that which was lost, then the love implanted by me in thee has grown, I have found balm for my heart hitherto burned.

687   "Fate treats every man like the weather, sometimes there is sunshine and sometimes the sky thunders forth in wrath; hitherto grief has been upon me, now this gladness is my lot; since the world has joy in it why should any be sad!

688 "Thou dost well not to break the oath thou didst swear; it is necessary to fulfil strong love for a friend, to seek for his cure, to know the unknown. (But) tell me, what shall I, luckless, do if the sun of my heaven be hidden!"

689 The knight replied: "By nearness (to thee) I have united to seven woes eight. Vain is it for one who is frozen to blow on water to warm himself therewith; vain is the love, the kiss from beneath, of the sun at its setting. If I be near thee, once is it woe, and if I go far from thee a thousandfold woe.

690 "Woe is me if I wander where, alas! the simoom burns the roamer; my heart is the target of an arrow, a dart is shot to pierce it; the term of my life seems by this day to be shortened to one-third; I long for a refuge, but the time is past for seeking shelter against troubles.

691 "I have heard your discourse, I have understood what you command; the rose reveals the thorn, why should I prick myself therewith? but, O sun, become altogether a sun for me, and let me carry with me some hopeful token of life."

692 The knight, sweetly and in sweet-sounding Georgian, giving good for good, spoke on this theme like a pleasant instructor to a pupil. The maiden gave him a pearl, she fulfilled his desire, and God grant that their present joy be perfected.

693 What is better than for a man to approach the jet to the crystal and ruby, or to plant in the garden the aloe near the cypress, to water it and make a tree of it, to cause joy to the gazer and sorrow to him who cannot look thereon? Woe to the parted lover! He will be groaning, moaning, groaning.

694 They found all their joy in gazing at each other. The knight went away, sundered from her he went dazed in heart;

the sun wept tears of blood more abundant than the sea, and said: "Fate is insatiable, alas! in the drinking of my blood!"

695   The knight went melancholy away, he beats his breast and so bruises it, for love makes a man weep and melts his heart. When a cloud hides the sun the earth is shadowed, so parting from his beloved makes twilight again, not morning.

696   Blood and tears mingled made channel upon channel on his cheeks. He said "My sun (T'hinat'hin) is by no means satisfied with me because I sacrifice myself to comfort the peerless (Tariel). I marvel how the black eyelash brands the heart of adamant. Until I see her, O world, I wish for no joy from thee.

697   "Him who yesterday was an aloe planted, watered and fully grown in Eden, him to-day Fate thrusts through with her lance, pierces with her knife. To-day my heart is caught in a net of unquenchable fire. Now know I the way of the world; it is a tale and nonsense."

698   Thus speaking, the tears gush forth, he trembles and shudders; with heart-sigh, with deep groan, his form bends and sways (as he goes). Converse with the beloved is a embittered by parting. Alas! O Fate! The end enshrouds and swathes the beginning.

699   The knight went and sat in his chamber; sometimes he weeps; sometimes he swoons, but in spirit he is near his beloved, he is not cut off from her. Like verdure in hoarfrost the hue of his face fades; see how soon lack of sun is apparent on the rose!

700   Accursed is the heart of man, greedy, insatiable; sometimes the heart desiring joys endures all griefs; blind is the heart, perverse in seeing, not at all able to measure itself; no king, nor even death itself, can master it.

701   While he spoke to his heart hearty words, he took the pearls, the love-token of his sun (T'hinat'hin), which had engirt the arm of his sun, and were comparable to her teeth; he put them to his mouth, he kissed them, his tears flowed like Pison.

702   When day dawned there came an inquirer calling him to the court; the knight went forth, proud, gentle, not having slept, unrefreshed by sleep. A host of spectators who had hastened stood crowding one upon another. The king was arrayed for the field; drum and clarion were prepared.

703   The king mounted. How can the pomp of those times be told now? By reason of the beating of the copper drums no word was heard by the ears. The hawks darkened the sun; hither and thither coursed the hound that day the fields were dyed purple with the blood shed by them.

704   They hunted, they returned joyful, having traversed the meadow; they took in with them magnates, princes and all the hosts. He (the king) sat down; he found the couches and all the pavilions adorned; harp harmonized with lute, there was a full choir.

705   The knight sat near the king, one questioned, the other replied; the crystal and ruby of their lips shone transparent, the lightning of their teeth flashed; those who were worthy sat near, they listened; afar off the hosts were grouped; none dared speak without mention of Tariel.

706   The knight departed sad at heart, his tears flowed on the fields; nought save his love passed before his eyes; sometimes he rises, sometimes he lies down. How can one sleep who is mad! Whose heart e'er hearkened to a prayer for patience!

707   He lies down; he says: "What can I imagine as, any consolation for my heart? I am sundered from thee, thou tree, in form as a reed, reared in Eden, thou joy of thy beholders, cause of woe to them that cannot gaze on thee. Since I am unworthy to see thee manifestly, would that I might behold thee in a dream."

708   Thus spake he, weeping, with flowing tears. Once more he addressed his heart: "Patience is like the fountainhead of wisdom. If we endure not what can we do? How can we adapt ourselves to anguish? If we desire happiness from God we must accept griefs also."

709   Again he says: "O heart, however much thou hast the desire for death it is better to bear life, sacrificing self for her; but hide it, let not the flame of thy fire be seen again. It ill befits a lover to expose his love."

AVT'HANDIL'S REQUEST TO KING ROSTEVAN, AND THE VIZIER'S DISCOURSE AND ENTREATY

710   When day dawned the knight arrayed himself and went forth early. He says: "I would that my love be not revealed, that I may conceal it!" For patience he prays: "Contrive something for my heart!" The moon-like one mounted his horse; he went to the house of the vizier.

711   The vizier heard of it, went to meet him: "The sun is risen upon my house; this day, meseems, a presentiment of joy announced to me this good news." He met (Avt'handil), saluted him, respectfully addressed to the perfect one perfect praise. A welcome guest should have a cheerful host.

712   This host, not listless, ill-disposed or idle, helped the knight to dismount; they stretched on the floor under his feet a Cathayan (rug). The knight illumined the house as the sun's beam the universe. They said: "To-day the western gale has wafted us the fragrant odour of roses."

713   He sat; they that looked on him truly maddened their hearts. They who gazed on him accounted it an honour to swoon for his sake; many sighs were uttered, not once but a thousand times; they were ordered to depart, they went away, the household was thinned out.

714   When the household was gone, the knight addressed the vizier; quoth he: "In the council chamber nought will ever be hidden from thee; in every matter of state the king does what

thou desirest, and agrees with thee. (Now) hearken to my woes; cure me with what will heal me.

715 "The fire of yon knight burns me, the flame that consumes him afflicts me; I am slain by longing and by not seeing the object of my desire; he would not grudge his life for me; what is due must be paid; one must love a generous ungrudging friend.

716 "The sight of him caught my heart as in a net, therein it stays; my patience, too, remains with him; in that he burns those near him, God created him indeed a sun. Moreover, Asmat'h is become a sister to me, more than a born sister.

717 "When I departed I swore with a fearful oath: 'I shall come again, I shall see thee not with a face despised of foes; thou art of darkened heart, I shall seek light for thee.' It is time for me to go, therefore am I burned with hot fire.

718 "All this I tell thee truly, not with braggart speech; he awaits me, and I cannot set forth. This it is that adds (fuel) to the hot fire; I cannot break my vow, I mad cannot abandon him mad. When and where did ever a breaker of oaths prevail?

719 "Go to the palace, report on my behalf to King Rosten what I have told thee. By his head I swear to thee, Vizier Ustasra, if he keep me not captive I shall not stay; if he keep me captive what can he make of me? Help me; let not the fire hurt and destroy my heart!

720 "Say from me: 'Let every mouth which is not speechless praise thee! Let God, the means of light, make known to thee how I fear thee. But that knight, an aloe-tree in form, burned

me with fire; forthwith he took away my heart, in no wise could I keep it.

721 "'Now, O king, for me existence lacking him is utterly impossible; he, the dauntless, has my heart. Of what avail am I here? If I can be of any service to him, to you first will the glory belong; if I fail to accomplish aught for him I shall set my heart at rest, mine oath will not have been broken.

722 "'Let not my going anger or grieve your heart. Let that befall my head (self) whate'er God wills. May He grant you the victory, and send me your (servant) back to you; but if I return not may you still reign, may your foes be affrighted.'"

723 Yet again the sun-faced one says to the vizier: "I have shortened my speech. Now speak thus to the king till (others) come in (to inform him), pleasantly entreat for me my congee, summon up thy courage, and a hundred thousand red (pieces) shall be bestowed on thee as a bribe."

724 The vizier said with a smile: "Keep thy bribe for thyself; for me it is sufficient favour from thee that thou hast found the road hither. How can I dare tell the king what I have now heard from you! I know of a truth he will fill me (with favours), and gain is not disagreeable!

725 "By his head! he will slay me straightway; I doubt whether he will delay even a moment. Thy gold will remain with thee, but for me, luckless, there will be earth for a grave. Slay me! What is of equal value with life to a man! The thing cannot be said and I cannot say it, however much anyone should reproach me.

726 "A road cannot go over (beyond) itself.? How can I, luckless, lay down my life for thee? He will despoil me or kill me.

He will say: 'How dost thou speak these words? Why didst thou not inform me there and then? Why art thou such a madman?' Life is better than loot; this I even now learn.

727   "Even if the king permit thee to depart, why should the hosts also be deceived? Why should they let thee go, why should they be hoodwinked, or why should they be removed far from their sun? If thou depart, our foes will become bold, will even themselves with us; but this must not be, as sparrows cannot change to hawks."

728   The knight wept; with tears he spoke: "Must I strike a knife into my heart! O vizier, it is apparent in thee thou knowst not what love is, nor hast thou in others seen friendship or oath. Or if thou hast seen such, how canst thou prove that without him my joy is possible?

729 "The sun has turned. I knew not what would make the sun turn. Now let us help him; it is better for us, in return he will warm our day. No one knows mine affairs like myself; what embitters me, what sweetens me... The discourse of idle men greatly grieves a man.

730   "Of what profit can I be to the king or his hosts, since I am mad now, (and) my tears flow unceasingly! It is better that I go away; I will not break my word; oaths prove a man. The griefs a man has not seen cannot, be comprehended by him at all (?).

731   "Now, O vizier, how can thy cursed heart be calm in this juncture! Iron in my place would become wax and not hard rock; I cannot repay his tears, even if Gihon flowed from mine eyes. Help me if thou wouldst, desire help from me.

732   "If he give me not leave I shall steal away, unknown shall I depart from him; as it entreats me so-shall I deliver my heart to be consumed by fire. I know he will do nothing to thee because of me, if he be not disposed to exile thee. Promise me-- whatever may happen to thee--'I shall sacrifice myself to be tortured!'"

733   The vizier said: "Thy fire consumes me also with fire. I can no longer look on thy tears, the world itself vanishes; sometimes speech is better than silence, sometimes by speaking we spoil (things). I shall speak; if I die it matters not, my life will be sacrificed for thee."

734   When the vizier had said this he arose and went to the palace. He saw the king arrayed; the sunlike face looked straight upon him. He was afraid, he dared not tell him unpleasing news; perplexed he stood, he thought not on warlike matters.

735   The king saw the vizier struck dumb by sadness. 'He said: "What grieves thee? What knowest thou? Why art thou come sad?" He answered: "I know nothing at all, but I am indeed wretched. You will be justified in slaying me when you hear the astounding news.

736   "My mourning neither adds to my grief nor surpasses it; I am afraid, though an envoy has no care for fear. Now Avt'handil bids thee farewell, he entreats, he wrangles not; (he says that) for him the world and life are nought without yon knight."

737   With timorous tongue he told him all he knew. He added, thereafter: "How canst thou know by such words in what a plight I saw him and how his tears flowed? Though you should let your wrath fall forthwith on me, you are just."

738   When the king had heard this he was wroth, he lost his senses, his colour whiled and he became terrible, he would have terrified onlookers. He cried: "What has made a madman of thee? Who else would have related this? It is the choice of a bad man to learn early what is evil.

739   "Traitor-like, thou hast told me of this as if it were a merry matter; what more could anyone do to me save slay me faithlessly, treacherously? Madman, how couldst thou employ thy tongue to dare to speak thus to me now! Such a madman as thou art is unworthy to be vizier or aught else.

740   "Should not a man spare his lord what is irksome, when he stupidly chatters stupid speech? Why were mine ears not deafened before hearing such a thing! If I kill thee, my neck must bear the responsibility for thy blood!"

741   Again he spake: "If thou hadst not now been sent hither by him, by my head! I had cut off thy head, let there be no doubt of this! Go, withdraw! Look at the mad, stupid, desperate, improper (fellow)! Brave word, brave man, brave the deed done by him!"

742   He bent down, he threw chairs, he hit the wall and shattered them; he missed his aim, but for his (the vizier's) sake he made them (the chairs) like adamant, not willowlike. "How couldst thou tell me of the going of him who plaited the aloe-tree branches!" (?). Hot tears hollowed out channels in the vizier's white cheeks (?).

743   The wretched vizier hurried away; he dared say no more. He crept off crestfallen like a fox; his wounded heart pains him. He comes in a courtier, he goes out gloomy, so

(much) does the tongue dishonour him. A foe cannot hurt a foe as a man harms himself.

744 He said: "What more will God show me like unto my woes? Why was I deceived? Why was I darkened? Would that someone might enlighten me! Whoever announces anything so boldly to a sovereign, my (evil) days stand upon him too; how can he ever enjoy peace!"

745 The disgraced vizier went away in black luck. Gloomily, sad-faced, he said to Avt'handil: "What thanks can I give thee! Thanks to thee, what a courtier am I become! Alas! I have lost my peerless self by mine own fault!"

746 He begs the bribe and behaves sportively, albeit his tears were not dry. I marvel why he spends his time in making jokes, why he is not grieved in heart! (Quoth he): "He who gives not what he promised quarrels with the Mourav [16]. It is said: 'A bribe settles matters even in hell.'

747 "How he took the matter, what he said to me, it is not to be told by me. What evil, what stupidity, what idiocy, what madness (he attributed to me)! I myself am no longer worthy of the name of man; no longer have I sense. At this I marvel--why he slew me not; God must have given him patience.

748 "I knew too what I did; it happened not to me by mistake. I had pondered, I knew he would be wroth with me, therefore is my grief increased. None can avoid vengeance for a deed done with forethought. Still, for thy sake death seems joy to me; my woes are not in vain."

749 The knight replied: "It is wholly impossible for me not to depart. When the rose withers the nightingale then dies; he

must seek a dewdrop of water, for the sake of this he must rove everywhere, and if he cannot find it what will he do or wherewith shall he soothe his heart?

750 "Without him I cannot bear to sit or lie. I will choose to roam like the beasts, with them to run. Why does he (Rostevan) desire me who am in such a state to fight his adversaries! It is better to have no man at all than to have a dissatisfied one.

751 "I will tell him once again; now, however angry the king may be, surely he can judge how my heart burns and flames. If he grant me not leave, I shall steal away when hope is gone. If I die, my portion and village will be uprooted."

752 When they had conversed, the vizier made a banquet befitting them; he played the host, gave fair gifts to the fair (guest), he enriched his attendants, both youths and grey-beards. They parted; the knight went home as the sun was setting.

753 He (Avt'handil) sent a message (to the king) saying: "How can I give or bestow on thee that which befits thee? What return can I think of for the debts I owe thee? If I survive I shall die for thee; I shall make myself thy slave.

I shall repay love with love, with a like weight."

754 How can I tell his peerlessness, valour, and praise him! He was a man fitting and worthy even of such a deed. Thus should service be, as much as lies in one's power (?). When a man is in trouble then needs he brother and kinsman.

AVT'HANDIL'S DISCOURSE WITH SHERMADIN WHEN HE STOLE AWAY

755   The sun-faced, dispenser of light, speaks to Shermadin and says: "This day is hope, the comforter of my heart, that thou wilt show what thou canst do for me." It needs a reader and a listener for the praise of this story of them.

756   He says: "Rosten did not grant me leave, he hearkened not even to a word from me; he knows not wherein one's being lies and how one's life is in another. Without him (Tariel) in truth I live not, neither abroad nor at home. What unrighteous deed has God ever forgiven to anyone?

757   "Though I resolved not to forsake him, and my decision is final--every liar and traitor insults God and thus lies--the heart seeing not him weeps and sighs, moans and groans, it comes not near to any joy, it shudders, grows sullen, cries clack! and alas!

758   "Three are the ways of showing friendship by a friend: First, the wish for nearness, impatience of distance; then giving and not grudging, unweariedness in liberality; and attention and aid, roaming in the fields td help him.

759   "But why should I lengthen speech; it is time to shorten it. Now to steal away is the healing of this bruised heart. Hearken to what I shall entreat so long as thou hast time in my company, and fortify thyself in observance of what I have already taught thee.

760   "Now prepare as first leader to serve the sovereigns, manifest thy valour and integrity in all things. Take care of my household, command my troops, repeat anew the service, the attention thou hast hitherto shown.

761   "Keep my foes out of the marches, let not thy might fail in aught, grudge no good to the loyal, may they that are false-hearted towards thee be slain; if I return, well shall thy due be repaid to thee by me; service to a master is never lost."

762   When he heard this, the hot tear flowed from Shermadin's eyes. Quoth he: "Wherefore should I be affrighted by sorrow in loneliness! But what shall I do without thee--twilight will fall on my heart! Take me with thee to serve thee; I will help thee however thou wishest.

763   "Who has heard of so great wandering by one alone! Who has heard of a knight holding back from his lord in trouble! Thinking thee lost, what shall I, useless, do here?" The knight answered: "I cannot take thee, however many tears thou sheddest.

764   "How can I disbelieve thy love for me! But the thing cannot be; thus Fate has taken up arms against me. To whom can I entrust my house; save thee, who is fit? Calm thy heart, believe me, I cannot take thee! I cannot! I cannot!

765   "Since I am a lover I must run mad alone in the fields. Should not one with blood-stained tears roam alone! Errantry is the business of lovers; how can one wait till he is grown old? This world is such, be thou assured thereof and submit.

766   "When I am far from thee, think of me, love me. I fear not my foes; I shall take care of myself. A brave man must be of

good cheer, he must not mope in grief; I hate when a man hesitates at no shameful deed.

767   "I am such an one as will not gather cucumbers in this world as an old man, one to whom death for a friend seems a sport and a play. I have left my sun, she grants me leave, why should I linger! Then, if I can bear to go from mine own home, whose can I not bear (to leave)?

768   "Now I give thee my testament addressed to Rosten. I will confide thee to him, and entreat him to care for thee as befits one brought up by me. Should I die, slay not thyself; do not the deed of Satan; weep thereupon, fill the channel [17] of the eyes."

THE TESTAMENT OF AVT'HANDIL TO KING ROSTEVAN WHEN HE STOLE AWAY

769   "He sat down to write the will, thus piteously inditing: "O king! I have stolen away in quest of him I must seek. I cannot remain sundered from him, the kindler of my fires. Forgive me and be merciful to me like as God.

770   "I know that in the end thou wilt not blame this my resolve. A wise man cannot abandon his beloved friend. I venture to remind thee of the teaching of a certain discourse made by Plato: 'Falsehood, and two-facedness injure the body and then the soul.'

771   "Since lying is the source of all misfortunes, why should I abandon my friend, a -brother by a stronger tie than born brotherhood? I will not do it! What avails me the knowledge of the philosophizing of the philosophers! Therefore are we taught that we may be united with the choir of the heavenly hosts.

772   "Thou hast read how the apostles write of love, how they speak of it, how they praise it; know thou it and harmonize thy knowledge: 'love exalteth us,' this is as it were the tinkling burden of their song: if thou conceive not this how can I convince ignorant men?

773   "He who created me, even He gave me power to overcome foes; He who is the invisible Might, the Aid of every earthly being, who fixes the bounds of the finite, sits immortal God as God, He can in one moment change a hundred into one and one into a hundred.

774 "What God wills not will not become fact. The violet fades, the rose withers, if they cannot gaze on the sunbeams; every lovely thing is desirable for the eye to gaze on. How can I endure the lack of him, or how can life please me!

775 "However angry thou art, forgive me that I have not kept your command; enthralled, I had no power to fulfil it. No! to go was the remedy for the flaming of my furnaces. Wherever I may be, what matters it to me if I have but my freewill?

776 "Sadness avails thee not, nor useless flow of tears. The deed which is inevitably decreed above cannot be avoided. It is a law with men that they should struggle and suffer woes, and no creature of flesh hath power to thwart Providence.

777 Whatever God has predestined to come to pass upon me let it be fulfilled, and when I return my heart will no longer remain ashes. May I see you also joyful in majesty and manifold wealth. What I can do for him is my glory, and this is sufficient booty for me.

778 "O king, this is my decision. Slay me! if anyone can disapprove! O king, can it be that my going grieves thee! I cannot be false, I cannot do a cowardly deed; he would shame me when we meet face to face in that eternity whereto we both shall come.

779 "Mindfulness of a friend ne'er doeth us harm. I despise the man who is shameless, false and treacherous. I cannot be false; I cannot do it for a mighty king. What is worse than a hesitant, tardy-going man!

780 "What is worse than a man in the fight with a frowning face, shirking, affrighted and thinking of death! In what is a

cowardly man better than a woman weaving a web! It is better to get glory than all goods!

781   "A narrow road cannot keep back Death, nor a rocky one; by him all are levelled, weak and strong-hearted; in the end the earth unites in one place youth and greybeard. Better a glorious death than shameful life!

782   "And now I fear, O king, to make this request to you: mistaken, mistaken is he who expects not death momentarily; it which unites us all comes alike by day and by night. If I see thee not living, life will be fleeting for me.

783   "If Fate, the destroyer of all, destroy me, an orphan I shall die travelling, unmourned by parent, nor will those who brought me up, nor the friend whom I trust, enshroud me; then indeed will your merciful, tender heart have pity on me.

784   "I have countless possessions weighed by none: Give the treasure to the poor, free the slaves; enrich every orphan without means; they will be grateful to me, remember me, bless me; I shall be thought of.

785   "Whatever is not worthy of being kept in your treasury, give part to build orphan homes, part to build bridges; be not sparing in the spending of mine estate for me; I have none save thee to quench the hot fires. [18]

786   "Henceforth thou shalt learn no more news from me, herewith I commit my soul to thee; this letter tells thee so, without flattering thee; the devil's deeds shall not seduce (my soul), it will prevail; forgive me and pray for me; what can be exacted from me dead?

787   "I entreat thee, O king, for Shermadin my chosen servant. This year he hath an added day of grief. Comfort him with the favour I was wont to favour him withal; make not the tears to flow from his eyes welling with blood.

788   "My testament is ended, written by mine own hand. Behold, mine upbringer, I have parted from thee; I am gone away with maddened heart. Let not the sovereigns be grieved for my sake, be ye not clad in gloom, but be ye in your sovereignty feared by foes."

789   When he had made an end of writing he gave the will to Shermadin. He said: "Convey this to the king discreetly; none can excel thee in any service." He embraced him and wept over him bloody-hued tears.

AVT'HANDIL'S PRAYER IN THE MOSQUE, AND HIS FLIGHT

790   "He prayed and said: "Great God of earths and heavens, who sometimes punishest, sometimes art ready to reward, Unknowable and Unspeakable, Lord of lordships, give me to endure longings, O ruler of heart-utterances!

791   "God, God, I beseech Thee, who govern'st the deeps and heights; Thou didst create love, Thou hast decreed its law; Fate has sundered me from mine excellent sun; uproot not the love sowed by her for me!

792   "God, God, merciful, I have none beside Thee; from Thee I beg aid on the road, however long I travel; shelter me from the mastery of foes, the turmoil of the seas, the evil one by night! If I survive, I shall serve Thee, I shall offer sacrifice to Thee."

793   When he had prayed, he mounted his horse (and) privily passed through the gates; he sent back Shermadin, albeit he made great lamentations. The vassal weeps and beats his breast; the wretched man sheds floods of tears. What can rejoice the vassal deprived of the sight of his lord!

794   Now will I begin another tale; I will attend the parting knight. There was no audience that day for the wrathful Rosten. When day dawned he rose sullen; he was as if he poured flame from his face; he commanded the vizier to be called; thither they led him pale with fear.

KING ROSTEVAN HEARS OF AVT'HANDIL'S SECRET FLIGHT

795 When he saw the vizier arrived with reverence in the hall of audience, Rosten said: "I recall not what thou saidst yesterday; thou didst annoy and enrage me, for a long time I could not compose my soul, therefore did I scold thee, vizier, heart of heart.

796 "I remember not what he (Avt'handil) wanted, (nor) why I treated thee so ill! Truly say the sages: Spite is a net of woes!' Never act in such a way! Consider the matter carefully. Now, tell me what thou saidst! Speak and repeat thy discourse!"

797 Again the vizier submitted his speech of yesterday. When he (Rosten) heard it, he made no lengthy answer: "If I think thee not mad may I be the Jew Levi! [19] Let me hear no more of this, else I wholly give thee up!"

798 When the vizier went forth to seek, he could not find the crystal one (Avt'handil); only the slaves with flowing tears told of his flight. He (the vizier) said: "I cannot go to court; I should remember former days. Whoever is daring let him dare; I repent what I have already said."

799 When the vizier came not, the king again sent a man; the man learned the news and stood outside, none dared report the departure. Rosten began to suspect, therefore grief increased tenfold. He said: "Doubtless he who alone overpowers hundreds has stolen away!"

800   With bent head he meditated; in his heart was great gloom. He sighed and looked up; he commanded a slave: "Go, let that villain come hither and tell me now; let him enter." When the vizier came back his colour paled and he was careful.

801   Again the vizier entered the audience chamber, gloomily, not gaily. The king inquired: "Is the sun gone away, become inconstant like the moon?" (The vizier) told him all, how he (Avt'handil) had gone away secretly: "The sun no longer shines on us; the weather is not bright!"

802   When the king heard this, he cried out with an exceeding great cry, he lamented, he said: "Alas, my foster-son, my dazed eyes shall see thee no more!" He made the onlookers to marvel by scratching his face and tearing his beard. "Whither art thou gone, and where hast thou lost those pillars of light?

803   "If thou hast thyself, none will think thee an orphan; but as for me, what can I do, O foster-son? Now plagues befit me as an abode; thou hast left me orphaned, me whose wretched heart longs for thee. Till I am reunited to thee, tongues cannot tell my sufferings!

804   "When shall I see thee joyous returning from the chase? I shall no longer see thee after the game of ball, graceful in form, a faultless gem! No more shall I hear thine alluring voice. Now without thee, alas! what shall I do with the throne and whole palace?

805   "I know that hunger will not kill thee, however far thou roamest; thy bow will provide thee, and thine arrowheads. Perchance God in His mercy will again lighten our woes; but if I die, O foster-son, by whom shall I be mourned!"

806 A noise was heard, a great host of men had assembled; there is a crowd of courtiers at the palace, seizing their beards with their hands; all rend and strike themselves, the sound of their slapping is heard. They said: "Darkness is upon us, accursed, since our sun is gone from the sky!"

807 When the king saw his magnates, he complained to them with tears and groaning. He said: "You see our sun has made his rays quite rare to us! In what have we annoyed him, wherein have we sinned, why has he parted from us, why forsaken us! How can any take for us the leadership of the hosts he maintained!"

808 All wept, lamented; then at length they grew calm. The king commanded: "Ask! is he alone, or with a squire?" The vassal Shermadin came fearfully, shamefacedly; he gave (the king) the testament, he wept, life seemed to him but loss.

809 He said: "I found this written by him in his chamber; weeping slaves stood there, they tore hair and beard; he is stolen away alone, neither youth nor greybeard is near him; if you slay me it will be just, an unseemly life irks me."

810 When they read the will, again they wept a long time. Then (the king) commanded: "Let not my troops don gay colours. Let us make the downtrodden, the orphans and widows, to pray; let us help them that God may give him paths of peace!"

AVT'HANDIL'S SECOND DEPARTURE AND MEETING WITH TARIEL

811 When the moon is far from the sun, distance makes her
[20] bright; when she is near, his ray consumes her--she is repelled, she cannot approach. But sunlessness dries up the rose and lessens its colour. Not seeing the beloved renews in us our old grief.

812 Now will I begin the story of that knight's departure. He goes away and weeps with boiling heart; it cannot be said that his tears diminished. Every moment he turned back; he prayed that he might find his sun-like one in sun-like beauty. He gazed, he could not detach his eyes; if he tore them away he lost consciousness.

813 When he was near fainting, he had no power to move his tongue, but tears run from his eyes, pouring forth as from a spring. Sometimes he turns; he looks for means (aid) to bear his pains. When he goes forward he knows not whither his horse has borne him.

814 He said: "O mine own! let him who is far from thee and yet silent be accursed; since my mind remains with thee, let my heart also return to thee; the weeping eyes, too, wish and long to see thee. It is better that the lover should be subjected as much as may be to love!

815 "What shall I do till I am united to thee, or in what thinkest thou I shall find joy! I would slay myself but that I doubt it would displease thee, but it would grieve thee to hear I was

no longer living. Come (then) and let us living give our eyes to the shedding of tears.

816   He said: "O sun, who art said to be the image of the sunny night of Him who is One in unity of being and Everlasting, whom the heavenly bodies obey to the jot of a second, turn not away my good fortune; hear my prayer till our meeting, mine and hers!

817   "Thou whom former philosophers addressed as the image of God, aid me, for I am become a captive, iron chains bind me! I, seeker of crystal and ruby, have lost coral and glass; formerly I could not endure nearness, now I regret absence."

818   Thus he lamented and cried out; like a candle he melted. The fear of being too late made him hasten; he wandered on. When night fell, he found delight in the rising of the stars; he compared them to her, he rejoiced, he gazed on them, he held converse with them.

819   He says to the moon: "I adjure thee in the name of thy God, thou art the giver of the plague of love to lovers; thou hast the balm of patience to make them bear it; hear my prayer to unite me with the face fair, through thee, like thine own."

820   Night rejoiced him, day tortured him, he awaited the sunset. When he saw a stream he dismounted; he gazed on the rippling of the water, with it he united the rivulet of blood from the lake of tears; again he set out, lie hasted onward on his road.

821   Alone he lamented; he who was like the aloe-tree in form wept. He killed a goat in the plain where he came to a rocky place, roasted and ate of it and went on, sun-faced,

martial in heart. He said: "I forsook roses, and behold me here woeful!"

822   I cannot now tell the words then spoken by that knight, or what he discoursed and lamented with such elegance. Sometimes his eyes reddened (with their tears) the rose (of his cheeks) scratched by his nail. When he saw the caves he was glad; he went up to the door of the cave.

823   When Asmat'h perceived him, she went to meet him, her tears fell fast; she rejoiced so greatly that she will never have such joy again. The knight dismounted, embraced her, kissed her, and conversed with her. When a man has waited for a man, the coming pleases him wondrously.

824   The knight said to the damsel: "Where and how is thy lord?" The damsel wept with tears which might have fed the sea. She said: "When thou wert gone, he roamed about, for it irked him to be in the cave; now I know nought of him, either by sight or tidings."

825   The knight was pained as if some lance had struck him in the midst of his heart. He said to Asmat'h: "O sister, not thus should a man be! How could he break his oath! I deceived him not; how could he be false to me If he could not keep it, why did he promise? If he promised me, why did he lie?

826   "Since save for him I counted not this world as grief, why did he forget me when I departed? Why could he not endure, what troubled him? How dared he break the oath he had sworn? But why should I marvel at evil from my fate!"

827   Again the maiden spoke: "Thou art justified in such sorrow; but when thou shalt judge aright--suspect me not of

complaisance--is not heart needed to fulfil oath and promise? He, bereft of heart, awaits only the curtailment of his days.

828 "Heart, mind and thought depend one upon another. When heart goes the others also go and follow it. A man deprived of heart cannot play the man; he is chased forth from men. Thou sawest not, thou knowest not, what fires consumed him.

829 "Thou art right in murmuring that thou art separated from thy sworn brother, but how can it be told into what plight he fell, how can I tell thee the fact? Tongue will fail, will be exhausted, the aching heart will ache (still more). Thus think I, for I saw, I luckless born.

830 "Hitherto none has heard in story of sufferings like unto his; such torture would affright' not only men, (but) even stones; sufficient for a fountain are the tears that have flowed from his eyes. Whatever you say, you are right; one is wise in another's battle.

831 "When he went forth, burned, consumed with fires, I asked him: 'Tell me, his adopted sister, what will Avt'handil do when he comes?' He replied: 'Let him come to seek me, me useless for his sake. I shall not leave this vicinage; I will not break my promise to him.

832 "'My vow I will not break, that oath will I not belie; I shall wait till the time appointed, however much the channels (of tears) may flow. If he find me dead, let him bury me, let him say Alas! and mourn. If I meet him living, let him marvel, (for my) life is doubtful.'

833 "Henceforth the sundering of the sun and the mountain-top hath befallen me, only I must shed tears moistening the

plains; maddened, I am tortured by the exceeding multiplication of groans; death has forgotten me, behold the deed of Fate!

834   "This true saying is written on a stone in China: 'Who seeks not a friend is his own foe!' Now that to which nor rose nor violet could be likened is become saffron. If thou seekest, then, seek him; do what befits thee."

835   The knight said: "Thou art right in not justifying me in murmuring against him. But bethink thee what service I have done as one prisoner (of love) to another: I fled from my home, like a stag seeking water I seek him and think of him, I wander from field to field.

836   "The crystal pearl-shells guard the ruby-hued pearl and apparel it; from her I have gone away, I could not stay near her, I could not make her happy, nor could I be happy; by my privy flight I have angered the equals of God, in return for their favours I have troubled their hearts.

837   "My lord and upbringer, by the grace of God living in might, paternal, sweet, merciful, a sky snowing graciousness, to him have I been faithless; I went away, verily I forgot all, and, guilty toward him, I no longer await any good thing from God.

838   "All this afflicts me thus, O sister, for his sake. I have not deceived him, but am come a wayfarer by night and day. Now he is gone somewhere, he for whom I am consumed with fire, wearied in vain and weeping I sit with a sad face.

839   "Sister, the hour and time give me no more leisure for converse. I repent not the past, early will I fulfil the word of the wises: I go, I will seek, either shall I find him or bring death early

upon me; otherwise, since I am thus doomed by Fate, what can I embolden myself to say to God."

840   No more than this he said; he wept and went his way. He passed the rocks, crossed the water, went through the reeds and came to the plain. The wind blowing over the fields froze the rose to a ruby hue. "Why givest thou me this plague?" He reproached Fate for this.

841   He said: "O God, wherein have I sinned against thee, the Lord, the All-seeing? Why hast Thou separated me from my friends? why didst Thou lure me on to such a fate? One thinking of two, I am in a parlous plight; if I die I shall not pity myself, my blood be on my head!

842   "My friend cast a bunch of roses on my heart, and so wounded it; that oath fulfilled by me he kept not. If, O Fate, thou partest me from him, my joy is past, to mine eyes another friend were reviled and shamed."

843   Then he said: "I marvel at the spleen of a man of sense; when he is sad, of what avail is a rivulet from the terrace of tears? It is better to choose, to ponder over the fitting deed. Now for me, too, it is better to seek that sun(-like one), reed-like in form."

844   The knight, weeping, besprinkled with tears, set himself to search; he seeks, he calls, he cries aloud, watching by night as by day; for three days he traversed many a glen, reedy thicket, forest and field; he could not find him; sad he went, unable to learn any tidings.

845   He said: "O God, wherein have I sinned against Thee? how have I displeased Thee so greatly? why bring this fate upon me? What torture hast Thou sent upon me! Judge me, O Judge,

hearken to my prayer; shorten my days, thus turn my woes to joy!"

846   Weeping and pale, the knight went his way and spoke; he mounted a certain hill, the plain appeared in sunshine and shadow. He saw a black (horse) standing with the reins on his neck on the edge of the rushes. He said: "Undoubtedly it is he; of that there can be no doubt."

847   When he saw, the heart of the knight leaped up and was lightened; here to him, distressed, joy became not tenfold, but a thousandfold; the rose (of his cheeks) brightened its colour, the crystal (of his face) became crystal (indeed), the jet (of his eyes) grew jetty; like a whirlwind he galloped down, he rested not from gazing at him.

848   When he saw Tariel he was indeed grieved; (Tariel) sat with drawn face in a state near unto death, his collar was rent, his head was all torn, he could no longer feel, he had stepped forth from the world.

849   On one side lay a slain lion and a blood-smeared sword, on the other a panther stricken down a lifeless corpse. From his eyes, as from a fountain, tears flowed fiercely forth; thus there a flaming fire burned his heart.

850   He could not even open his eyes, he had wholly lost consciousness, he was come nigh to death, he was far removed from joy. The knight calls him by name, he tries to rouse him by speech; he cannot make him hear; he leaped about; the brother shows his brotherliness.

851   He wipes away (Tariel's) tears with his hand, he cleansed his eyes with his sleeve; he sits down near by and only

calls him by name; he says: "Know'st thou not me, Avt'handil, for thy sake wandering and mad?" But he heard little, staring with fixed eyes.

852   This is all thus, even as related by me. He wiped away the tears from his eyes, he somewhat recalled him to consciousness; then only he knew (Avt'handil), kissed him, embraced him, treated him as a brother. I declare by the living God none like him was ever born.

853   He said: "Brother, I was not false to thee, I have done what I swore to thee; unparted from my soul I have seen thee, thus have I kept my vow; now leave me; till death I shall weep and beat my head, but I entreat thee for burial, that I be not yielded to the beasts for food."

854   The knight replied: "What ails thee? Why doest thou an evil deed? Who hath not been a lover, whom doth the furnace not consume? Who hath done like thee among the race of other men! Why art thou seized by Satan, why kill thyself by thine own will?

855   "If thou art wise, all the sages agree with this principle: 'A man must be manly, it is better that he should weep as seldom as possible; in grief one should strengthen himself like a stone wall.' Through his own reason a man falls into trouble.

856   "Thou art wise, and (yet) knowest not to choose according to the sayings of the wise. Thou weepest in the plain and livest with the beasts; what desire canst thou thus fulfil? If thou renounce the world thou canst not attain her for whose sake thou diest. Why bindest thou a hale head, why openest thou the wound afresh?

857   "Who hath not been a lover, whom hath the furnace not consumed? Who hath not seen pains, who faints not for somebody? Tell me, what has been unexampled! Why should thy spirits flee! Know'st thou not that none e'er plucked a thornless rose!

858   "They asked the rose: 'Who made thee so lovely in form and face? I marvel why thou art thorny, why finding thee is pain!' It said: 'Thou findest the sweet with the bitter; whatever costs dear is better; when the lovely is cheapened it is no longer worth even dried fruit.'

859   "Since the soulless, inanimate rose speaks thus, who then can harvest joy who hath not first travailed with wee? Who hath ever heard of aught harmless that was the work of devilry? Why dost thou murmur at Fate? What hath it done unexampled?

860   "Hearken to what I have said, mount, let us go at ease. Follow not after thine own counsel and judgment; do that thou desirest not, follow not the will of desires; were it not better thus I would not tell thee, mistrust not that I shall flatter thee in aught."

861   (Tariel) said: "Brother, what shall I say to thee? Scarce have I control of my tongue; maddened, I have no strength to hearken to thy words. How easy to thee seems patience of the suffering of my torments! Now am I brought close to death; the time of my joy draws nigh.

862   "Dying, for her I pray; never shall I entreat (her) with my tongue. Lovers here parted, there indeed may we be united, there again see each other, again find some joy. Come, O friends, bury me, cast clods upon me!

863 "How shall the lover not see his love, how forsake her! Gladly I go to her; then will she wend to me. I shall meet her, she shall meet me; she shall weep for me and make me weep. Inquire of a hundred, do what pleaseth thine heart, in spite of what any may advise thee.

864 "But know thou this as my verdict, I speak to thee words of truth: Death draws nigh to me, leave me alone, I shall tarry but a little while; if I be not living, of what use am I to thee? If I survive, what canst thou 1 make of me, mad? Mine elements are dissolved; they are joining the ranks of spirits.

865 "What thou hast said and what thou speakest I understand not, nor have I leisure to listen to these things. Death draws nigh me maddened; life is but for a moment. Now the world is grown distasteful to me--more than at any time (heretofore). I, too, go thither to that earth whereon the moisture of my tears flows.

866 "Wise! Who is wise, what is wise, how can a madman act wisely? Had I my wits such discourse would be fitting. The rose cannot be without the sun; if it be so, it begins to fade. Thou weariest me, leave me, I have no time, I can endure no more."

867 Avt'handil spoke again with words of many kinds. He said: "By my head! by these empty words I shall do thee some good! Do it not! It is not the better deed. Be not thine own foe!" But he cannot lead him away; he can do nothing at all by speech.

868 Then he said: "Well, since thou wilt by no means hearken to me, I will not weary thee; my tongue has hitherto spoken in vain. If death be better for thee, die! Let the rose

wither--they all wither! One thing only I pray thee, grant me this"--for this his tears were flowing--

869 "Where the Indians (black lashes) engird the crystal (brow) and rose (cheeks) with a hedge of jet--from this am I parted; hastily I went, not quietly. The king cannot keep me by his paternal converse. Thou wilt not unite with me, thou wilt renounce me; now how can I speak my joy!

870 "Send me not heart-sore away, grant me one desire: Mount once thy steed, let me see thee, ravisher of my soul, on horseback; perchance then this present grief will flee away, I shall go and leave thee, let thy will be done!"

871 He entreated him, "Mount!" He begged and prayed him, and said not Alas! He knew that riding would chase away his sadness, that he would bend the reedy stems (of his form), and make a tent of the jet (eyelashes). He (Avt'handil) made him (Tariel) obedient; it pleased (Avt'handil); (Tariel) sighed not nor moaned.

872 He said plainly: "I will mount; bring forward my horse." (Avt'handil) brought (the horse) and gently I helped him to mount; he did not make him pant with haste; he took him towards the plain, he made his graceful form to sway. Some time they rode; going made him seem better.

873 He (Avt'handil) entertains him, and speaks fair words to him; for (Tariel's) sake he moved his coral-coloured lips in speech. To hear him would make young the aged ears of a listener. He put away melancholy; he took unto himself patience.

874   When the elixir of grief (Avt'handil) perceived the improvement, joy not to be depicted lightened his rose-like face--(joy which is) the physician of the reasonable, the sigh and moan of the foolish. He who had formerly spoken senselessly now spoke reasonably.

875   They began to converse; he spoke a frank word: "One thing will I say to thee: Open to me what is secret. This armlet of her by whom thou art wounded--how much dost thou love it? How dost thou prize it? Tell me, then let me die!"

876   He said: "How can I tell thee the likeness of that incomparable picture! It is my life, the giver of my groans, better to me than all the world--water, earth and tree. To hearken to that to which one should not listen is more bitter than vinegar!"

877   Avt'handil said: "I truly expected thee to say this. Now, since thou hast said it, I will answer thee, and think not I shall flatter thee; to lose Asmat'h were worse than the loss of that armlet. I commend not thy behaviour in choosing the worsen.

878   "This armlet thou wearest is golden, molten by the goldsmith, inanimate,' lifeless, speechless, unreasoning; thou no longer wantest Asmat'h! Behold a true judgment! First, she, luckless, was with her (Nestan); then she is thine own adopted sister.

879   "Between you (and Nestan) she formed a bond, by thee she has been called sister; she was the servant who contrived your meeting, (while) she herself was worthy of being summoned by thee; she, upbringer of her and brought up by her, she is mad for (Nestan), (and) thou forsakest her, wretched (woman), (and) wilt not see her? Bravo! a just judgment (indeed)!"

880   He said: "What thou sayest is only too true. Pitiable is Asmat'h, who thinks of (Nestan) and sees me. I thought not to live; thou are come in time to quench the fires. Since I still survive, come, let us see, albeit I am still dazed."

881   He obeyed. Avt'handil and the Amirbar set out. I cannot achieve the praise of their worth: teeth like pearls, lips cleft roses. The sweetly discoursing tongue lures forth the serpent from its lair.

882   Thereupon (Avt'handil) says: "For thy sake will I sacrifice mind, soul, heart; but be not thus, open not thy wounds afresh. Learning avails thee not if thou do not what the wise have said; of what advantage to thee is a hidden treasure if thou wilt not use it?

883   "Grieving is of no use to thee; if thou art sorrowful what good will it do thee? Know'st thou not that no man dies undesignedly? Awaiting the sunbeams the rose fades not in three days. Luck, endeavour and victory, if God will, shall be thy lot."

884   The knight (Tariel) replied: "This teaching is worth all the world to me. The intelligent loves the instructor; he pierces the heart of the senseless. But what shall I do, how can I endure when I am in excessive trouble? My griefs have hold of thee too. If, then, thou justify me not shall I not wonder?

885   "Wax hath an affinity with the heat of fire, and therefore is lighted; but water hath no such affinity, if (wax) fall into (water) it is quenched. Whatever thing afflicts someone himself, in that will he be bold for the sake of others too. Why know'st thou not once for all in what way my heart melts?

886   "With my tongue will I relate to thee in detail all that hath befallen me; then indeed with wise heart judge the truth. I expected thee, awaiting thee was irksome to me, I could no longer endure the cave, I wished to ride in the plain.

887   "I came up that hill, I had traversed these reeds; a lion and a panther met, they came together; they seemed to me to be enamoured, it rejoiced me to see them; but what they did to each other surprised me, horrified me.

888   "I came up the hill, the lion and panther came walking together; they were to me like a picture of lovers, my burning fires were quenched. They came together and began to fight, embittered they struggled; the lion pursues, the panther flees. They were not commended by me.

889   "First they sported gaily, then they quarrelled fiercely; each struck the other with its paw, they had no fear of death; the panther lost heart, even as women do; the lion fiercely pursued, none could have calmed him.

890   "The behaviour of the lion displeased me. I said: Thou art out of thy wits. Why annoy'st thou thy beloved? Fie on such bravery!' I rushed on him with my bared sword, I gave him to be pierced by the spear, I struck his head, I killed him, I freed him from this world's woe.

891   "I threw away my sword, I leaped down, I caught the panther with my hands, I wished to kiss it for the sake of her for whom hot fires burn me. It roared at me, and worried me with its blood-shedding paws. I could bear no more; with enraged heart I killed it too.

892 "However much I soothed it, the panther became not calm. I grew angry, I brandished it, dashed it on the ground, shattered it. I remembered how I had striven with my beloved. (Yet) my soul tore not itself altogether out of me. Why, then, art thou astonished that I shed tears!

893 "Behold, brother! I have told the woes that grieved me. Life itself befits me not. Why didst thou wonder that I am thus fordone? I am sundered from life, death is become shy of me." So the knight ended his story, sighed, and wept aloud.'

HERE IS THE GOING OF TARIEL AND AVT'HANDIL TO THE CAVE, AND THEIR SEEING OF ASMAT'H

894   Avt'handil also wept with him and shed tears. He said: "Be patient, die not, rend not altogether thy heart. God will be merciful in this, though sorrow hath not shunned thee; if He had willed to part you, He would not first have united you.

895   "Mischance pursues the lover, embitters life for him; but to him who at first bears woe it yields joy at last. Love is grievous, for it brings thee nigh unto death; it maddens the instructed, it teaches the untaught."

896   They wept and went on; they wended their way to the cave. When Asmat'h saw them she rejoiced indeed; she met them, she wept, her tears wore channels in the rocks. They kissed and wept aloud; each pressed the other to tell his news again.

897   Asmat'h said: "O God, Thou who canst not be expressed by man's tongue! Thou art the fulness of all; Thou fillest us with Thy sun-like radiance. If I praise Thee, how can I praise Thee? What can I say in praise of Thee, who art not to be praised by the intellect? Glory to Thee! Thou hast not slain me by the shedding of tears for them."

898   Tariel said: "Ah, sister! for this have my tears flowed here. For that she erstwhile made us smile, Fate makes us weep in turn; 'tis an old law of the world, not one newly to be heard of! Alas! were it not for pity of thee, death would be my joy.

899 "If he be athirst, what sane, reasonable man would pour away water! I marvel why I am soaked in tears from mine eyes! Lack of water slays, water flows never dried. Alas! the opened rose, the beauteous pearl, is lost!"

900 Avt'handil, too, was reminded of his sun and beloved. He said: "O mine own, how can I remain living without thee! Apart from thee my life is for me pitiable. Who can tell thee how I suffer, or how sore a fire burns me!

901 "How can the rose think, 'If the sun go away I shall not wither'? Or what, alas! will be our lot when the sun sets behind the hill? Heart, it is better for thee to harden thyself, petrify thyself wholly. Perchance it may happen to thee to see her; let not thy spirit be utterly spent!"

902 They calmed their souls, they were silent, fire burned both. Asmat'h followed, went in; like them, a furnace consumed her. She stretched out the panther's skin he formerly used. They both sat down; they spoke of whatever pleased them.

903 They roasted meat and made a meal fitting the occasion; there the meal was breadless, and there was no multitude of guests. They begged (Tariel) to eat; he had not power to eat; he chewed a morsel, spat it out, he hardly swallowed the weight of a drachm.

904 Pleasant it is when man converses agreeably with man; he will listen to what is said, not let it pass in vain; thus the fire which burns so greatly is somewhat quenched; great comfort it is to speak of troubles when a man has the opportunity.

905 That night those lions, those heroes, were together, they conversed, and each revealed to the other his woes; when day dawned they began again many-worded conversations; they heard (again) from each other the oath formerly sworn.

906 Tariel said: "Why speak many words? For that which thou hast done for me, God is surety for the debt. Oath for oath is enough; remembrance, friendship for a departing friend, are not the deed of a drunken man.

907 "Now be merciful to me, make me not burn again in hottest fires; the flame which consumes me is not kindled by a steel; thou canst not extinguish it for me, thou thyself shalt be burned by the law of the creation of the world. Go, return, go back thither, to the place where thy sun is.

908 "To cure me seems hard even to Him who created me--understand, ye who hear!--therefore I roam mad in the fields. Once I too was a doer of what befits the reasonable; now the turn of madness has fallen to my lot, and so I am mad."

909 Avt'handil said: "What can I say in answer to this thou hast said? Thou thyself hast spoken as a man sagely instructed. How is it not possible for God again to cure the wound! He is the upbringer of everything planted or sown.

910 "Why should God do this, create such as you and not unite you, part you, madden thee with weeping? Mischance pursues the lover. Look well into the matter, know it. If you meet not each other again, then slay me!

911 "Who else is a man save he that will endure what is grievous? How can one let himself be bent by grief! What subject of conversation is this! Fear not, God is generous though

the world be hard! Learn then what I teach thee; I make bold to tell thee that he who will not learn is an ass.

912 "Heed what thou hearest; let this suffice for teaching. I asked leave of my sun to come away to you; I said to her: 'Since he made cinders of my heart I am no longer of use to thee, I will not stay; what else need I tell thee in many (words)?'

913 "She said: 'I am content, thou art doing well and bravely, the attention thou showest to him I accept as a service to me.' At her request I came away. I am not drunk nor intoxicated! If I now return what shall I say? 'Why art thou come back like a coward?' (will be her greeting).

914 "Better than such discourse is this: hearken to what I say: The man who is to do a difficult deed must be reasonable, the rose withered for lack of sun cannot make provision for itself; (if) thou art no longer of any, use to thyself, be of use to me; brother must act brotherly to brother.

915 "Wherever thou wilt, stay there after thy rule: if thou wilt with wise heart, if thou wilt with maddened mind. With that loveliness of mien, that grace of form, do but strengthen thyself, die not, be not consumed by the flame!

916 "I beg no more than leave for a year and a week. Here in the cave look for me when I have gathered news from every quarter. As a token of that time I give thee the season when these roses shall again bloom abundantly; the sight of the roses will make thee start as at the bark of a dog.

917 "If I exceed that time and come not hither to the cave, then know that I am not alive, undoubtedly I shall have died. It

will be a sufficient token of this if thou shed tears for me. Then rejoice if thou wilt, or if thou wilt increase thy grief.

918   "Now perchance wilt thou sorrow for the sake of what I have told thee? I go far from thee, and I know not whether horse or ship may fail me. No! lack of speech avails not. I am not quick-scented like a beast; I know not what God will do to me, nor the ever-revolving sky."

919   He (Tariel) said: "I will weary thee no more, nor say too much; thou wilt not listen to me however much I lengthen my discourse. If a friend will not follow thee, follow thou him; do whatever he wills. In the end every bidden thing shall come to light.

920   "When thou art convinced, then thou shalt know the difficulty of mine affairs; for me it is all one, roaming or not roaming; what thou hast told me that will I do, however much madness torture me. (But) if shortness of days (i.e., death) befall me in thine absence, what shall I do?"

921   They ended their discourse; they gave that promise to each other. They mounted, rode out, each killed game in the plain. They returned, their tearful hearts wept again; the thought of the parting on the morrow added grief to grief.

922   Readers of these verses, your eyes also are shedding tears! What, alas! shall heart do without heart, if heart part from heart! Absence and parting from a friend are the slayers of a man. Who, indeed, knows not, understands not, how hard is that day!

923   Morning dawned; they mounted and said farewell to the maiden. From the eyes of Tariel, Asmat'h and Avt'handil

tears flowed. The cheeks of all three hung out flags of crimson. Those lions ever made wild (by grief went out to the beasts.

924   They descended (from) the caves and went away crying aloud with flowing tears. Asmat'h weeps and laments: "O lions! whose tongues can chant lamentations for you! The sun has burned and consumed you heavenly stars. Alas for my woes so great! Alas the sufferings of life!"

925   Those knights, departed thence, travelled that day together. They came to the seashore, there they tarried, they travelled not through dry land (?) That night they parted not; again they shared their fire. They wept for the absence from each other; they bewailed it.

926   Avt'handil said to Tariel: "The channel of the flow of tears is dried! Why didst thou separate from P'hridon, the giver of this steed? Thence are tidings and means to be learnt regarding that beautiful sun. Now I go thither; teach me the way to thy sworn brother."

927   Tariel teaches him by word the direction of the road to P'hridon's. He made him understand as well as he could by his power of speech: "Go towards the east; fare even unto the seashore. If thou seest him tell him of me; he will ask news of his brother."

928   They killed a goat and dragged it after them, they made a fire on the seashore, they sat down and ate such a meal as was fitting to their grief. That night they were together; they lay together at the root of a tree. I curse treacherous Fate, sometimes generous, sometimes niggardly.

929   At dawn they rose to part, they embraced each other. The things said by them then would have melted anyone who heard. They shed on the fields tears from the eyes like waters from a spring. Long they stand in a close embrace; breast was welded to breast.

930   With tears and face-scratching and tearing of hair they parted; one goes up, the other goes down; roadless they ride by bridle-paths through the rushes; as long as they saw each other, with drawn faces they shouted; looking upon their frowns the sun would frown too.

OF THE GOING OF AVT'HANDIL TO P'HRIDON'S WHEN HE MET HIM AT MULG-HAZANZAR

931   Alas! O world (Fate), what ails thee? Why dost thou whirl us round? What (? ill) habit afflicts thee? All who trust in thee weep ceaselessly like me. Whence and whither earnest thou? Where and whence uprootest thou? But God abandons not the man forsaken by thee.

932   Avt'handil, parted from (Tariel), weeps; his voice reaches to the heavens. Quoth he: "The stream of blood which flowed anew flows once again. Now is parting as hard as union will be till (we meet) in heaven. Men are not all equal; there is a great (difference) between man and man."

933   Then the beasts of the field drank their fill of the tears he shed there; he could not quench the furnace, he burned with frequent fire. Again the thought of T'hinat'hin fills him all the more with grief; the coral-rooted crystal shines on the rose of the lips.

934   The rose is faded, it drips, the branch of the aloe-tree quivers, the cut crystal and ruby are changed into lapis-lazuli. He strengthened himself against death; against him it vaunted not itself. He said: "Why should I wonder at darkness since thou, O sun, hast abandoned me!"

935   He said to the sun: "O sun, I compare thee to the cheeks of T'hinat'hin, thou art like her and she is like thee, ye light mountain and valley. The sight of thee rejoices me a madman,

therefore unweariedly I gaze on thee; but why have you (both) left my heart cold, unwarmed?

936   The absence of one sun for a month in winter freezes us; I, alas! have parted from two; how, then, should heart not be harmed? Only a rock perceives not, is never hurt! A knife cannot cure a wound; it cuts or causes a swelling."

937   Wending his way he laments to the sky, he speaks; to the sun he says: "O sun, to thee I pray, thou mighty of the mightiest mights, who exaltest the humble, givest sovereignty, happiness (?); part me not from my beloved, turn not my day to night!" [21]

938   "Come, O Zual, [22] add tear to tear, woe to woe; dye my heart black, give me to thick gloom, heap upon me a heavy load of grief as on an ass; (but) say to her: 'Forsake him not! Thine he is, and for thee he weeps.'

939   "O Musht'har, [23] I entreat thee, thou just, perfect judge, come and do justice, heart takes counsel with heart; twist not justice, destroy not thus thy soul. I am righteous, judge me, why wouldst thou wound afresh me

940   "Come, O Marikh, [24] mercilessly pierce me with thy spear, dye me and stain me red with the flow of blood; tell her my sufferings, let her hear them with the tongue; thou knowest what I am become, no longer my heart path joy."

941   "Come, Aspiroz, [25] aid me somewhat; she has consumed me with the flame of fires, she who encircles the pearl (of her teeth) with lip of coral; thou beautifiest the fair with such charm (? as thine); one like me thou abandonest and maddenest."

942 "Otarid![26] save thee none other's fate is like to mine. The sun whirls me, lets me not go, unites with me and gives me over to burning. Sit down to write my woes! For ink I give thee a lake of tears, for pen I cut for thee a trim form, slim as a reed."

943 "Come, O Moon, take pity on me; I shrink and am wasted like thee; the sun fills me, the sun, too, empties me; sometimes I am full-bodied, sometimes I am spare. Tell her my tortures, what afflicts me, how I faint. Go, say: 'Forsake him not!' I am hers, and for her sake I die.

944 "Behold, the stars bear witness, even the seven confirm my words: the sun, Otarid, Musht'har and Zual faint for my sake; moon, Aspiroz, Marikh, come and bear me witness; make her hear what fires consume me without thee (her)."

945 Now he says to his heart: "As the tear still flows, and is not dried, what avails it to slay thyself! It is clear thou hast fraternized with the devil as a brother. I myself know that she who maddened me has for hair the tail of a raven; but if thou bearest not grief what is the enduring of joy?

946 "If I remain, this is better for me"--he speaks of the uncertainty of life--"perchance it will be my lot to see the sun (T'hinat'hin), I shall not forever cry Alas!" He sang with sweet voice; he checked not the channel of tears. Compared to his voice even the voice of the nightingale was like an owl's.

947 When the knight's song was heard, the beasts came to listen; by reason of the sweetness of his voice even the stones came forth from the water, they hearkened, they marvelled, when he wept they wept; he sings sad songs, tears flow like a fount.

947a All living creatures on earth came to applaud: game from the forest, fishes in the water, crocodiles in the sea, birds from the sky, from India, Arabia, Greece, Orientals and Occidentals, Russians, Persians, Franks and Egyptians from Misret'hi. [27]

OF AVT'HANDIL'S GOING TO P'HRIDON'S WHEN HE PARTED FROM TARIEL

948   Weeping the knight went seventy days along the road to the seashore. Afar off he saw in the sea sailors approaching; he waited and asked: "Who are you, I beg you to tell me this: Whose realm is this or whose voice doth it obey?"

949   They dutifully answered: "O fair of face and form, strange and pleasing to us thou seemest, therefore with praise we address thee; hereunto is the boundary of the Turks, marching with the border of P'hridon, whose (men) we are; of him shall we tell thee, if we faint not from gazing on thee.

950   "Nuradin P'hridon is king of this our land, a knight brave, generous, mighty, on horseback a swift racer; none has power to harm so fair a sun; he is our lord, he like the beams spread forth from heaven."

951   The knight said: "My brethren, in you have I happed upon good men. I seek your king, teach me whither I should go. How shall I go, when shall I come thither, how long is the road?" The sailors guided him; they left not the shore.

952   They reported to him: "This is the road going to Mulghazanzar, there our king will meet thee, he of the swift arrow, the keen sword. Thou shalt arrive there ten days hence, O thou of the cypress form, ruby in hue. Alas! why dost thou, a stranger, burn us strangers, why consumest thou us like a flame of fire!"

953 The knight said: "I marvel, brethren, why you are heart-slain for me, or how the faded winter roses can please you thus! If you had seen us then when we sat proud, uncrippled, we charmed them that gazed on us, with us they sat joyful."

954 They departed, the knight turned to pursue his road, he whose form is like the cypress, whose heart is like iron. He puts his horse to a canter, he discourses, he speaks aloud to comfort himself; the narcissi (his eyes) thunder, it rains tears, they lave the crystal and glass (of his face).

955 Whatever strangers he met on the road served him, were subservient to him; they came to gaze on him, they courted him, it was hard for them to let him go, scarce could they bear parting, they gave him a guide for the road, whatever he asked they told him.

956 He neared Mulghazanzar; soon he ended the long road. In the plain he saw an army of soldiers, and they were seen to be destroying game; on all sides a chain was formed, they encircled the outside of the field; they shot and shouted, they mowed down beasts like standing corn.

957 He met a man, he asked him tidings of that host; he said: "Whose is this sound of trampling and stir?" He answered: "P'hridon the monarch, King of Mulghazanzar, hunts, he holds the edge of the sedgy plain engirt."

958 Matchless in mien he went towards the troops, he became merry, how can I ever tell the beauty of that knight! Those who are parted from him he makes to freeze, like the sun he burns them that are met with him; he renews, if they look on him, those who gaze, his form sways like a tree.

959   In the very midst of the hosts an eagle soared from somewhere. The knight urged on his horse, he emboldened himself, he feared not; he drew his bow and let the arrow fly; (the eagle) fell and blood flowed (from it); he dismounted and clipped its wings; calmly he remounted, he panted not.

960   When they saw him, the archers ceased to shoot; they broke the circle, they came, they pressed upon him, they fainted, from all sides they surrounded him, some followed behind. They dared not ask him: "Who art thou?" nor could they say aught to him.

961   In the meadow was a hill, on it stood P'hridon; forty men worthy to shoot with him attended him; thither Avt'handil made his way, after him followed the centre of the host. P'hridon marvelled. "What are they doing?" said he; he was angry with his armies.

962   P'hridon sent out a slave, saying: "Go, see the armies, what they are doing, why they have broken the circle, whither blind like they go." The slave swiftly reached them, he saw the cypress, the sapling form; he stood, his eyes became dazed, he forgot the words he had to say.

963   Avt'handil perceived that this (man) was come to learn news of him. He said: "I beg thee to convey this message to thy lord from me: 'I am a stranger, lonely, far removed from my home, sworn brother to Tariel, sent to you.'"

964   The slave went to P'hridon to tell him his message. He said: "I have seen a sun arrived, he seems like the lightener of day. I think even sages would be maddened if they saw him anywhere. Quoth he: 'I am Tariel's brother (thus come) rudely to join P'hridon.'"

965   When he heard (the name of) Tariel, P'hridon's woes were lightened, from his eyes tears sprang forth, his heart grew more agitated, a blast froze the rose, from his eyelids whirled snowstorms (of tears). They met each other, each was praised by the other, not dispraised.

966   Hastily P'hridon came down from the ridge; he descended to meet (Avt'handil). When he looked on hint he said: "If this be not the sun, who is it?" (Avt'handil) outdid the praise (P'hridon) had heard from the slave. They both dismounted; joy made tears gush up.

967   They embraced; they were not shy for being strangers. The knight seems peerless to P'hridon, and P'hridon pleases the knight. Any onlookers who saw them (would) despise the sun. Slay me! if another like them will ever be bargained for or sold in the bazaar.

968   What knights are there like P'hridon! But near him is one whom praises still more befit; the sun makes the planets invisible when they come near; a candle gives no light by day, but its rays shine by night.

969   They mounted their horses and set out for P'hridon's palace. The chase was broken up; they made an end of the slaying of beasts. From all sides the troops thronged to gaze on Avt'handil; they said: "What creature can compare with him?"

970   The knight said to P'hridon: "Thou art eager, I know, to hear my tidings. I will tell thee who I am, whence I come, inasmuch as thou wishest to know, also whence I know Tariel and why I spoke of our brotherhood. He calls me brother; 'Thou art my brother,' quoth he, though I am scarce worthy to be his slave.

971   "I am King Rosten's vassal, a knight nurtured in Arabia, Grand Commander-in-Chief; by name they call me Avt'handil, I am a noble of great family, reared as son of the king, one to be respected, bold, none dares meddle with me.

972   "One day the king mounted, went forth to hunt; in the plain we saw Tariel, he poured forth tears watering the fields; we were astonished, he surprised us, we called and he came not, he made us angry; we knew not how fire consumed him.

973   "The king shouted to the troops to seize him, and he was irritated; without trouble he slew, battle was not grievous to him; of some he broke the arms and legs, some he slew outright; there they learned that the course (chariot) of the moon is not to be turned back.

974   "The king, greatly indignant, perceived that the troops could not capture him; himself he mounted and went against him, the haughtily unfearing. When Tariel knew it was the king, then he avoided his sword, he gave the reins to his horse, he was lost to our eyes.

975   "We sought and could find no trace; we believed it devilry. The king was sad, forbad drinking, feast and banquet. I could not endure lack of certainty about his story. I stole away in quest of him, fire burned me, and smouldering.

976   "Three years I sought him; I enjoyed not even sleep. I saw Khatavians he had mauled; they showed him to me. I found the yellowish rose, faint-rayed, pale-tinted; he welcomed me and loved me like a brother, like a son.

977 "He took the caves from the Devis after great bloodshed. There Asmat'h attends the solitary, none else is with him; ever the old fire burns him, it is not newly roused. Groaning befits one parted from him, a black mourning kerchief bound round the head.

978 "Alone in the cave the tearful, tear-stained damsel weeps. The knight hunts game for her as a lion for its whelp; he brings it, and thus he feeds her. He cannot rest in one place. Save her (Asmat'h) he desires not the sight of any of man's race.

979 "To me, a stranger, he pleasantly narrated his wondrous and pleasing (story); he told me his tale, and his beloved's. What woe he has suffered this tongue of a madman cannot now tell; longing slays him, and lack of the sight of his grave-digger.

980 "Like the moon he unceasingly roams, he rests not; he sits on that horse thou gayest him, he never alights; he sees no speaking being, like a wild beast he shuns men. Woe is me, remembering him; alas for him dying for her sake!

981 "The fire of that knight burns me, I am consumed with hot fire; I pitied him, and I became mad, my heart grew furious; I wished to seek remedies for him by sea and land. I returned and saw the sovereigns, whose hearts were gloomy.

982 "I entreated leave of absence; the king was enraged at me, and fell into sadness. I deserted my soldiers, therefore they there cried, 'Woe!' I stole away, I freed myself from the flood of tears of blood. Now I seek balm for him; I turn about hither and thither.

983 "He told me tidings of thee, how he had made brother-hood with thee. Now have I found thee, peerless, worthy to be praised by the tongue; counsel me where it is better to seek

that heavenly sun, the joy of those who gaze on her, the disturber of those that cannot see her."

984   Now P'hridon speaks, utters the words spoken by that knight (Tariel); both in unison lamented in a threnody worthy of praise; sobbing, they wept with impatient hearts, there the roses were sprinkled by the water of tears dammed up in the jungle.

985   Among the soldiers there arose the sound of great weeping, the scratching of the face by some, from others comes a torrent (of tears). P'hridon weeps, laments aloud the seven years' separation. Alas! the inconstancy and falsity of this vain world!

986   P'hridon laments: "How can we tell forth thy (i.e., Tariel's) praise, thou who canst not be praised, thou inexpressible one! O sun of the earth, who transferrest the sun of the firmament from its course, joy, life, quickener of them that are near thee; light of the planets of heaven, consumer and swallower up!

987   "Since I was removed from thee life has been hateful to me. Though thou hast no leisure for me I long for thee; to thee lack of me seems joy, it oppresses me greatly. Life without thee is empty; the world is become hateful to me."

988   P'hridon uttered these words in a beautiful lament. They grew calm, they were silent; they rode with no sign of song. Avt'handil is fair to beholders in his ethereal loveliness; he covers the inky lakes (of his eyes) with the jet ceiling (of his lashes).

989   They entered the city, there they found the palace adorned in perfection, with all the officers of state mustered, the slaves delicately apparelled were in faultless order; they were enraptured and ravished in heart with Avt'handil.

990   They entered and held a great court, not a privy council; on this side and on that side ten times ten magnates were ranged; apart sat the two together; who can tell forth their praise? Here glass, there jet, adorned the crystal and ruby (of their faces).

991   They sat, they banqueted, they multiplied the best liquor; they entertained Avt'handil as kinsman (treats) kinsman; they brought beautiful vessels, all quite new. But the heart of those who looked on that youth, alas! was given to flame.

992   That day they drank, they ate, there was a banquet for the tribe of drinkers. Day dawned; they bathed Avt'handil; there lies abundance of satin; they clad hint in raiment worth many thousands of dracanis; [28] they girded him with a girdle of inestimable worth.

993   The knight tarried some days, though he could not brook delay; he went out hunting with P'hridon and sported, he slew alike from far and near whatever offered itself to his hand; his archery put every bowman to shame.

994   The knight said to P'hridon: "Hear what I have now to tell thee. Parting from you seems to me like death, and thereby shall I harm myself; but I, unhappy, have not time to stay; another fire also consumes me. A long road, an urgent deed I have to do, I shall be very late.

995   "Right is he who sheds tears at parting from thee. To-day without fail I depart, therefore it is that another fire burns

me; to tarry is a mistake of a traveller, he will do well to teach himself this; lead me to the seashore where thou sawest that sun (Nestan)."

996   P'hridon answered: "Nothing shall be said by me to hinder thee. I know thou hast no more time; another lance pierces thee. Go! God will guide thee, may thy foes be destroyed! But tell me, how shall I bear the lack of thee?

997   "This I venture to tell thee: It is not fitting that thou go away alone, I will give thee knights with thee to serve and attend thee, armour and beasts, a mule, a horse. If thou take not these thou wilt have trouble, tears will flow on the rose cheeks."

998   He brought out four slaves, trustworthy in heart, complete armour for each man, with armpieces and greaves, sixty pounds of the red (gold), full weight, not with any shortage, a peerless stallion with complete harness."

999   On a strong-legged mule he packed bedding. He set out, and P'hridon mounted and went forth with him also. Now fire burned and consumed him who awaited the parting. He laments: "If the sun were near us, winter could not freeze us!"

1000   The rumour of the knight's departure spread, they gave themselves up to grief; the burgesses flocked together, those who sold silk goods like those who sold fruit; the voice of their lamentation was like thunder in the air; they said: "We are removed from the sun; come, let us close our eyes."

1001   They passed through the city, they went on, they came to the seashore where P'hridon had formerly seen the sun (Nestan) seated (? landed); there they shed a rivulet of blood from the lake of tears. P'hridon tells the story of that shining captive.

1002 "Hither the two slaves brought by ship the sun, white-teethed, ruby-lipped--a black sight! I spurred my horse, I determined to steal her by sword and arm; they saw me from afar, they soon fled from me, the boat seemed like a bird."

1003 They embraced each other, they multiplied the springs of tears; they kissed, and both their fires were renewed; the inseparable sworn brothers parted like brothers. P'hridon remained, the knight went away, the form the slayer of gazers.

AVT'HANDIL'S DEPARTURE FROM P'HRIDON TO SEEK NESTAN-DAREDJAN

1004   The knight speaks as he goes on his way (majestically) like the full moon; there is the thought of T'hinat'hin to gladden his heart. He says: "I am far from thee; alas! the falseness of cursed Fate! Thou hast the healing balsam for my wound.

1005   "Why doth the ardour of grief for the heroes continually burn me? why is my heart of rock and cliff become a hard rock? even three lances cannot show a bruise on me. Thou art the cause that this world is thus envenomed for me."

1006   Avt'handil fares on alone to the seashore with the four slaves, with all his might he seeks balm for Tariel; weeping by day and night he pours forth pools of tears; all the world seems to him as straw, even as straw in weight.

1007   Wherever he sees travellers walking by the shore he addresses them, he asks tidings of that sun (Nestan). He roamed a hundred days. He went up a hill; camels loaded with stuff appeared; merchants distressed stood in perplexity on the shore.

1008   A countless caravan was there on the seashore, they were distressed, they were gloomy, they could neither stand nor go forward. The knight greeted them; they hailed him with praise. He asked: "Merchants, who are ye?" They began to converse.

1009   Usam was the chief of the caravan, a wise man. He uttered respectfully a perfect eulogy, he invoked blessings on (Avt'handil) and praised his manners; he said: "O sun, thou art come as our life and comforter. Dismount; we will tell thee our story and business!"

1010   He dismounted. They said: "We are Bagdad merchants, holders of the faith of Mahmad; we never drink new wines; we haste to trade in the city of the Sea-King; we are rich in wholesale goods, we have no cut pieces of stuff.'

1011   "Here on the seashore we found a man lying senseless; we succoured him till he could speak clearly with his tongue. We asked him: 'Who art thou, stranger? What business dost thou follow after?' He said to us: If ye go in they will slay you. It is well that I still live!'

1012   "He said: 'From Egypt we set out with a caravan and a guard, we embarked upon the sea laden with many kinds of stuff, there pirates (in ships) with sharp (iron) pointed wooden rams slew us. All was lost; I know not how I came hither.'

1013   "O lion and sun, this is the reason of our standing here. If we return, our loss will be a hundredfold; if we embark, alas! they may slay us, we have no strength for battle. We cannot stay, we cannot go, the power to maintain ourselves is gone from us."

1014   The knight said: "Whoever grieves is nought, and strives in vain; whatever comes from above, we cannot avoid its coming. I am surety for your blood, I take upon myself what you shall shed; whoever fights with you, my sword will wear itself out on your foes."

1015 They of the caravan were filled with great joy; they said: "He is some knight, some hero, not timid like us, he has self-confidence, let us be calm in heart." They embarked, they went on board ship, they set out from the coast.

1016 With pleasant weather they journeyed without hardship; their convoyer, Avt'handil, leads them with brave heart. A pirate ship appeared with an exceedingly long flag; that ship had an (iron-shod) plough with (beam of) wood for shattering ships.

1017 (The pirates) yelled and came on, they shouted and trumpeted; the caravan was afraid of the multitude of those warriors. The knight spoke: "Fear not their hardihood; either I slay them all or this is the day of my death.

1018 "Nought undecreed can they do to me, even if all the hosts on earth engage me: if it be decreed, I shall not survive, the spears are ready for me, neither strongholds nor friends, not even brothers, can save me; he who knows this is stout-hearted like me.

1019 "You merchants are cowards, unskilled in war. Lest they slay you with the arrow from afar, shut the doors behind you. Behold me alone how I fight, how I use my lion-like arms; see how I make the blood of the corsair's crew flow."

1020 With gesture like a swift panther he clad his form in armour; in one hand he held an iron mace. He stood forth with dauntless heart in the front of the ship, and as he slew onlookers with his gaze, so he slew foes with his sword.

1021 Those warriors yelled; their voices were uninterrupted. They thrust the beam upon which was the plough. The knight stood fearless at the head of the ship, he trembled not; he struck with the mace, he broke the beam, the lion's arm swerved not.

1021a   The beam was destroyed, and Avt'handil remained with ship unshattered. Those warriors feared, they sought a way to shelter, they could not contrive it in time; he leaped on his foes, threshing them down round about him; there was not left there living man unhacked by him.

1022   With intrepid heart he slew those warriors like goats; some he threw down on the ship, some he cast into the sea; he threw one upon another, eight upon nine and nine upon eight; those who were left were hidden among the corpses, they stifled their cries.

1023   As much as his heart desired was he victorious in the fight with them. Some humbly adjured him: "Slay us not, by thy faith!" Those he slew not, he enslaved them, whoever survived his wounds. Truly saith the Apostle: "Fear makes love."

1024   O man! boast not of thy strength, brag not drunken like! Might is of none avail if the power of the Lord aid thee not. A tiny spark overcomes, and burns up great trees. If God protect thee, it cuts alike well whether thou strike with a log or a sword.

1025   There Avt'handil saw their great treasures. He grappled twin-like ship to ship. He called the caravan. Usam was merry when he saw, he rejoiced, he lamented not, he spoke a eulogy in his praise, he gave form to great imaginings.

1026   Praisers of Avt'handil need even a thousand tongues; even they could not tell how fair he appeared after the fight. The caravan shouted, saying: "Lord, thanks to Thee! The sun has shed down on us his beams; the dark night has broken into day for us."

1027   They came up to him, they kissed his head, face, feet, hand; they spoke praise unstinted to the fair, the praiseworthy; the sight of him maddens the wise man as well as the fool!" We all are saved by thee in so hard a mischance."

1028   The knight said: "Thanks to God, the Creator, Maker of all, by whom the heavenly powers decree what is to be done here; 'tis they that do all deeds hidden and some revealed. It is necessary to everyone to believe; a wise man has faith in the future.

1029   "God hath deigned to spare your blood, so many souls! I, alas! vain earth, what am I? Of myself, what have I done? Now I have slain your foes, I have fulfilled what I spoke; I have brought you the ship complete with its wealth as a gift."

1030   Pleasant it is when a good knight has won the battle, when he has surpassed his comrades who were with him. They congratulated him, they praised him, in this state they were ashamed. The wound becomes him well, but little was he hurt.

1031   That day they looked at that ship of the corsairs, they put not off till the morrow. How could they count the quantity of treasure lying there! They conveyed it to their ship, they completely emptied the (pirate) ship; they smashed it up and burned some of it; the wood they bartered not for sixpence.

1032   Usam conveyed to Avt'handil a message from the merchants: "We are strengthened by thee; we know our baseness. Whatever we have is thine, of this there can be no doubt; whatever thou givest us, let it be ours, we have made an assembly here."

1033   The knight announced: "O brothers, but now ye heard it: the stream which flowed from your eyes has been perceived by God, He hath saved you alive. What am I? What joy, alas! have I given you? What could I do with whatever you gave me? I have myself and my horse!

1034   "As much treasure as I desired to amass I had of mine own, countless priceless coverlets of silk. What use could I make of yours? What do I want? I am but your companion. Moreover, I have some other dangerous business.

1035   "Now, of this countless treasure I have found here, take what you each wish; I shall be a claimant against none. One thing I entreat: grant my request, one not to be mistrusted; I have a certain matter to be kept hidden within you.

1036   "Till the time comes, speak not of me as if I were not your master. Say, 'He is our chief,' call me not knight. I will clothe myself as a merchant, I will begin chaffering; keep the secret, by the brotherhood between us."

1037   This thing very greatly rejoiced the caravan; they came and saluted him, saying: "It is our hope--the very request we should have made to you, you yourself have made to us--that we may serve him whose face we acknowledge as the face of the sun."

1038   Thence they departed and travelled on, they wasted no time; they met fair weather, they sailed ever pleasantly; they delighted in Avt'handil, they sang his praises; they presented him with a pearl of the tint of the knight's teeth.

THE STORY OF AVT'HANDIL'S ARRIVAL IN GULANSHARO

1039   Avt'handil crossed the sea; with stately form went he. They saw a city engirt by a thicket of garden, with wondrous kinds of flowers of many and many a hue. In what way canst thou understand the loveliness of that land!

1040   With three ropes they moored the ship to the shore of those gardens. Avt'handil clad his form in a cloak and sat on a bench. They brought out men that were porters, provided with drachmas. That knight bargains, acts as chief (of the caravan), and thereby conceals himself.

1041   Thither came the gardener of him at whose garden they had landed; with ecstasy he gazes at the knight's face flashing like lightning. Avt'handil hailed him, he spoke to the man with faultless words: "Whose men are ye, who are ye? how call they the king reigning here?

1042   "Tell me all in detail," quoth the knight to that man; "what stuff is dearer, or what is bought up cheap?" He said: "I see, thy face seems to me like the face of the sun. Whatever I know I will tell thee truly; I will by no means inform thee crookedly.

1043   "The Sea Realm is this, ten months' (travel) in extent, this is the city of Gulansharo [29], full of much loveliness. Hither everything fair cometh by ships sailing from sea to sea. Melik Surkhavi rules, perfect in good fortune and wealth.

1044   "Even if he be old, a man is rejuvenated by coming hither; drinking, rejoicing, tilting and songs are unceasing; summer and winter alike we have many-hued flowers; whoever knoweth us envieth us, even they who are our foes.

1045   "Great merchants can find nought more profitable than this: They buy, they sell, they gain, they lose; a poor man will be enriched in a month; from all quarters they gather merchandise; the penniless by the end of the year have money laid by.

1046   "I am gardener to Usen, chief of the merchants. I shall tell thee somewhat of the manner of his ordinance: This is his garden, your resting-place for the day; first it is necessary to show him all the fairest of your goods.

1047   "When great merchants arrive they see him and give him gifts, they show him what they have, elsewhere they cannot unpack their goods; for the king they set aside the best, they straightway count out the price; thereupon he frees them to sell as they please.

1048   "His duty it is to receive such honourable folk as you, he orders the caterers how to entertain them fitly; he is not now here, what avails it me to speak of him To meet you and carry you away with him, pressing you politely, is the way he should treat you.

1049   "P'hatman Khat'hun, the lady, his wife, is at home, a hospitable hostess, amiable, not rough. I shall inform her of your arrival, she will take you in as one of her own folk, she will send a man to meet you, you shall enter the city by daylight."

1050   Avt'handil said: "Go, do whatever thou desirest." The gardener runs, he rejoices, sweat pours down to his breast. He tells his tidings to the lady: "I boast of this: a youth comes, to them that look on him his rays seem like the sun.

1051 "He is some merchant, chief of a great caravan, well-grown like a cypress, a moon of seven days, his coat and the fold of his coral-hued turban become him; he called me, asked me tidings and the tariff for the purchase of goods."

1052 Dame P'hatman rejoiced; she sent ten slaves to meet him; they prepared the caravanserais, she stored their wares. The rose-cheeked, crystal and ruby, glass, jet, entered; they who looked on him compared his feet to the panther's, his palms to the lion's (paws).

1053 There was a hubbub, the hosts of the town all assembled; they pressed on this side and on that, saying: "We will gaze on him till sleeptime." Some were carried away by desire, some had their souls reft from them; their wives grew weary of them, their husbands were left contemned.

AVT'HANDIL'S ARRIVAL AT P'HATMAN'S; HER RECEPTION OF HIM AND HER JOY

1054   P'hatman, Usen's wife, met him in front of the door, joyful she saluted him, she showed her pleasure; they greeted each other, they went in and seated themselves. As I have observed, his coming annoyed not Dame P'hatman.

1055   Dame P'hatman was attractive to the eye, not young but brisk, of a good figure, dark in complexion, plump-faced, not wizened, a lover of (female) minstrels and singers, a wine-drinker; she had abundance of elegant gowns and head-dresses.

1056   That night Dame P'hatman entertained him right well. The knight presented beautiful gifts; they that received them said: "They are worthy!" P'hatman's entertainment of him was worth while; by God! she lost not. When they had drunken and eaten, the knight went outs to sleep.

1057   In the morning he showed all his wares, he had them all unpacked; the fairest were laid aside for the king, he had the price counted out; he said to the merchants: "Take them away!" He loaded them, (and) had them carried away. He said: "Sell as ye will; reveal not who I am!"

1058   The knight was clad as a merchant; he was by no means dressed in his proper raiment. Sometimes P'hatman calls on him, sometimes he visits P'hatman. They sat together; they conversed with refined discourse. Absence from him was death to P'hatman, as Ramin's was to Vis. [30]

P'HATMAN BECOMES ENAMOURED OF AVT'HANDIL; WRITES HIM A LETTER AND SENDS IT

1059   Better, for him who can bear it, is aloofness from woman; she plays with thee and pleases thee, she wins thee over and trusts thee; but in a trice she betrays thee, she cuts whatever pierces; so a secret should never be told to a woman.

1060   Desire of Avt'handil went into the heart of Dame P'hatman, love grew from more to more, it burned her like fire, she essayed to conceal it, but could not hide her woes, she said: "What am I to do, what will avail me?" She rained, she poured forth tears.

1061   "If I tell him this, alas! he will be wroth, even the sight of him will become rare to me; if I tell him not, I cannot endure it, the fire will become more intense. I will speak, let me die or live, let one (or other) be my lot! How can the physician cure him who tells not what hurts him?"

1062   She wrote a piteous letter to be presented to that youth concerning her love, revealing her sufferings, moving and shaking the listeners' heart, a letter to be kept, not to be idly torn up.

THE LETTER OF LOVE WRITTEN BY P'HATMAN TO AVT'HANDIL

1063   "O sun, since it pleased God to create thee a sun, thus a joy and not a desirer of woes to them removed from thee, a burner of those near united, a consumer of them with fire, thy glance seems sweet to the planets, a thing to be boasted of.

1064   "They that gaze on thee become enamoured of thee; for thy sake piteously they faint. Thou art the rose I marvel why nightingales quiver not on thee. Thy beauty withers the flowers, and mine too are fading. If the sunbeams reach me not timely I am quite scorched.

1065   "God is my witness that I fear to tell you this, but, luckless, what can I do for myself? I am quite parted from patience; the heart cannot constantly endure the piercing of the black lashes! If by any means thou canst help me, then help, lest I lose my wits.

1066   "Till an answer to this letter reaches me, till I know if thou wilt slay me or reassure me--till then shall I endure life, however much my heart pains me. Oh for the time when life or death will be decided for me!"

1067   Dame P'hatman wrote and sent the letter to the knight. The knight read it as if it were from a sister or kinswoman; he said: "She knows not my heart. Who is she who courts the lover of her whose I am? The beloved I have--how can I compare her (beauty) to this one's?"

1068 Said he: "What hath the raven to do with the rose, or what have they in common? But upon it the nightingale has not yet sweetly sung. Every unfitting deed is brief, and then it is fruitless. What says she? What nonsense she talks! What a letter she has written!"

1069 This kind of thought he thought in his heart. Then said he to himself: "Save thee I have no helper. For the sake of that for which I am a wanderer, since I wish to seek her (Nestan) I will do everything by which I can find her; what else should my heart heed!

1070 "This woman sits here seeing many men, a keeper of open house and a friend to travellers coming hither from all parts. I will consent, she will tell me all; however much the fire burns me with its flames, perchance she will be of some use to me; I shall know how to pay my debt to her."

1071 He said: "When a woman loves anyone, becomes intimate with him and gives him her heart, shame and dishonour she weighs not, being wholly accursed; whatever she knows she declares, she tells every secret. It is better for me, I will consent; perchance I shall somewhere find out the hidden thing."

1072 Again he said: "None can do aught if his planet favour him not; so what I want I have not, what I have I want not. The world is a kind of twilight, so here all is dusky. Whatever is in the pitcher, the same flows forth."

AVT'HANDIL'S LETTER IN ANSWER TO P'HATMAN'S

1073   "Thou hast written to me; I have read thy letter in praise of me. Thou hast anticipated me, but the burning of the fire (of love) afflicts me more than thee. Thou wishest, I too want thy company uninterrupted. Our union is agreed since it is the desire of both."

1074   I cannot tell thee how P'hatman's pleasure increased. She wrote: "The tears I, absent from thee, have shed suffice. Now I shall be unaccompanied, here shalt thou find me alone; hasten my union with thee, to-night when evening falls. Come!"

1075   That very night when the letter of invitation was presented to the knight, when twilight was falling and he was going, another slave met him on the way (with the message): "Come not to-night; thou shalt find me unready for thee." This vexed him, he turned not back, he said: "What sort of thing is this?"

1076   The invited guest went not back again on the withdrawal of his invitation. P'hatman sits troubled. Avt'handil the tree-like went in alone. He perceived the woman's uneasiness, he saw it forthwith on his going in; she could not reveal it from fear, and also out of complaisance for him.

1077   They sat down together and began to kiss, to sport pleasantly, when a certain elegant youth of graceful mien appeared standing in the doorway. He entered; close behind followed a slave with sword and shield. When he saw Avt'handil he was afraid. "It looks," quoth he (to himself), "as if the road were rocky."

1078   When P'hatman saw, she was afraid, she shook and fell a-trembling. (The stranger) gazed with wonder at them lying caressing; he said: "I will not hinder, O woman . . . but when day breaks I shall cause thee to repent that thou hast had this youth.

1079   "Thou hast shamed me, O wicked woman, and made me to be despised, but to-morrow thou shalt know the answer to be paid for this deed; I shall make thee to devour thy children with thy teeth; if I fail to do this, spit upon my beard 1, let me run mad in the fields!"

1080   Thus he spake, and the man touched his beard [31] and went out of the door. P'hatman began to beat her head, her cheeks were scratched, the gurgling of her tears flowing like a fountain was heard. She said: "Come, stone me with stone, let the throwers approach!"

1081   She laments: I have, alas! slain my husband, I have killed off my little children, I have given away as loot our possessions, the peerless cut gems! I am separated from my dear ones! Alas! the upbringer! Alas! the upbrought! I have made an end of myself; shameful are my words!"

1082   Avt'handil hearkened to all this in perplexity. He said: "What troubles thee, what say'st thou, why dost thou thus lament, why did that youth threaten thee, what fault found he in thee? Be calm; tell me who he was and on what errand he roved!"

1083 The woman replied: "O lion! I am mad with the flow of tears; ask me no more tidings, nought can I tell thee with my tongue. I have slain my children with mine own hand, therefore can I no more be gay; impatient for thy love I have slain myself.

1084 "This kind of thing certainly should happen to the utterer of idle words, the chatterer who cannot hide a secret, the witless, mad, raving. 'Help me with your lamentations!" This will I say to all who see me. A physician cannot cure one who drinks his own blood!

1085 "Do one thing of two: desire nothing more than this: If thou canst kill that man, go, slay him secretly by night; thus shalt thou save me and all my house from slaughter; return, I will tell thee all, the reason why I shed tears.

1086 "If not, take away thy loads on asses this very night, escape from my neighbourhood, gather everything for flight. I doubt my sins will fill thee too with woe. If that knight go to court he will mare me eat my children with my mouth."

1087 When Avt'handil, the proud, gifted with bold resolve, heard this, he arose and took a mace--how fair, how bold is he! "To ignore this matter would be remissness on my part!" said he. Think not any living is his like; there is none other like unto him!

1088 To P'hatman he said: "Give me a man as instructor, as guide, let him show me the road truly, else I want no helper; I cannot look on that man as a warrior and mine equal. What I do I shall tell thee; wait for me, be calm!"

1089 The woman gave him a slave as guide and leader. Again she cried out: "Inasmuch as the hot fire is to be cooled, if thou slay that knight to assuage the irritation of my heart, he has my ring, I entreat thee to bring it hither."

1090 Avt'handil of the peerless form passed the city. On the seashore stood a building of red-green stone; in the lower part fair palaces, then above terrace upon terrace, vast, beautiful, numerous, hanging one over the other.

1091 Thither is the sun-faced Avt'handil led by his guide, who says to him in a low voice: "This is the palace of him thou seekest." He shows it to him, and says: "Seest thou him standing on yonder terrace? There he lies to sleep; know this, or thou shalt find him sitting."

1092 Before the door of that luckless youth lay two guards. The knight (Avt'handil) passed, he stole in without making a sound; he put a hand on each of their throats, forthwith he slew them, he struck head upon head, brain and hair were mingled.

HERE IS THE SLAYING OF THE CHACHNAGIR AND HIS TWO GUARDS BY AVT'HANDIL

1093 That youth lay alone in his chamber with angry heart. Bloody-handed Avt'handil, strong in stature, entered, he gave him no time to rise, privily he slew him, we could not have perceived it; he laid hold of him, struck him on the ground, slew him with a knife.

1094 He is a sun to them that gaze on him, a wild beast and a terror to those that oppose him. He cut off the finger with the ring, he hurled him down to the ground; he threw him from the window towards the sea, he was mingled with the sands of the sea; for him nowhere is there a tomb, nor spade to dig his grave.

1095 Not a sound of their slaughter was heard. The sweet rose came forth; whereby could he have been so embittered? This is a marvel to me, how he could thus steal his blood! As he had lately come, by the same road went he away.

1096 When the lion, the sun, the sweetly-speaking knight, came into P'hatman's (house), he announced: "I have slain him; no more will that youth see sunny day; thy slave himself I have as witness; make him swear an oath in God's name (that I did the deed); behold the finger and the ring, and I have my knife bloodied.

1097 "Now tell me of what thou spakest, why thou wert so furiously enraged. With what did that man threaten thee? I am in great haste (to know it)." P'hatman embraced his legs: "I am not worthy to look on thy face; my wounded heart is healed; now am I ready to extinguish my fires.

1098   "I and Usen with our children are now born anew. O lion, how can we magnify thy praises! Since we may boast that his blood is spilt, I will tell thee all from the beginning; prepare to listen.

P'HATMAN TELLS AVT'HANDIL THE STORY OF NESTAN-DAREDJAN

1099   "In this city it is a rule that on New Year's Day no merchant trades, none sets out on a journey; we all straightway begin to deck and beautify ourselves; the sovereigns make a great court banquet.

1100   "We great merchants are bound to take presents to court; they (the sovereigns) must give gifts befitting us. For ten days there is heard everywhere the sound of the cymbal and tambourine; in the public square, tilting, ball-play, the stamping of horses.

1101   "My husband, Usen, is the leader of the great merchants, I lead their wives; I need none to invite me; rich or poor, we give, presents to the queen; we entertain ourselves agreeably at court, we come home merry.

1102   "New Year's Day was come, we gave our gifts to the queen; we gave to them, they gave to us, we filled them, we were filled. After a time we went forth merry, at our will; again we sat down to rejoice, we were not of their company.

1103   "At eventide I went into the garden to sport; I took the ladies with me, it behoved me to entertain; them; I brought with me minstrels, they discoursed sweet song; I played and gambolled like a child, I changed veil and hair.

1104   "There in the garden were fair mansions beautifully built, lofty, with a prospect on every side, overhanging the sea.

Thither I led the ladies, them that were with me; anew we made a banquet, we sat pleasantly, joyously.

1105 "Merry, I entertained the merchants' wives, pleasantly, in a sisterly way. While drinking, without any cause a distaste came upon me. When they perceived me thus, they separated, all that sat at meat. I was left alone; some sadness fell on my heart like soot.

1106 "I opened the window and turned my face to the sea, I looked out, I shook off the sadness growing within me. Far away I saw something small, it floated in the sea, methought a bird or beast; to what else could I liken it?

1107 "From afar I could not recognize it; when it came near it was a boat; two men clad in black, and black also of visage, on either side stood close; only a (? woman's) head appeared; they came ashore, that strange sight astonished me.

1108 "They beached the boat; they landed in front the garden. They looked thither, they looked hither, (to see if any anywhere observed them, they saw no creature, nothing alarmed them. Secretly I watched them; I was quiet indoors.

1109 "What they landed from the boat in a chest—they took off the lid—was a maiden of wondrous form, who stepped forth; on her head was a black veil, beneath she was clad in green. It would suffice the sun to be like her in beauty.

1110 "When the maiden turned towards me, rays rose upon the rock; the lightning of her cheeks flashed over land and sky; I blinked mine eyes, I could no more gaze on her than on the sun; I closed the curtain of the door on my side; they could not perceive that they were watched.

1111 "I called four slaves who waited upon me; I pointed: 'See what beauty the Indians hold captive! Steal down, go forth, quietly, not racing hastily. If they will sell her to you, give them the price, whatever they may be wanting.

1112 "'If they will not give her to you, let them not: take her away, capture her from them, slay them, bring hither that moon, do the errand well, use your best endeavour!' My slaves stole down from above as if they flew; they chaffered, they sold not. I saw the blacks looked right ill pleased.

1113 "I stood at the window; when I saw they would not sell her, I cried: 'Slay them!' They seized them and cut off their heads, they threw them out into the sea; they turned back, they guarded the maiden. I went down to meet her, I took her, she had not tarried long on the. seashore.

1114 "How can I tell thee her praise! what loveliness! what delicacy! I swear she is the sun; 'tis untrue that the sun is sun! Who can endure her rays, who can delineate her! If she consume me, lo! I am ready, no preparation is needed for this."

1115 When she had ended these words, P'hatman rent her face with her hands; Avt'handil, too, wept, he shed hot tears; they forgot each other, for her (Nestan's) sake they became as mad; the spring (of tears) flawing down from above melted the slight new-fallen snow (of the cheek).

1116 They wept. The knight said: "Break not off! Conclude!" P'hatman said: "I received her; I made my heart faithful to her. I kissed her every part, and thereby I wearied her. I seated her on my couch, I caressed her, I loved her.

1117 "I said to her: 'Tell me, O sun, who thou art or of what race a child! Whither were those Ethiops taking thee, lady of the Pleiads of heaven?' To all these words she made me no answer. I saw a hundred springs of tears dropping from her eyes.

1118 "When I pressed her with questions, with much discourse, she wept with gentle voice, sobbing from the heart; a stream flowed through the jetty trough (of her lashes) from the narcissus (eyes), upon the crystal and ruby (of her cheeks). Gazing at her I burned, I became dead-hearted.

1119 "She said to me: 'To me thou art a mother, better than a mother. Of what profit can my story be to thee? It is but the tale of a chatterer. A lone wanderer am I, overtaken by an unhappy fate. If thou ask me aught, may the might of the All-seeing curse thee!' (?)

1120 "I said (to myself), 'It is not fitting untimeously to carry off and summon the sun; the captor will become mad and wholly lose his wits. A request should be timely, the making of every entreaty. How know I not that it not a time to converse with this sun!'

1121 "I led away that sun-faced one, (already) praise I cannot call her unpraised. By the longing I have for her, and by her sun (life), I hardly could hide the ray that sun! I enveloped her in many folds of heavy brocade, not thin stuff." The tear hails down, the rose is frostbitten, from the lashes blows a snowy blast.

1122 "I led into my home that sun-faced one, an aloe-tree in form. For her I furnished a house, therein I put her very secretly, I told no human being, I kept her privily, with precaution; I caused a negro to serve her; I used to enter, I saw her alone.

1123 "How, alas! can I tell thee of her strange behaviour! Day and night weeping unceasing and flowing of tears! I entreated her: 'Hush!' For (but) one moment would she submit. Now without her how do I live; alas! woe is me!

1124 "(When) I went in, pools of tears stood before her; in the inky abyss (of her eyes) were strewn jetty lances (eyelashes), from the inky lakes into the bowls full of jet there was a stream, and between the coral and cornelian (of her lips) glittered the twin pearls (rows of teeth).

1125 "By reason of the ceaseless flow of tears I could not find time for inquiry. If I asked even, 'Who art thou? what brought thee into this plight?' like a fountain, a rivulet of blood gushed forth from the aloe-tree. No human being could endure more, unless made of stone.

1126 "No coverlet she wanted, nor mattress to lie upon, she was ever in her veil and one short cloak, her arm she placed as a head-rest and reposed thereon. With a thousand entreaties I could scarce persuade her to eat a little.

1127 "By-the-by, I will tell thee of the wonder of the veil and cloak: I have seen all kinds of rare and costly things, but I know not of what sort of stuff hers were made, for it had the softness of woven material and the firmness of forged (metal).

1128 "Thus that lovely one tarried long in my house. I could not trust my husband; I feared he would inform. I said to myself: 'If I tell him, I know the rascal will betray my secret at court.' Thus I thought at my frequent goings in and comings out.

1129 "I said to myself: 'If I tell him not, what am I to do, what can I do for her? I know not in the least what she wants, nor what any could do to help her. If my husband finds out, he will slay me, nothing can save me; how can I hide that sunlike light!

1130 "'I, alas! what can I do alone! The burning of my fires increases. Come, I will trust him, I will not wrong Usen; I will make him swear not to betray me; if he give me full assurance, he cannot doom his soul, he will not be an oath-breaker!'

1131 "Alone I went to my husband; I frolicked and fondled him. Then I said to him: 'I will tell thee something, but first swear to me thou wilt tell no human being, give me a binding oath.' He swore a fearful oath: 'May I beat my head on the rocks!

1132 "'What thou tellest me I will reveal to no soul, even unto death, neither to old nor young, friend nor foe!' Then I told all to that kind-hearted man, Usen: 'Come, I will lead thee to a certain place here; come, I will show thee the sun's peer.'

1133 "He rose to accompany me, we departed, we entered the palace gates. Usen marvelled; he even quaked when he saw the sunbeams. He said: 'What hast thou shown me, what have I seen, what is she, of what stuff? If she be verily an earthly being, may God's eyes look upon me with wrath!'

1134 "I said: 'Nor know I aught of her being a creature of flesh; I have no knowledge more than I have told thee. Let me and thee ask who she is, and who is at fault that such madness afflicts her; perchance she will tell us somewhat, we will pray her to do us this great kindness.'

1135 "We went in, we both had a care to show her respect. We said: 'O sun, for thy sake a furnace of flame burns us. Tell us what is the cure for the waning moon, what hath ensaffroned thee who art ruby-like in hue?'

1136   "Whether she heard or hearkened not to what we said we know not; the rose was glued together, it showed not the pearl; the serpents (her locks) were twined in disorder; the garden was built with its front to the back; the sun was obscured (eclipsed) by the dragon, it dawned not upon us.

1137   "By our converse we could not induce her to answer. The coursing-panther sits sullen-faced, we could not comprehend her wrath; again we annoyed her, she wept tears flowing like a fountain, and, 'I know not! Let me alone!' quoth she; this only with her tongue she said to us.

1138   "We sat down and wept with her and poured forth tears. What we had spoken to her made us sorry; how could we venture to say aught else? We could scarce persuade her to be quiet, we calmed her, we soothed her; we offered her some fruit, but we could not make her eat at all.

1139   "Usen said: 'She has wiped away a multitude of woes from me. Those cheeks are fit for the sun; how can they be kissed by man! Most right is he who sees not her if his sufferings be increased a hundred-and-twenty-fold. If I prefer my children may God slay them!'

1140   "A long time we gazed at her, (then) we went forth with sighs and moans; to be with her seemed to us joy, parting grieved us greatly. When we had leisure from affairs of trade we used to see her. Our hearts were inextricably prisoned in her net.

1141   "After some time had passed, and nights and days were sped, Usen said to me: 'I have not seen our king since the day before yesterday; if thou advisest me, I will go and see him, I will go and pay my court and present gifts.' I replied: 'Certainly, by God, since such is your desire.'

1142   "Usen set out pearls and gems on a tray. I entreated him, saying: 'At court thou wilt meet the drunken court folk. Kill me! if thou be not wary of the story of that maid.' Again he swore to me: 'I will not tell it, may swords strike my head!'

1143   "Usen went; he found the king sitting feasting. Usen is the king's boon companion, and the king is his well-wisher. (The king) called him forward; he accepted the gifts he had brought. Now behold the tipsy merchant, how hasty, rash and ill-bred he is!

1144   "When the king had drunk before Usen many great goblets, still they quaffed and again filled more tankards and beakers; he forgot those oaths; what (to him were) Korans and Meccas! Truly is it said: 'A rose befits not a crow, nor do horns suit an ass!'

1145   "The great king said to the witless, drunken Usen: 'I marvel much whence thou gettest these gems to give us, (where) thou findest huge pearls and peerless rubies. By my head! I cannot return thee one-tenth for thy gifts!'

1146   "Usen saluted, and said: 'O mighty sovereign, shedder of beams from above, O nourisher of creatures, O sun! Whatever else I have, whose is it, be it gold or treasure? What brought I forth from my mother's womb? By you it has been granted to me.

1147 "'By your head! I make bold to say that gratitude for gifts beseems you not. I have somewhat else, a daughter-in-law for you, a bride to unite to your son; for this undoubtedly you will thank me when you see the sun's like; then will you oftener say: "Happiness is ours!"'

1148 "Why should I lengthen (speech)? He brake his oath, the power of religion; he told of the finding of the maid portrayed by gazers as a sun. This pleased the king greatly; it gave gaiety to his heart. He ordered her conveyance to court and the fulfilment of Usen's utterance.

1149 "Pleasantly I was sitting here at home; hitherto I had not sighed. At the door appeared the chief of the king's slaves, he brought with him sixty slaves, as is the custom of kings; they came in, I was much astonished, I said: 'This is some high affair (of state).'

1150 "They greeted me: 'P'hatman,' said they, 'it is the command of the equal of the sun: that maid like two suns whom Usen presented to-day, now bring her to me, I shall take her with me; we have not far to go.' When I heard this, the heavens overwhelmed me, with wrath hill struck hill (or heap fell on heap).

1151 "Thereupon in amazement I inquired: 'What maid do you want, which?' They said to me: 'Usen presented (one with) a face flashing with lightning.' There was nought to be done; the day of the taking away of my soul (i.e., Nestan) was fixed. I trembled, I could not rise, neither could I remain sitting.

1152 "I went in; I saw that lovely one weeping and flooded in tears. I said: 'O sun, seest thou fully how black fate hath played me false! Heaven is turned towards me in wrath, I am despoiled, I am wholly uprooted; I am denounced, the king asketh for thee, therefore am I heartbroken.'

1153 "She said to me: 'Sister, marvel not, however hard this may be! Luckless Fate hath ever been a doer of ill upon me; if some good had befallen me thou mightest have wondered, what marvel is evil? All kinds of woe are not new to me, old are they.'

1154 "Her eyes poured forth frequent tears like pearls. She rose as fearless as if she were a panther or a hero; joy no longer seemed joy nor did woe seem woe to her. She begged me to cover her form and face with a veil.

1155 "I went into the treasure-house; I took out gems and pearls on which no price was set, as much as I could, every single separate one was worth a city. I went back; I girded them round the waist of her for whose sake my black (sad) heart was dying.

1156 "I said: 'O my (dear one)! Perchance this sort of thing may somewhere be of use to thee!' I gave that face, the sun's peer, into the hands of the slaves. The king was warned, he met her; the kettledrum was beaten, there was hubbub. She went forward with bent head, calm, saying nought.

1157 "Onlookers flocked upon her, there was trampling and uproar; the officers could not hold them back, there was no quiet there. When the king saw her, cypress-like, coming towards him, he said in amazement: 'O sun, how art thou brought hither (from heaven)?' (or, 'how contest thou hither?')

1158 "Sun-like, she made those who gazed on her to blink. The king deigned to say: 'I have seen (sights), she hath turned me into (one) who has seen nought. Who but God could imagine her? Right is he who is in love with her if he, wretched, roam mad in deserts!'

1159 "He seated her at his side, he talked to her with sweet discourse; quoth he: 'Tell me who art thou, whose art thou, of what race art thou come?' With her sun-like face she gave no answer; with bowed head, of gentle mien, sorrowful she sits.

1160 "Whatever he said, she hearkened not to the king. Elsewhere was her heart; of somewhat else she thought. The roses were glued together; she opened not the pearl. She made them that looked on her wonder of what she thought.

1161 "The king said: 'What can we think of? with what can we comfort our heart? There can be no opinion save these two: Either she is in love with someone, she is thinking of her beloved, save him she has no leisure for any, to none can she speak;

1162 "'Or she is some sage, lofty and high-seeing ; joy seems not joy to her, nor sorrow wheal it is heaped on sorrow, as a tale she looks on misfortune and happiness alike; she is elsewhere, elsewhere she soars, her mind is like a dove's.

1163 "'God grant my son come home victorious. I will have for his home-coming this sun ready for him; perchance he will make her say something, and we also shall know what is revealed; till then, let the moon rest with waning ray far sundered from the sun.'

1164 "Of the king's son I will tell thee: a good, fearless youth, peerless in valour and beauty, fair in face and form; at that time he was gone forth to war, there had he tarried long; for him his father prepared her, the starlike one.

1165 "They brought her and apparelled her form in maidenly garb; on it was seen many a ray of glittering gems, on her head they set a crown of a whole ruby, there the rose was beautified by the colour of the transparent crystal (of her face).

1166 "The king commanded: 'Deck the chamber of the princess royal.' They set up a couch of gold, of red of the Occident. The great king himself, the lord of the whole palace, arose and set thereon that sun, the joy of the heart of beholders.

1167 "He commanded nine eunuchs to stand guard at the door. The king sat down to a feast befitting their race; to Usen he gave immeasurable (gifts) as a return for that peer of the sun; they made trumpet and kettledrum to sound for the increasing of the noise.

1168 "They prolonged the feasting; the drinking went on exceeding long. The sun-faced maiden says to Fate: 'What a murderous fate have I! Whence am I come hither, to whom shall I belong, for whose sake am I mad? What shall I do? What shall I undertake? What will avail me? A very hard life have I!'

1169 "Again she says: 'I will not wither the rose-like beauty. I will attempt somewhat; perchance God will protect me from my foe. What reasonable man slays himself before death (comes)? When he is in trouble, then it needs that the intelligent should have his wits!'

1170 "She called the eunuchs, and said: 'Hearken, come to reason! You are deceived, mistaken as to my royalty; your lord is in error in desiring me for a daughter-in-law. In vain, alas! sounds he for me the trumpet, the kettledrum and clarion.

1171   "'I am not suited to be your queen; elsewhither leads my path. God keep man far from me, be he sun-faced, cypress-formed! You beg of me something different; my business is of another kind. With you my life beseems me not.

1172   "'Without fail I shall slay myself, I shall strike a knife into my heart; your lord will kill you, you will have no time of tarrying in the world. This then is better: I will give you the weighty treasure wherewith my waist is girded, let me steal away, let me go free, lest you regret.'

1173   "She undid the pearls and gems that girdled her; she doffed, too, the crown, transparent, of a whole ruby; she gave them, she said: 'Take them, with burning heart I implore you; let me go, and you will have paid a great debt to your God!'

1174   "The slaves were greedy for her costly treasure, they forgot the fear of the king as of a bellman, they resolved to let her of the peerless face escape. See what gold doth, that crook from a devilish root!

1175   "Gold never gives joy to them that love it; till the day of death greed makes them gnash their teeth. (Gold) comes in and goes out, they murmur at the course of the planets when it is lacking; moreover it binds the soul here (in this world), and hinders it from soaring up.

1176   "When the eunuchs had ended the matter as she wished, one took off his garment and gave it to her; they passed through other doors (because) the great hall was full of drunken men. The moon remained full, unswallowed by the serpent.

1177   "The slaves, too, disappeared; they stole forth with her. The maiden knocked at my door, and asked for me, P'hatman. I went, I knew her, I embraced her, was I not surprised! She would not come in with me at all, saying: 'Why dost thou invite me?' I regretted it.

1178 "She said to me: 'I have bought myself with what thou gavest me. May God in return reward thee with heavenly favour! No longer canst thou hide me, let me go, send me off swiftly on horseback ere the king get wit and send men to gallop in pursuit.'

1179 "Swiftly I entered the stable, I loosed the best steed, I saddled it, set her upon it; cheerful was she, not sighing. She was like the sun, the best of heaven's lights, when it mounts the Lion [32] My labour was lost; I could not harvest what I had sown.

1180 "The day drew down to evening, the rumour spread, her pursuers came; inside the city was a state of siege, they raised a hue and cry; they questioned me, I said: 'If you find her there in the house where I am, may I be guilty towards the kings and answerable for their blood-money.'

1181 "They sought, nought could they discover, they returned abashed. From that time the king and all his familiars mourn. Behold the palace folk; they go in (clad in raiment) dyed violet colour [33]. The sun went away from us; since then we lack light.

1182 "Now I shall narrate to thee anon the whereabouts of that moon, but first of all I will tell thee why that man threatened me. I, alas! was his doe; he was my buck; Timidity slurs a man, and wantonness a woman.

1183 "I am not content with my husband, for he is lean and ill-favoured; this man, the Chachnagir, was a gentleman high at court; we loved each other, though I shall wear no mourning weeds for him; would that one might give me a cup of his blood to sip!

1184 "Like a woman, like a fool, I told him this story of the coming of that sun to me, and of her stealing away like a fox; he threatened me with exposure, not like a friend, like a foe. Now when I think of him as a corpse, ah! how relieved am I!

1185 "Whenever we quarrelled alone he menaced me. When I called thee I did not think he was at home; he had arrived, he told me of his coming. Thou also wert coming; I was afraid, so I begged thee: 'Do not come!' I sent a slave to meet thee.

1186 "You turned not back, you came, you brought beams of light to me; you both met, you were assembled to fight over me, so I feared, I could think of no way. He, alas! desired my death in his heart, and not (only) with his tongue.

1187 "If thou hadst not slain him, and if he had gone forthwith to court, in his wrath he would have denounced me, (for) his heart was burned as with fire; the angry king would have cleared away my house at one swoop, he would, O God! have made me eat my children, then he would have stoned me with stone.

1188 "God reward thee in return--what thanks can I render thee! thee who hast delivered me safe from that serpent's gaze! Now henceforth I can be happy in my star and fate! No longer do I fear death. Ha! ha! . . ."

1189 Avt'handil said: "Fear not! even in the book is it thus written: 'Of all foes the most hateful is the friend-foe; if a man be wise, he will not heartily confide.' Fear I no more from him, now is he corpse-like.

1190 "Tell me the same story--since thou spedst the maiden, all the tidings thou hast learned or heard of her." Again P'hatman spoke weeping; again the tear flowed from her eyes. Quoth she: "The ray which sun-like illumined the fields was brought to nought."

THE STORY OF THE CAPTURE OF NESTAN-DAREDJAN BY THE KADJIS, TOLD BY P'HATMAN TO AVT'HANDIL

1191   Woe, O Fate, in falsehood thou art like Satan, none can know aught of thine, where thy treachery is. That face apparent as a sun--where hast thou it hidden? Whither hast thou taken it? Therefore I see that in the end all seems vain (desolate), wherever anything may be.

1192   P'hatman said: "The sun was departed from me, the light of all the world, life and existence, the gain of my hands; from that time unceasingly the burning of hot fires. afflicted me, I could not dry the spring of tears flowing forth from mine eyes.

1193   "House and child became hateful to me, I sat with cheerless heart; waking I thought of her, when I fell asleep (I thought of her) in my drowsiness. The oath-breaker Usen seems to me of the infidels in faith; the accursed one cannot approach me, to be near me with his cursed face.

1194   "One day at eventide, just at sunset, I passed the guards, the door of the asylum caught mine eye; I was in a reverie, sadness at the thought of her was slaying me; I said: 'Cursed is the vow of every man!'

1195   "From somewhere there came a wandering slave with three companions, the slave clad as a slave, the others in coarse travelling garb; they brought food and drink which they had bought in the city for a drama. They drank, they ate, they chattered, thus they sat merry.

1196   "I hearkened to them, I watched them. They said: 'Pleasantly we rejoiced, but (though) here we are joined as comrades, (yet) are we strangers, none of us knows who another is or whence we are come; we must at least tell one another our stories with our tongues.'

1197   "Those others told their tales as is the wont of wayfarers. The slave said: 'O brothers, providence is a celestial thing; I harvest for you pearls, you sowed but millet; my story is better than your stories:

1198   "'I am the slave of the exalted king, the ruler of the Kadjis. It chanced that he was struck by a sickness which prevailed over him; the helper of the widow, the comforter of the orphan, was dead to us; now his sister, better than a parent, rears his children.

1199   "'Dulardukht is a woman, but a rock, like a cliff, her slave is wounded by none, but he wounds others. She had little nephews: Rosan and Rodia; now she is seated as sovereign of Kadjet'hi, "the Mighty" is she called.

1200   "'We heard news of the death overseas of her sister. The viziers were distressed, they refrained from assembling a privy council: "How can we venture to report the extinction of a face which was the light of the lands?"--Roshak is a slave, the chief of many thousand slaves.

1201   "'Roshak said: "Even if I be killed (for mine absence), I shall not be at the mourning! I go into the plain, I will reive, I will fill myself with booty; I shall come home enriched, I shall be back in good time. When the sovereigns goes forth to bewail her sister, I too will accompany her."

1202 "'He said to us, his underlings: "I will go, come with me!" He took of us a hundred slaves, all chosen by him. By day in the sunlight we reived, by night also we watched; many a caravan we broke up, we unloaded the treasure for ourselves.

1203 "'One very dark night we were wandering over the plains; there appeared to us certain great lights in the midst of the field; we said: "Is it the sun strayed down from heaven to earth!" Perplexed, we gave our minds to torturing thought.

1204 "'Some said: "It is the dawn!" others said: "It is the moon!" We, drawn up in fighting array, moved towards it--I saw it from very near--we made a wide circuit round it, we came and surrounded it. From that light came a voice speaking to us.

1205 "'It said to us: "Who are you, O cavaliers? Tell me your names! From Gulansharo I go, a messenger to Kadjet'hi; have a care of me." When we heard this we approached, we formed a circle round about. A certain sun-faced rider appeared before our eyes.

1206 "'We gazed at the brilliant face flashing out lightning, its glittering spread itself over the surroundings like the sun; rarely she spoke to us with some gentle discourse, (then) from her teeth the ray lighted up her jetty lashes.

1207 "'Again we addressed that sun with sweet-discoursing tongue; she was not a slave, she spoke falsely, this we perceived. Roshak discovered that it was a damsel; he rode by her side; we did not let her go, we made bold to keep her in our hands.

1208 "'Again we asked: "Tell us the true story of that sun-like light of thine. Whose art thou, who art thou, whence comest thou, enlightener of darkness?" She told us nought; she shed a stream of hot tears. How pitiable is the full moon swallowed by the serpent!

1209 "'Neither plain tale nor secret, she told us nought, neither who she was, nor by whom she had been treacherously treated; angrily she spoke with us, sullen, on the defensive, like an asp attacking onlookers with her eye.

1210 "'Roshak ordered us: "Ask not, it seems nought is to be said now; her business is a strange one and difficult to be told. The good fortune of our sovereign is to be desired by creatures, for God giveth her whatever is most marvellous.

1211 "'"This (damsel) has been destined to us by God that we might bring her; we will take her as a gift, she (Dulardukht) will render us very great thanks; if we conceal it, we shall be found out, (and) our sovereign is. proud: first, it is an offence to her, then it is a great disgrace."

1212 "'We agreed, we prolonged not the discussion. We returned, we made for Kadjet'hi, leading her with us; we ventured not to speak directly to her, nor did we annoy her. She weeps; with embittered heart she laves her cheeks in flowing tears.

1213 "'I said to Roshak: "Give me leave; soon again shall I attend you. At present I have some business in the city of Gulansharo." He granted me leave. Hereabout I have some stuff to be carried off, I will take it with me, I will go and overtake them.'

1214 "This story of the slave greatly pleased those men. I heard it; the stream from the pool of tears dried up in me. I guessed, I recognized every sign of (her who is my) life this gave me a little comfort, like a drama's weight.

1215 "I laid hold of that slave and set him close before me. I asked him: 'Tell me what thou wert saying; I, too, wish to hear.' He told me again the same as I had heard thence (i.e., from my hiding-place). This story enlivened me; me, struggling in soul (with death), it preserved alive.

1216 "I had two black slaves full of sorcery, by their art they go and come invisible; I brought them out, I despatched them to Kadjet'hi, I said: 'Tarry not; give me tidings of her by your deeds.'

1217 "In three days they came and told me, swiftly had they trod the road: 'The queen, who was ready to go over the sea, has taken her. None can fix his eyes to gaze upon her, as upon the sun. She (the queen) has betrothed? her (Nestan) as wife to the little boy Rosan.

1218 "'"We shall wed her to Rosan," this is the decree of Queen Dulardukht, "at present I have not leisure for the wedding, now is my heart consumed with fire; when I return home I will make a daughter-in-law of her who is praised as heaven's sun." She has set her in the castle; one eunuch attends her.

1219 "'She (Dulardukht) took with her all those skilled in sorcery, for perilous is the road, her foes are ready for the fray; she has left at home all her bravest knights. She will tarry; but little time has already passed.

1220 "'The city of the Kadjis has hitherto been unassailable by foes; within the city is a strong rock, high and long; inside that rock is hollowed out a passage for climbing up. Alone there is that star, the consumer of those who come in touch with her.

1221 "At the gate of the passage are continually on guard knights not ill-favoured, there stand ten thousand heroes all of the household, at each of the three city gates three thousand.' O heart, the world hath condemned thee; I know not, alas! what binds thee."

1222 When Avt'handil the sun-faced but woeful (?) heard these tidings he was pleased, he showed nothing else. The lovely creature rendered thanks to God: "Somebody's sister has told me joyful news!" (?)

1223 He said to P'hatman: "Beloved, thou art worthy to be loved by me, thou hast let me hear a welcome story, not with louring looks; but let me hear more fully about Kadjet'hi [34]; every Kadj is fleshless, how can it become human?

1224 "Pity for that maiden kindles me and burns me with flame; but I marvel what the fleshless Kadjis can do with a woman!" P'hatman said: "Harken to me! Truly I see thee here perplexed (? timorous). They are not Kadjis, but men (who) put their trust in steep rocks," quoth she.

1225 "Their name is called Kadji because they are banded together, men skilled in sorcery, exceeding cunning in the art, harmers of all men, themselves unable to be harmed by any; they that go out to join battle with them come back blinded and shamed.

1226 "They do something wondrous, they blind the eyes of their foes, they raise fearful winds, they make the ship to founder midst the seas, they run as on dry land, (for) they clean dry up the water; if they wish they make the day dark, if they wish they enlighten the darkness.

1227   "For this reason all those that dwell round about call them Kadjis, though they, too, are men fleshly like us." Avt'handil thanked her: "Thou hast extinguished my hot flames; the tidings just told me have pleased me greatly."

1228   Avt'handil, shedding tears, magnifies God with his heart; he said: "O God, I thank Thee, for Thou art the Comforter of my woes, who wast and art, Unspeakable, Unheard by ears: Your mercy is suddenly spread forth over us!"

1229   For the knowledge of this story he magnified God with tears. P'hatman thought of herself; therefore she was again burned up. The knight kept his secret, he lent himself to love; P'hatman embraced his neck, she kissed his sun-like face.

1230   That night P'hatman enjoyed lying with Avt'handil; the knight unwillingly embraces her neck with his crystal neck; remembrance of T'hinat'hin slays him, he quakes with secret fear, his maddened heart raced away to the wild beasts and ran with them.

1231   Avt'handil secretly rains tears, they flow to mingle with the sea; in an inky eddy floats a jetty ship. [35] He says: "Behold me, O lovers, me who have a rose for mine own! Away from her, I, the nightingale, like a carrion-crow, sit on the dungheap!"

1232   The tears which flowed there from him would have melted a stone, the thicket of jet dammed them up there is a pool on the rose-field. P'hatman rejoiced in him as if she were a nightingale; if a crow find a rose it think itself a nightingale.

1233 Day dawned; the sun (Avt'handil) whose rays were soiled by the world went forth to bathe. The woman gave him many coats, cloaks, turbans, many kinds of perfumes, fair clean shirts. "Whatsoever thou desirest," said she, "put on; be not shy of me!"

1234 Avt'handil said: "This day will I declare mine affair." The wearing of merchant garb had hitherto been his resolve. That day wholly in knightly raiment he apparelled his brave form; he increased his beauty, the lion resembled the sun.

1235 P'hatman prepared a meal, to which she invited Avt'handil. The knight came in adorned, gaily, not with louring looks. P'hatman looked, she was astonished that he was not in merchant garb; she smiled at him: "Thus is it better for the pleasure of them that are mad for thee."

1236 P'hatman exceedingly admired his beauty. He made no answer, he smiled to himself: "It seems she does not recognize me!" How foolishly he behaved, how he invited (her)! Though he took some liberty he did not go farther.

1237 When they had eaten they separated, the knight went home; having drunk wine, he lay down merry, pleasantly he fell asleep. At eventide he awoke; he shed his rays across the fields. He invited P'hatman: "Come, see me, I am alone, quite alone!"

1238 P'hatman went, Avt'handil heard her voice making moan; she said: "Undoubtedly I am slain by him whose form is like an aloe-tree." He set her at his side; he gave her a pillow from his carpet. The shade from the eaves of the eyelashes overshadows the rose-garden (of the cheeks).

1239 Avt'handil said: "O P'hatman, I know thee; thou wilt tremble at these tidings like one bitten by a serpent; but hitherto thou hast not heard the truth concerning me: my slayers are black lashes, trees of jet.

1240 "Thou thinkest me some merchant, master of a caravan; I am the Commander-in-Chief of the exalted king Rostevan, chief of the great host befitting him; I have the mastery over many treasuries and arsenals.--

1241 "I know thee to be a good friend, faithful, trusty.--He has one daughter, a sun the enlightener of lands; she it is who consumes me and melts me; she sent me, I forsook my master, her father.

1242 "That damsel thou hadst--to seek that same damsel, that substitute for the sun, I have gone over the whole world; I have seen him who roves for her sake, where he, pale lion, lies wasting himself, his heart and strength."

1243 Avt'handil told all his own tale to P'hatman, the story of the donning of the panther hide by Tariel. He said: "Thou art the balm of him thou hast not yet seen, the resource of (him of) frequent eyelash, ruffled like a raven's wing.

1244 "Come, P'hatman, and aid me, let us try to be of use to him, let us help them, perchance those stars shall receive joy. All men who shall know it, all will begin to praise us. Surely again will it befall the lovers to meet.

1245 "Bring me that same sorcerer slave, I will send him to Kadjet'hi, we will make known to the maiden all the tidings known to us, she also will inform us of the truth, we will do what she chooses. God grant you may hear that the kingdom of the Kadjis is vanquished by us."

1246 P'hatman said: "Glory to God, what things have befallen me! This day I have heard tidings equal to immortality!" She brought the sorcerer slave, black as a raven, and said: "I send thee to Kadjet'hi; go, thou hast a long journey.

1247 "Now will appear advantage for me from thy witchcraft, speedily quench the furnace of the burning of my fires, tell that sun the means for her cure." He said: "To-morrow I shall give you full news of what you wish."

LETTER WRITTEN BY P'HATMAN TO NES-TAN-DAREDJAN

1248   P'hatman writes: "O star, heavenly sun of the world, consumer and griever of all them that are afar from thee, elegant and eloquent in words, lovely, fair-tongued, crystal and ruby both welded in one!

1249   "Though thou gayest me not to hear thy story, I have learnt the truth, thereby hath my heart been comforted. Console with news Tariel, who is become mad for thee! May you both attain your desire, may he be a rose and thou a violet!

1250   "His sworn brother is come in quest of thee, Avt'handil, an Arab knight renowned in Arabia, Commander-in-Chief of King Rosten, to be contemned of none. Write news of thyself, thou proud one, wise in understanding!

1251   "For this purpose have we sent this slave to your presence: We would know tidings of Kadjet'hi. Have the Kadjis come home? We wish to know in detail the number of warriors there. Who are thy guards, and who is their chief?

1252   "Whatever thou knowest concerning that place, write to us, make it known. Then send some token for thy lover. All the sorrow thou hast had hitherto, change (it) into joy! May it please God that I unite the lovers so befitting each other!

1252a   "Go, O letter, hasten, if swift be thy knee! I envy thee, thou goest to see the crystal, jet and rubies. In fate thou art happier than I, O letter; the eyes of her who consumes me will look upon thee. If thou hearest of my life after thee, shalt thou not pity me!"

1253   P'hatman gave the letter to that cunning sorcerer: "Give this letter to the sunlike maiden!" The wizard donned a certain green mantle over his form; in that very moment he was lost to view, he flew over the roofs.

1254   He went like an arrow shot by a swift-bowed archer. When he reached Kadjet'hi it was just dusk twilight. Invisible he passed the multitude of knights guarding the gates. He gave to that sun the greeting of her who longed for her.

1255   He passed the closed gates of the castle as if they had been open; the negro entered, the black-faced, long-haired,cloaked; that sun was affrighted, she thought it was somewhat to harm her; the rose was changed to saffron and the violets to sky blue.

1256   The Kadj said: "Whom think'st thou me to be, and why faintest thou thus? I am P'hatman's slave despatched to thy presence, this letter will justify me, I speak not falsely to thee. Let the sun's rays come forth, O rose, fade not so soon."

1257   The sun-faced marvelled at P'hatman's wonderful news; she split her almonds (opened her eyes), the jets (? black pupils) quivered with the rod of jet (her lashes). The slave gave her the letter with his own hand. She sighs, she reads the letter, she wets it with her hot tears.

1258   She asked the slave: "Tell me, who is my seeker, or who knows me to be alive, treading the earth?" He said: "I will venture to tell you only what I know. When thou wentest forth, since then hath our sun been darkened.

1259   "Henceforth P'hatman's heart hath been torn by lances; the tears she shed are (such as) to be united to the seas. Once already I brought news of thee to her. I call God to witness that for her since then the tear hath not ceased.

1260   "Now there came a certain knight? fair of face; in detail she told him all, what trouble you are in; he with hero-like arm is thy seeker; they sent me, they entreated me to hasten with ceaseless haste."

1261   The maiden said: "What thou hast said, O man, seems to me to be truth. How could P'hatman know from whom I was carried away! Doubtless somewhere is he who burns me with fire. I will write to her; thou also shalt tell how my heart boils."

THE LETTER WRITTEN BY NESTAN-DAREDJAN TO P'HATMAN

1262 "I, the sun-faced, write: O dame, O mother, better than a mother to me! See what the world (Fate) hath done to me its thrall! Alas! there is added to those griefs of mine still another! Now that I have seen thy missive it hath greatly encouraged me.

1263 "Thou didst save me from two sorcerers; thou didst alleviate my woes. Now I am thus held here by the whole force of the Kadjis; a whole realm, many thousand heroes, guard me alone. Ill befell my counsels and resolves (to flee from P'hatman).

1264 "What other tidings hence can I write to thee? The king (i.e., queen) of the Kadjis is not come, nor will the Kadjis yet come; but countless hosts guard me, and with what bravery! (?) What! the quest for me! It is not possible, believe me!

1265 "Whoever is come seeking me is wearied in vain he suffers, he is consumed, he is kindled for me, a flame like fire burns him. But I envy him, he hath seen the sun, thus is he not frozen. Without him, alas! what great pity my life is

1266 "Formerly I told thee not my story, I hid it from thee for that my tongue could not speak it; I spared myself woes. I entreat thee, beg my beloved to have pity and not come in search of me, write to him, send him a message.

1267 "What afflicts me is enough, let him not slay me with (a woe) equal to this: I should see him a corpse, I should die a double death. None can help me, I know this for a truth; this is no gossip. If he (Tariel) will not hearken to thee, stone me with a heap of black stone!

1268   "Thou didst ask me to send a token, show this: I send a cutting from the veils he gave me; these (veils) for his sake are a fair sight to me, though in colour they are black, like my fate."

THE LETTER WRITTEN BY NESTAN-DAREDJAN TO HER BELOVED

1269 "Now will I, sobbing, weeping, write to my beloved; by the tear of that one who burns him is a man's fire quenched." She wrote a letter piercing the heart of the hearers. She splits the rose (opens her mouth); there appears the translucent crystal.

1270 "O mine own! this letter is the work of my hands; for pen I have my form, a pen steeped in gall; for paper I glue thy heart even to my heart; O heart, black (sad) heart, thou art bound, loose not thyself, now be bounds!

1271 "Thou seest, O mine own! of what deeds the world is a doer. However much light shines, for me it is but darkness. The wise know it (the world), therefore they despise it, to them it is contemptible. My life without thee, woe is me! how exceeding hard it is!

1272 "Thou seest, mine own! how Fate and cursed time have parted us; no longer do I glad see thee, my glad loved one; what, indeed, can the heart rent by thee do without thee! Secret thought manifests to thee what is hidden (?).

1273 "By thy sun (life)! until now I thought not thou wert alive; as for me, methought my life and all my resource had passed away. Now when I hear (news of thee), I magnify the Creator and humble myself before God. All mine erstwhile grief I weigh as joy.

1274 "Thy life is sufficient for my heart to hope in, a heart all wounded and so consumed! Think of me, remember me as one lost to thee; I sit nursing the love I planted.

1275 "Now, O mine own, my story is not to be written to thee by me; the tongue will tire, none that hear will believe! P'hatman took me from sorcerers; may God protect her! Now again Fate hath done what befits it.

1276 "Fate hath now added worse woe to my woe, my ill luck was not appeased by these manifold afflictions; and again it delivered me into the hands of the Kadjis, hard to combat; Fate hath done to us, mine own, all that hath befallen us.

1277 "I am sitting in a castle so lofty that eyes can scarce see the ground; the road enters by a passage, over it stand guards; day and night knights miss not their turn as sentries, they will kill those that engage them, like fire will they envelop them.

1278 "Surely thou thinkest not that these are of the same kind as other warriors? Slay me not with woes worse than the present! I shall see thee dead, I shall be burnt up like tinder by steel. (Since) I am sundered from thee, renounce me with a heart harder than rock itself.

1278a "Beloved, sorrow not with such grief! Tell me, can there be for me another with the form of an aloe-tree! Life without thee is nought for me, henceforth I should be full of regret; either I would cast myself down from the rock or slay myself with a knife.

1279 "By thy sun (life)! thy moon [36] will fall to the lot of none save thee! By thy sun! to none shall she fall though triple suns shone forth! Here would I dash myself down; the great rocks are very nigh to me. To thee would I commit my soul; perchance wings would be given to me by Heaven.

1280 "Entreat God for me; it may be He will deliver me from the travail of the world and from union with fire, water, earth and air. Let Him give me wings and I shall fly up, I shall attain my desire--day and night I shall gaze on the sun's rays flashing in splendour.

1281 "The sun cannot be without thee, for thou art an atom of it; of a surety thou shalt adhere to it as its zodiac (Leo), and not as one rejected. There shall I see thee; I shall liken thee to it, thou shalt enlighten my darkened heart. If my life was bitter, let my death be sweet!

1282 "Death is no longer grievous to me, since it is to thee I commit my soul; but I have laid thy love in my heart, and there it rests. When I think of parting from thee, for me wound is added to wound. Weep not and mourn not for me, O mine own, for love of me!

1283 "Go, betake thyself to India, be of some help to my father, who is straitened by foes, helpless on all sides; comfort the heart of him who suffers separation from me. Think of me weeping for thy sake with undrying tears.

1284 "Whatever complaint I have made against my Fate is sufficient complaint. Know this, that true justice goeth from heart to heart; for thy sake will I die, I shall become the prey of ravens! But as long as I live I shall weep and suffer enough for thee, too.

1285 "Lo, mark the token from the veil that was thine; from one end I have cut off a strip, O mine own; this (the veil) is all that is left to me in place of that great hope; in wrath the wheels of the seven heavens has turned upon us."

1286 When she had finished this letter written to her beloved, she cut off a fringe from those veils; bareheaded, the thick, long locks of her hair became her well, the scent blows from the aloe, breathing through the raven's wings.

1287 That slave departed, journeying to Gulansharo; in one instant he reached P'hatman's, he travelled not many days. When this matter so dear to him had been accomplished, Avt'handil with hands upraised thanks God, with full understanding, not as one bemused.

1288 He said to P'hatman: "The thing desired is timely finished for me; thy great zeal for my sake is (still) unrecompensed. I go, I have no leisure to tarry longer, last year's time is come. Swiftly shall I lead into Kadjet'hi him who will annihilate and destroy them."

1289 The lady said: "O lion, the fire now becomes hotter; (my) heart will be sundered from (thee) its light, thereby will it be darkened; hasten, grieve not for me, the madman will thus become furious. Should the Kadjis arrive before you, going thither will be made difficult for you."

1290 The knight called P'hridon's slaves who attended him. He said: "Corpses hitherto, now indeed are we enlivened; we are renewed by the hearing of what we wished. I shall show you our enemies wounded and thereby woe-stricken.

1291 "Go and tell P'hridon this unvarnished story. I cannot see him, I am hurried, my road is one of haste. Let him strengthen his great voice to make it still more bold. I will give you all the treasure taken by me as booty.

1292 "Great is the debt laid upon me by you; I will show my gratitude in another way when I join P'hridon again. For the nonce, take away all that was reft from the pirates; I can give you no more than this, I know that so I shall seem to you niggardly.

1293 "I have no home near; I have no power to dispense gifts." He gave them a ship full, beautiful things, a host in number. He said: "Go, take them away, travel the road to that same region. Give this letter from me, his sworn brother, to P'hridon."

AVT'HANDIL'S LETTER TO P'HRIDON

1294   He wrote: "Exalted P'hridon, supremely blest, king of kings, lion-like in stout-heartedness, O sun, recklessly shedding rays, mighty, joyous, spiller of the blood of foes--thy youngest brother from far, far away barks thee a greeting.

1295   "I have seen troubles, and I have, too, received recompense for what pains I have suffered. Well hath fallen out the matter planned by me: I have truly learned the story of that face likened to a sun, the sustainer of that lion who was buried under the earth.

1296   "The sovereign of the Kadjis has that sun; she is captive in Kadjet'hi. To go thither seems to me sport, though the road is one of battle. From the narcissi a rain of crystal falls; the rose is wet with rain. The Kadjis are not yet with the maid, but countless is their host.

1297   "Glad in heart I rejoice, for this my tear will not flow in channels. Wherever thou and thy brother (Tariel) are the difficult will be made easy; whatever you may desire you will certainly do it, you shall not fail; not only no man can stand against you, I trow that even a rock will soften before you.

1298   "Now pardon me, I cannot see thee, so I have passed afar off; I have no leisure to linger on the road, for that moon is captive. Soon shall we come merry; rejoice at the sight of us! What more than this can I say to thee: help thy brother in brotherly fashion?

1299 "The attachment of these slaves is beyond reward; pleasantly have they served me, and your heart, too, will be pleased at this. Why should he be praised who hath sojourned long with you? Every like gives birth to like; this is a saying of the sages."

1300 He wrote this letter, he tied it up and rolled its; the rose, the violet-haired, gave it to P'hridon's slaves; he communicated through them by word of mouth all that was needful, how he should do; the open door of coral showed its pearls to them.

1301 Avt'handil searched; he found a ship of that region (where Tariel was). That sun with the face of a full moon prepared to set out; but to leave the woeful-hearted P'hatman was a heaviness to him; those who parted from him shed a rivulet of blood.

1302 P'hatman, Usen and the slaves weep with hot tears. They said: "O sun, what hast thou done to us? Thou didst burn us with hot fires, why darkenest thou us with the gloom of thine absence? Bury us with thy hands which have (already) buried us! (i.e., by thy departure)."

AVT'HANDIL'S DEPARTURE FROM GULAN-SHARO, AND HIS MEETING WITH TARIEL

1303   Avt'handil has crossed the seas in a certain ship for travellers. He rides glad-hearted all alone. To meet Tariel with such tidings rejoices him. With hands uplifted, with his heart he hopes in God.

1304   Summer was come, from the earth came forth verdure, the token of the rose bursting into bloom, the time of their tryst, the change of course by the sun, the setting out of the cypress-formed. He sighed when he saw the flower long time unseen by him.

1305   The sky thundered and the cloud rained crystal dew; he kissed the rose with his rose-like lips; he said: "I gaze on you with tenderly-observant eye; I rejoice to have converse with you in her (T'hinat'hin's) stead."

1306   When he thought on his friend, the bitter tears flowed; he travelled those weary ways towards Tariel, deserted and pathless, unknown regions; lion and panther of the reedy thickets he slew wherever he saw them.

1307   The caves came in sight, he was glad, he recognized them. He said: "These be the rocks where my friend is, he for whom my tears have flowed. I am indeed worthy to see him face to face, to relate to him what I have heard. If he be not come, what shall I do? Vain will have been my travail.

1308   "If he be come, doubtless he would not tarry within; he would go somewhere into the plain, like a wild beast he would roam in the fields; it is better for me to go round by the rushes." He bethought himself, he looked about; thus he spoke and turned, he went towards the plains.

1309   He canters along and sings with merry heart; he shouts to him by name with cheerful voice. He went a little farther, there appeared the sun in full splendour, at the edge of the rushes stands Tariel with sharp sword.

1310   Tariel had slain a lion; its blood anointed his sword. He stood dismounted at the edge of the rushes; his horse was not with him. He heard Avt'handil's shout, he was astonished; he looked at him, recognized him, started, ran towards him, bounded.

1311   Tariel flung aside his sword and went towards his adopted brother. The knight alighted from his horse; it seemed to him that he had attained his goal (?). They kissed each other; their necks were as if riveted together. There was the sugary sound of the rose frequently opening.

1312   Tariel, weeping, uttered polished, exquisite words--the tear of blood dyed the jetty thickets crimson, the fountain of tears, many streams, waters the aloe: "Since I have seen thee, what matters it to me if eight pains oppress me?"

1313   Tariel weeps and Avt'handil was speaking to him laughing, he smiles, he opens his coral (lips), the flash from his teeth quivers; he said: "I have learned tidings which will please thee; now the flower will be renewed, the rose hitherto fading."

1314 Tariel said: "O brother, that which rejoices me to-day is enough, in seeing thee I have seen all my comfort, whatever other balm God gives; hast thou not heard: How can man find in the world that which is not of Heaven's doing!" (?)

1315 When Tariel was not convinced, Avt'handil was ill at ease, he could no longer delay to tell the tale; he hastened, he drew forth the veil of her on whose lips the rose blooms; when Tariel saw, he recognized it, seized upon it, started.

1316 He recognized the letter and the fringe of the veil and unfolded them, he pressed them to his face; he fell, a rose pale in hue, his spirits fled, the watchman of jet bowed his head. Neither Caen nor even Salaman could bear sorrows like his.

1317 Avt'handil gazes at Tariel lying lifeless; he flew to him, he set about helping him, the sweetly-speaking; he could not be of avail to the consumed one, completely burned up with fire; her tokens had laid hold of his life.

1318 Avt'handil sat down to weep; he mourns with melodious voice, full oft he tears his raven locks, he rouses them by seizing them with his crystal (hand), he brake the ruby polished with a hammer of adamant, thence issue streams which I likened to coral in hue.

1319 He scratches his face; blood flows from his cheeks while gazing at (Tariel). "What I have done neither madman nor fool hath done. Why did I in my haste pour water on a fire difficult to quench! The heart struck hastily by exceeding joy cannot bear it.

1320 "I have slain my friend! What befits me disgraced? I blame myself for a deed not thought out with heed. A stupid man cannot do well in a difficult matter. It is said: 'Chidden slowness is better than praised haste.'"

1321   Tariel lay unconscious, as if scorched, Avt'handil rose, he passed through the rushes in search of water; he found the lion's blood, he carries it to quench the flame, he sprinkled it on (Tariel's) breast; the lapis-lazuli became ruby-hued.

1322   Avt'handil sprinkled the breast of that lion (Tariel) with the lion's blood. Tariel started up, the ranks of the race of India moved, he opened his eyes, he received power to sit up; blue seems the ray of the moon diminished in ray by the sun.

1323   Winter makes the roses fade, their leaves fall; the ardour of the summer sun burns them, they bemoan the drought, but upon them nightingales complain with lovely voice; heat consumes, frost freezes; the wounds hurt them in either case.

1324   Even so is it hard to deal with the heart of man; it is mad alike both in grief and in joy; it is always wounded, its fate is never whole. He only can trust this world who is his own foe.

1325   Tariel gazed again on the writing of his slayer; he reads, though the reading of her letter maddens him; his tears blind him to the light, dark seems the beam of day. Avt'handil rose, he began to speak with rough? words.

1326   He said: "Such behaviour is unworthy of an instructed man! Why should we weep now? It behoves us to set about the making of smiles. Arise, let us go in quest of that lost sun. Soon shall I lead thee to her; I must bring thee to thy desired one.

1327 "What joy befits us, therewithal let us first rejoice. Then let us mount and set out, let us wend towards Kadjet'hi. Be our swords our guides, let us sheath them in their (the Kadjis') backs; untroubled shall we return, we shall reduce them to carrion."

1328 Then Tariel asks for tidings; he no longer fainted. He looked up, he raised his eyes, the black and white lightning glittered, as a ruby by the sun so was his colour increased. Who is worthy that towards him the sky turn ever in mercy?

1329 To Avt'handil he gave thanks; he conversed with him: "How shall I speak thy praise, worthy to be praised by the wise! Like a spring up on a mountain thou hast watered the flower of the plain; thou hast cut off for me the flow of tears of the pool of the narcissi (the eyes).

1330 "I can never make thee a return; may the God of heaven repay thee! May He in my stead reward thee from His height!" They mounted and went home; they made great rejoicing. Now the world (Fate) will indeed sate Asmat'h so long hungering.

1331 At the door of the cave Asmat'h sits alone, not fully dressed; when she had looked she recognized Tariel, and with him a knight on a white horse; both were sweetly singing like songster nightingales. Immediately she recognized them she rose hastily, bare but for her smock.

1332 Hitherto she had ever seen him come to the cave weeping, now she wondered to behold him singing, laughing; seized with fear she arose, her understanding was like a drunkard's; she heard not yet the news she so longed for.

1333 When they saw her they shouted to her, laughing and showing their teeth: "Ho! Asmat'h! God's mercy is come down on us from on high; we have found the lost moon; what we desired that have we done; now we shall have our fires quenched by Fate, our sorrows turned to joy."

1334   Avt'handil alighted from his horse to embrace Asmat'h; she laid hold of the aloe, pliant to the touch was its branch (his arm); she kisses his neck and face; she sheds tears. "Tell me what thou hast discovered, what thou hast done. Beseeching thee, I weep on the field."

1335   Avt'handil gave to Asmat'h the letter of her charge, the aloe with faded branch, the pale moon. He said: "See the writing of her who hath passed through troubles; the sun approaches us, it hath given us the putting away of shadow."

1336   When Asmat'h saw the letter she knew (Nestan's) hand; she marvelled, fear seized her, she quakes like one possessed, from head to foot overwhelming wonder laid hold on her; she says: "What have I seen, what do I heard is it indeed true?"

1337   Avt'handil said: "Fear not, this story is true, joy is given to us, all sore grief is put away from us, the sun is come nigh us, darkness is no longer dark for us. Good hath overcome ill; the essence of (good) is lasting."

1338   The King of the Indians merrily spoke somewhat with Asmat'h; they embraced each other, joy made them weep; the raven's tail (eyelashes) dropped light dew upon the rose (cheeks). God forsaketh not man if man comprehend this.

1339   They gave God great thanks. They said: "Thou hast done to us what was best; now we recognize that your mouth would not have adjudged to us the worst." The King of the Indians, with uplifted hand, joyously shouted this. Merry they went into the caves; Asmat'h made ready somewhat for their refreshment.

1340   Tariel said to Avt'handil: "Hearken to these words: I will tell thee something, think me not a tedious narrator. Since the time when I captured the caves (and) slew droves of Devis, their precious treasury lies here.

1341   "Never have I seen it, for I have not wished to do so. Come and let us open it; let us see how much treasure there is." It pleased him; both arose, nor did Asmat'h stay seated. They broke down forty doors; it was no great struggle for them.

1342   They found unequalled treasure, hitherto unseen by their eyes. There stood a heap of jewels of fair workmanship. There were seen pearls each as big as a ball for play. Who could make account of the gold not to be numbered by any!

1343   Inside those forty rooms were full. They found an armoury newly made for armour; there all kinds of armour were placed like preserves (in a store cupboard); therein was a coffer, sealed, unopened.

1344   Upon it was written: "Here lieth wondrous armour: chain helmet, habergeon, steel-cutting sword. If the Kadjis attack the Devis it will be a hard day. Whoever openeth at any other time is a slayer of kings!"

1345   They opened the coffer; they found in it three suits of armour fit for three warrior knights to don; coats of mail, swords, helmets, greaves of like sort; they were in emerald nests, as it were shrines.

1346   Each clothed himself with each, they tested them on themselves; chain helmet and habergeon nought could dint;

they struck the swords on iron, they cut it like cotton-thread. I tell you they prize them more than all the world; they would not barter them for it.

1347   They said: "As a sign this is enough for us; we are in good luck. God has gazed on us with His eye, looking down from above." They took up that armour, each put it on his neck; they bound up one (set) with leather thongs to present to P'hridon.

1348   They took with them some gold, some rare pearls; they went forth, they sealed up the forty treasuries. Avt'handil said: "Henceforth will I fasten my palm to the sword; nowhere shall I go to-night, when day dawns I shall not tarry."

1349   Now, painter, limn the sworn brothers more steadfast than brothers, these lovers of stars, excelled by none, both heroic knights renowned in bravery. When they go to Kadjet'hi you shall see a battle of piercing lances.

TARIEL AND AVT'HANDIL GO TO P'HRIDON

1350   When day dawned they set out; they took Asmat'h with them. Till they came to Nuradin's land they mounted her behind them; there a merchant gave them a horse for a price in gold, he made not a gift of it. As guide Avt'handil sufficed; whom else need he take!

1351   They wended their way and met with Nuradin's herdsmen, they saw the herd (of horses); it pleased them, who had come for P'hridon. There said the Hindoo to Avt'handil: "I will have thee do a good piece of fooling: Come, let us play a joke on P'hridon, let us chase his herd.

1352   "We will carry off the herd, he will come and hear that the herd is reived; he will prepare to do battle, to dye the plain with gore. Suddenly he will recognize us, he will be surprised, he will calm his heart. Pleasant is good joking; it makes even the proud merry."

1353   They began to seize the steeds, P'hridon's finest. There the herdsmen made a torch, they struck steel. They shouted: "Who are ye, knights, who do such high (-handed) deeds? This herd is his who strikes the foe with his sword without making him to sigh."

1354   They seized their bows, they pursued the herdsmen; the herdsmen shrieked aloud, they raised their voices: "Help, help! brigands are massacring us!" They made an outcry, they united, they appealed to P'hridon, they were not bashful.

1355　P'hridon arrayed himself, he mounted, he rode forth in full array. They made an outcry, they united, the regiment covered the fields. Those suns whom winter could not freeze came forward; they were covered up, helmets hid their faces.

1356　When Tariel knew P'hridon, "Now have I seen him I want," said he; he raised his helm, he smiled, he laughed; he said to P'hridon: "What dost thou wish? Why doth our coming annoy thee? Bad host! Thou meetest us to fight."

1357　P'hridon swiftly dismounted; he fell down and saluted. They also alighted, they embraced--ay, kissed him. P'hridon with upraised hand gave God measureless thanks. The magnates also kissed them, whoever knew them.

1358　P'hridon said: "Why tarried ye? I expected ye sooner. I am ready; I shall not lag in any service of yours!" It seemed as if two suns and a moon were united there; they beautified one another. They set out, they departed.

1359　At P'hridon's fairly-built house they both alighted; he sits down beside his sworn brother Avt'handil; Tariel sat on a throne covered in cloth of gold. To P'hridon, renowned as a hero, they presented that armour.

1360　They said: "At this time we have no other gifts for thee, but we have many other fair things lying in a place (we wot of)." He laid his face to the ground, he wasted not time: "Such a gift to me is worthy of you."

1361　That night they rested as P'hridon's guests; baths he gave them, he gave them gifts of garments in plenty, he clad their beauty in beauty, each (garment) fairer than the other; he gave them rare jewels and pearls in a golden basin.

1362 He said: "This (that I am about to say) is the speech of a bad host; 'tis as if hospitality to you wise (ones) wearied me as if you were mad (ones); but tarrying now avails not, it is better to travel the long road; if the Kadjis outstrip us there is a risk of trouble.

1363 "Why should we use great hosts? We want good and few; three hundred men suffice us, let us go (swift) like runaways; in Kadjet'hi for fighting the Kadjis we shall put basket-hilts on our swords; soon shall we find her whose pleasant aloe form will slay us.

1364 "Once aforetime I was in Kadjet'hi; you shall see it, and you, too, shall find it strong; on all sides round about is rock, a foe may not come up to it; if we may not go in privily, it is impossible to engage openly; so we need no army, the squadron cannot follow us secretly."

1365 With what he said, they too agreed. They left there the maiden Asmat'h; P'hridon bestows a gift upon her. They took with them three hundred horsemen equal to heroes. At the last God will give the victory to all who have been distressed.

1366 All three sworn brothers crossed the sea. P'hridon knows the way; going day and night they travel. P'hridon said: "Now are we coming nigh the regions of Kadjet'hi; henceforth we must travel by night so that we be not discovered."

1367 The three behaved according to this advice of P'hridon's; when it was daylight they stopped, and by night they went swiftly on. They arrived; the city appeared; they could not count the guards; outside was a rock, the noise of the sentinels in crowds increased.

1368 At the gate of the passage ten thousand braves kept guard. Those lions saw the city; the shining moon stood upon it. They said: "Let us advise what is best, now is choice difficult; a hundred can overcome a thousand if they choose the best way."

THE COUNCIL OF P'HRIDON, AVT'HANDIL AND TARIEL AS TO THE ASSAULT ON THE CASTLE OF KADJET'HI

1369   P'hridon said: "I will speak a word, I think I am not at fault: We are few, the city is only expugnable by many; we have not strength for a direct attack--this is no time for boasting--in a thousand years we could not anywhere win in if they shut the gate against us.

1370   "In my childhood my tutors instructed me in gymnastics, they taught me their tricks, they made me leap, they trained me, I used to go along a rope so that eyes could not follow me; whatever little boys looked at me they also desired to do it.

1371   "Now, whichever of you knows best how to cast a noose, let us throw the end of a long rope to that tower, it seems as easy for me to cross as a field; I shall make it a trouble to you to find a sound man inside.

1372   "To me it seems nought to cross in armour, no trouble to bear a shield; nimbly shall I leap down inside, strike like a wind, slay the soldiers; I shall open, you will see the opening of the gate, you too come thither where you hear the uproar of alarm."

1373   Avt'handil said: "Ha, P'hridon! friends cannot complain of thee; thou hast hope in thy lion-like arms, wounds hurt not thee; thou counsellest hard counsel to make foes lament; but hearest thou not how very near the garrison shouts!

1374 "When thou goest over, the garrison will hear the clatter of thine armour, they will perceive thee, they will cut the cord, of this thou must be assured. Everything will turn out ill for thee; only the vain attempt will remain to thee. That counsel is of no value; let us help ourselves in some other way.

1375 "This is better: you stay hidden in ambush. These men will not lay hands on a traveller coming into the town. I will dress myself as a merchant, I will do a treacherous deed; I will load a mule with helmet, hauberk and sword.

1376 "It is of no use for the three of us to go in, there is risk that they would perceive it; I shall go alone as a merchant, and well shall I win in unnoticed; secretly shall I don mine armour, I shall appear, I shall deceive them. God grant that I may make channels of blood to flow generously in there!

1377 "Without any difficulty I shall remove the guards inside; you strike outside the gate, all like heroes; I shall shatter the locks, I shall open, you will see the opening of the gate. If aught else would be better, say so; I am for a plan of this sort."

1378 Tariel said: "I recognize your heroism exceeding that of heroes; your counsel and advice is like your own stout-heartedness; I know you desire fierce fight, not a vain brandishing of swords, when the battle becomes perilous then are ye men.

1379 "But let me too have some choice in the matter. The sound will be heard by her who maddens me; like the sun she will be standing aloft; you will have fierce fight, she will see me as a non-combatant! This will be a slur on me. Nay, speak no flattering words!

1380   "Better than that counsel is this--let us do as I say: Let us divide the men by hundreds; when night turns to dawn let the three of us start out from three places, swiftly let us urge on our horses; they will send out to encounter us, we shall seem insignificant to them, we shall lend a powerful palm to the sword.

1381   "Swiftly shall we engage them, we shall get round them; they will not be able to shut the gates against us; one of the three will go in, the others from outside will strike with battering-rams (?); that one who is inside will fall on those within, making their blood flow; again let us lay hold of the arms mightily used by us!"

1382   P'hridon said: "I understand, I perceive, I know what (it is). None could forestall at the gates that horse that once was mine; when I gave it I knew not that we should want to mount guard over the Kadjis in Kadjet'hi; if so, I tell thee I would by no means have given it to thee, such is mine avarice!"

1383   P'hridon the gay jests with such discourse as this; thereupon they, the eloquent, wise-worded ones, laugh, they joke one with another, with merriment beseeming them. They dismounted and arrayed themselves; they mounted their excellent steeds.

1384   Again they interchanged words, not tart to the mouth. They resolved on that plan proposed by Taria. They divided among them by hundreds the men, all equal to heroes. They mounted their horses; their helmets they raised.

1385   I saw those heroes shining with rays excelling the sun; those three are covered by the seven planets with a column of light. Tariel with slender form sits on the black (horse); they consumed their foes in fight as their admirers by gazing.

1386   Now, this is what I shall say is their image and likeness: When clouds rain down, and the stream pours from the mountains, it comes and glides through the glens, turmoil and uproar is heard; but when it unites with the sea then is it even so calm.

1387   Though P'hridon and Avt'handil are unrivalled in valour, yet to engage with Taria is to be desired of none; the sun hides even the planets, nor do the Pleiads shine. Now give heed, O listener; thou shalt hear of fierce fights.

1388   The three split up into three, one for each gate; with them they had three hundred men all equal to heroes. That night they hastily made a reconnaissance, not illusory. Day dawned, they appeared, they set forth, they each had his shield.

1389   First they went quietly in the guise of some travellers; those inside could not perceive, they could not meet them alertly, they had no fear in their hearts, quietly they stood at ease. They approached; for the time being they covered over their helmets.

1390   Suddenly they spurred their horses, their whips swished. When they saw, they opened the gates, a tumult came forth from the city. The three set out in three different directions, thus risking their lives (?). They played on fifes and drums; they made the trumpets sound shrill.'

1391   Then the measureless wrath of God struck Kadjet'hi. Cronos, looking down in anger, removed the sweetness of the sun; to them (the Kadjis) also in wrath turned round the wheel and circle of heaven. The fields could not contain the corpses; the army of the dead was increasing.

1392 The sound of Tariel's mighty voice made men unwounded faint, he rent the armour, the strength of the chainmail was brought to nought; they attacked the gates on three sides, they found no difficulty in cutting them down; when they entered the city they began swiftly to destroy the castle.

1393 Avt'handil and the lion P'hridon met inside, they had wholly destroyed the enemy, whose blood flowed in streams; they shouted and saw each other, they rejoiced greatly; they said: "How goeth it with Tariel?" Their eyes roved round seeking him.

1394 None of them knew; they could hear nought of Tariel. They wended to the castle gate, no care had they for the foe; there they saw a bank of armour, shattered chips of swordblades, the ten thousand guards lifeless, like dust.

1395 All the castle guard lay like sick men, every one wounded from head to foot, their armour rent in pieces, the castle gates open, the fragments of the gates flung aside. They recognized Tariel's handiwork, they said: "This is his doing."

1396 They found the roads prepared, they entered and crept up the passages; they saw: the moon was freed from the serpent to meet the suns; he raised his helmet, his reedy hair thrown back became him (well), breast was glued to breast, neck was riveted to neck.

1397 They (Nestan and Tariel) embraced each other, they kissed and shed tears; they were like when Musht'har and Zual are united. When the sun surrounds the rose they become fair and reflect the rays. They that have hitherto seen griefs will henceforth rejoice.

1398   They kissed each other, they stood neck-welded; again full oft they glued the roses of the opened lips. Now those also (Avt'handil and P'hridon) came forth, the three sworn brothers were gathered together; they gave greeting to that sun, they presented themselves as they were called on.

1399   The sun (Nestan) met them with lovely, laughing face, the proud one kissed her helpers with gentle mien, she humbly gave them thanks with dainty words; both together talked with fair discourse.

1400   They greeted Tariel too, that tree like an aloe sapling, they wished him joy of the victory, they asked news of one another; it irked them not, they regretted not, for their armour had not failed them; they themselves had quit themselves as lions, those that fought against them had been as hinds and goats.

1401   Out of the three hundred men, a hundred and sixty came in with them; it grieves P'hridon for his troops, but on the other hand he rejoiced; they sought out and suffered not to live whatever adversaries were left. What treasures they found, now how can their number be told!

1402   They collected mules, camels, whatever they could find that was swift, they loaded three thousand with pearls and gems, every gem cut, jacinths and rubies; they placed that sun in a palanquin, precautions are taken by them.

1403   They appointed sixty men to guard the castle of Kadjet'hi. They led away that sun--hard would it be to ravish her from them--they set out for the City of the Seas, though long is the way thither. They said: "We must see P'hatman; we owe her a due recompense."

THE GOING OF TARIEL TO THE KING OF THE SEAS AND TO P'HRIDON'S

1404   To the presence of the King of the Seas he sent a messenger (of good tidings); he bade him announce: "I, Tariel, come, vanquisher of foes, their destroyer and slayer; from Kadjet'hi I bring my sun, piercer of me with arrows; I desire to see thee with honour, as father and parent.

1405   "Now I have the land of the Kadjis and their hoards. O king, all that is good hath happened to me from you: my sun was freed by P'hatman, she was a mother and a sister to her. What can I give thee in return for this? I hate vain promises.

1406   "Come, see us before we have passed thy land. I present to thee outright the kingdom of the Kadjis, accept it from me; let thy men be posted there, hold the castle strongly. I am in haste, I cannot come to see thee, come thou forth, wend towards me.

1407   "On my behalf tell Usen, P'hatman's husband, to send her, the sight of her will please her she freed; whom else can she desire to see more than her who is brighter than the sun, even as crystal is brighter than pitch?"

1408   When Tariel's man was received by the ruler of the seas--it is the custom that the heart is agitated by startling tidings--he gave thanks and glory to God the Just Judge. Straightway he mounted; he needed no other messenger (or invitation).

1409   He loaded baggage, he appointed the making of their wedding, he takes a number of pretty things, not a great quantity of jet. He has P'hatman with him, they made a journey of ten days; the sight of the lion and the sun, the light of the lands, rejoices him.

1410   Afar off the three met the great King of the Seas, they dismounted, he humbly kissed them, they were encompassed by a host of troops; they rendered praise to Tariel, he gave a thousand thanks, when they saw the damsel he (the King of the Seas) was fascinated by her crystal-halo rays.

1411   Slow fire consumed Dame P'hatman at the sight of her, she embraced her, she covered with kisses her hand, foot, face, neck; she said: "O God, I will serve Thee, since my darkness is lightened for me; I recognize the shortness of evil, Thy goodness is everlasting."

1412   The maiden embraced P'hatman; sweetly she speaks, not angry: "God hath enlightened my rent, faded heart; now am I as full as formerly I was waning; the sun hath shed his beams upon me, therefore I appear a rose unfrozen."

1413   The King of the Seas celebrated there an exceeding great wedding; he thanked (Tariel) too for Kadjet'hi; he would not let them go for seven days; generously he dispensed gifts, the treasure he had loaded; they wore out (by treading) upon (it) the scattered gold coin as if it were a bridge.

1414   There stood a heap of silk, brocade and satin. He gave to Tariel a crown, a price could not be set on it, of a whole jacinth, yellow, exceeding pure, likewise a throne of gold, red, refined.

1415   He presented to Nestan-Daredjan a mantle adorned with gems, red jacinths, rubies of Badakhshan and rubies; they both sat, the maid and the youth, with faces flashing lightning; they that looked on them burned with new fire.

1416   He presented to Avt'handil and P'hridon measureless great gifts, a valuable saddle, an excellent horse, to each a jewelled coat shedding rare-hued rays; they said: "What thanks can we utter! Prosperous be your state!"

1417   Tariel rendered thanks with his tongue in fair words: "Greatly have I been pleased, O king; first at seeing you, then you have filled us with many fair kinds of gifts; I wot we did well not to pass by afar off from you."

1418   The King of the Seas says: "O king, lion, valorous, life of those near you, slayer from afar of those that cannot look on you, what can I give you like unto yourself, O fair to look upon! When I am away from you what shall avail me, O desirable to be gazed on!"

1419   Tariel said to P'hatman: "I adopt thee as my sister. O sister, great is mine unpayable debt to thy heart! Now whatever treasure of the Kadjis I have brought with me from Kadjet'hi I give it to thee, take it, I sell it not."

1420   Dame P'hatman made obeisance, she proffered exceeding great thanks: "O king, parting from thee burns me with unquenchable fire. When I shall be away from thee what shall I do! Thou wilt leave me like one bereft of sense. Ah, blessed are those near thee; woe to him that cannot gaze on you."

1421   The two radiant ones spoke to the King of the Seas; their teeth were crystals, their lips as pearl-shells. "When we are deprived of you we desire not merrymakings, harps and kettledrums. But give us leave, it is time, let us depart, we are in haste.

1422   "Be our father, parent and hope! But this indeed we beseech of thee: grant us a ship!" The king said: "I grudge not to give myself as earth for you (to tread on); since thou art in haste, what can I say to thee! Go! Thine arm be thy guide!"

1423   The king fitted out a ship on the shore. Tariel set out; those who were parted shed tears, they beat their heads, they tore their hair and beards (and) cast them away. P'hatman's tears in their flow even augmented the sea.

1424   The three sworn brothers crossed the seas together, again they confirmed by their word what they formerly affirmed; singing and laughter were beseeming to them, who were not ignorant thereof; the ray from their lips shone upon the planks of crystal (their teeth).

1425   Thence they sent a man to Asmat'h as a messenger of good tidings; also to the households of P'hridon's chiefs who had been in the fight, to announce to them: "He comes hither, as the sun he rises high, reinforcing (?) the planets; we erstwhile frozen shall be frozen now no more."

1426   They seated that sun (Nestan) in a palanquin; they wended their way along the coast. They sported like children; the passing away of woe gladdened them. They came where was the land of the hero Nuradin, they were met, they heard the sound of frequent song.

1427 There all P'hridon's magnates met them. Asmat'h, full of joy, whose wounds no longer appeared, was riveted to Nestan-Daredjan so that axes could not unloose them. Now she had ended all her faithful services.

1428 Nestan-Daredjan embraces her, kisses her face with her mouth. She said: "Mine own, woe is me, I have filled thee too with grief. Now God hath granted us grace, I acknowledge His (boundless) bounty. I know not with what I can repay so great a heart as thine!"

1429 Asmat'h said: "Thanks be to God, I have seen the roses unfrozen. At length understanding hath thus revealed things hidden. Death itself seems to me life when I see you happy. Better than all friends are suzerain and vassals that love one another!"

1430 The magnates did homage, they rendered great praise: "Since God hath caused us to rejoice, blessed is His divinity; He hath shown us your face, no longer doth the burning of fires consume us; even He that gave the wound, He hath the power to heal it."

1431 They came and put their mouths on their hands; thus they kissed them. The king (Tariel) said: "For our sake have your brethren sacrificed themselves. They have found joy in eternity a reality and no dream. They have attained communions with the One; their glories are increased an hundred and twenty fold."

1432 "Though their death is sore to me and grievous, yet the great immortal gift hath there fallen to their lot." This he spake, gently he wept, and the rain (of tears) was mingled with the snow (of his cheeks). Boreas blows from (? shakes) the narcissi; January freezes the rose.

1433 There all wept when they saw him in tears; whoever had lost any (kinsman) moaned, weeping and sobbing. All were hushed. Then they said respectfully (to Tariel): "Since sages liken thee to the sun, it befits them that look upon you to be merry; wherefore should they lament!

1434 "Who is worthy of your so great weeping and sorrow? Death for your sake is far better than walking upon the earth!" Then P'hridon said to the king: "Make not bitterness to thyself from aught. May God in return render to thee a thousand joys!"

1435 Avt'handil also sympathized; he speaks with great sorrow. They rendered praise, and said: "Let us now yield ourselves to smiling; since the lost lion has found the vanished sun, no more will we weep what is deplorable, no longer will we set canals in our eyes."

1436 Thither they went where is the great city Mulghazanzar. They played trumpet and kettledrum, there was trampling and uproar; the sound of drums and copper drum blended fairly; the burgesses crowded round, they left the bazaar.

1437 The merchants came from their rows, on all sides there is a host of onlookers; the officers kept a wide space round them, they had arms in their hands; families came crowding in, causing trouble to the officers; their entreaty is to be allowed there to look upon them.

1438 At P'hridon's they alighted, they saw a pleasing palace, many slaves with golden girdles met them, they have nought but gold brocades as a carpet for their feet; they threw up gold above their heads, the crowd marching there picked it up in heaps.

THE WEDDING OF TARIEL AND NESTAN BY P'HRIDON

1439   He placed for the maid and the youth a throne white and coral-hued, prettily sprinkled with red and yellow gems; for Avt'handil one of mingled yellow and black; they came, they sat down. The spectators, I ween, were impatient for them.

1440   The minstrels came forth; the sound of sweet singing was heard. They made the wedding; the presentation of soft silk stuffs was multiplied by P'hridon, the good entertainer, not an abashed host. A smile, a tooth-glimpse, beautifies Nestan-Daredjan.

1441   They brought out incomparable gifts from the wealthy P'hridon: nine pearls in size like a goose's egg; also one gem like to the sun with augmented ray; before it at night a painter could have painted a picture.

1442   Likewise he presented to each a necklace to throw over the neck, of gems cut into spheres, of whole jacinths. He also brought a tray scarcely to be held in the hand, a gift for the lion Avt'handil from the generous P'hridon.

1443   That tray is full of plump pearls; he gave all to Avt'handil, with not unseemly words. The house was filled with brocade and soft cloth of gold; Tariel the proud gave thanks with sweet words.

1444   For eight days P'hridon made measureless wedding festivities, every day they offer priceless presents prepared; day and night lute and harp ceased not to sound. Behold a youth and a maiden worthy each of other have attained each other.

1445 Tariel one day spake to P'hridon words of the heart: "Your heart is more mine than that of a complete (i.e., born) brother; my life would not be a fitting return, nor the gift of my soul; dying I found from you the balm for my wound.

1446 "Thou knowest of Avt'handil's self-sacrifice for my sake; now I would serve him in return; go, ask, he will reveal what he wants; as he hath quenched my furnace, even so hath his burned enough.

1447 "Say to him: 'O brother, what will repay thee for the grief thou hast seen for my sake? God will grant thee His grace imaged forth from on high. If I cannot do something desirable for thee, contrived for thy sake, I will not see my house, nor hall, not hut.

1448 "'Now tell me what thou wishest of me, or in what I can help thee. I choose that we go to Arabia; be thou my guide. Let us bring to reason the sweet with words, the warlike with swords. If thou be not united to thy wife I will be no husband to mine.'"

1449 When P'hridon told Avt'handil Taria's message, he laughed, he smiled, mirth beautified him. He said: "Why want I a helper? I am not hurt by a wound from any. The Kadjis possess not my sun, nor doth lack of joy afflict her.

1450 "My sun sits upon a throne, powerful by the will of God, respected and honoured, proud, harmed by none, she is by no means oppressed by Kadjis, nor by the sorcery of wizards. Why should I want help with regard to her? Expect me not to speak flattering words.

1451 "When Providence shall come for me, heavenly beings from above, (if) God wills, shall visit my heart, consolations for the furnace; then indeed the radiances of the flashing of the sun will be my lot (when I am) dying; till that time be come, vain are my runnings to and fro.

1452 "Go and report to Tariel the answer spoken by me: 'What thanks are needed, O king, however great is thy compassion; even from my mother's womb am I born to be your servant, and, by God, let me be but earth till thou be recognized as king.'

1453 "Thou hast said: 'I desire thy union to thy beloved!' This is like your compassionate heart. There my sword cuts not, nor breadth of tongue. It is better for me to await the deed of yon celestial Providence.

1454 "This is my wish and my desire, that I may see thee powerful in India, enthroned upon the thrones, the heavenly light (Nestan), too, sitting by thy side, the face flashing lightning; that your foes be exterminated, that no adversary appear there.

1455 "When these the desires of my heart have been fulfilled to me, then indeed shall I go to Arabia, it will befall me to be near that sun; when she wills she shall quench the burnings of this fire for me. Nought else do I wish from you; I hate all kinds of flattery."

1456 When P'hridon reported to Tariel these words of the knight, he said: "That will I not do; for that it needs no wizard. As he found the cause of the existence of my life (Nestan), even so he too shall see the valour of a brother (used) in his favour.

1457 "Go, speak on my behalf words not of adulation: I will not remain without seeing thy foster-father. I suspect I slew many servants beloved by him. I will only beg forgiveness, and so I shall return.'

1458 "Speak thus: 'Send me no more messages. Tomorrow I shall not fail to set out; I shall have no more of the word "if"; the King of the Arabs will not make my words to be of no avail; pleasantly shall I beg his daughter, I shall entreat of him, I shall persuade him."

1459 P'hridon told Avt'handil Taria's message: "He will not stay," quoth he; "vain is it for thee to speak of waiting!" It oppressed him; again the smoke and glow burned his heart. Thus respect is due to kings, devotion from knights.

1460 Avt'handil went to beseech Taria on bonded knee; he embraces his feet, he kisses them, he no longer looks up to his waist. He says: "What I have sinned against Rosten this year is enough; make me not again to be a breaker, a shatterer of loyalty.

1461 "What thou desirest God's justice will not give thee. How can I dare do a treacherous deed to my foster-father, how can I undertake aught against him who for my sake is become pale, how can the servant use his sword upon his master!

1462 "Such a deed will make discord between me and my beloved. Woe is me if she become angry, displeased, if wrath compel her heart! (Then) will she even stint me of tidings, and make me languish for a sight of her. No man of flesh can exact forgiveness for me."

1463 Tariel, that radiant sun, spake laughing. He took Avt'handil's hand, raised him, set him on his feet: "Thy help hath done me every good, but it is better that thou also shouldst rejoice my joy with thine.

1464 "I greatly hate too much fear, respect and ceremony in a friend, I hate unbroken sternness, gloominess, majesty; if one be a hearty friend let him tend towards me; if not, I for myself, he for himself, separation is much better.

1465 "I know the heart of thy beloved with regard to thee; the visit of me who have met thee will not displease her. Now I can venture to speak somewhat plausibly to the king: I only desire to see the desirable sight of them.

1466 "This only will I say to him entreatingly and respectfully: that he should give thee his daughter of his free will. Since the end is union, how can you endure separation? Beautify each other; fade not apart."

1467 When Avt'handil knew from Taria that he would not be hindered from going, he ventured not to dispute, he added thereto assent. P'hridon counted over select men as a convoy; he set out with them, of course he travelled the road with them.

TARIEL GOES AGAIN TO THE CAVE AND SEES THE TREASURE

1468   This hidden thing Divnos the sage reveals: "God sends good, He creates no evil, He shortens the bad to a moment, He renews (? repeats) the good continuously (? for a long time), His perfect self He makes more perfect, He degrades not Himself."

1469   Those lions, those suns, set out from P'hridon's (country). They lead with them the sun-faced, the maiden, the amazing to beholders; the raven's tail (of her hair), ordered, hangs coiled by the crystal (of her brow or cheek); beauty, tenderness, there adorned the (fine) ruby.

1470   That sun sat in a palanquin, and thus they made her fare. They followed the chase; there caused they blood to flow. Wherever they came upon a land they were the joy of beholders, they went forth to meet them, gave gifts, eulogized, reviled them not.

1471   It was as if the sun sat in the firmament amid moons. Many days they journeyed, merry, sagely discoursing, within those great plains on all sides unattained of men. They reached the neighbourhood of that rock where Tariel had been.

1472   Tariel said: "It is seemly that I should be your host this day. Thither will I go where I was while madness afflicted me. There will Asmat'h entertain us; she hath (store of) smoked meat. When I give you fair gifts you shall praise the variety of the treasure."

1473 They went in; they dismounted in that cave of the great rocks. Asmat'h had venison; she carves it for the guests. They were merry, they joked at the passing of those deeds; they thanked God that He had turned their. days of woe to joy.

1474 They explored the hollow hill, merry they played; they found those treasures sealed up by Taria, uncounted by any, apprehended by none; they say not with dissatisfied hearts: "We lack!"

1475 He gave many fair gifts, to each what was fitting; then he enriched P'hridon's people, army and generals alike; every man was enriched, (all) those who came with them, but there lay so much treasure it seemed still untouched by man.

1476 He said to P'hridon: "Hard will it be for me to pay the debt I owe thee; but it is said: 'A man who is a doer of good loseth not in the end.' Now the treasure, as much as lieth here or is to be found, let it all be thine, take it away, as it belongs to thee." so

1477 P'hridon humbly did homage, he expressed exceeding gratitude: "O king, why thinkest thou me stupid and thus mazed? Every enemy seems to thee as straw, however much he may be like a thick cudgel. My joy lasts but so long as I shall be a gazer on thee."

1478 P'hridon made men go back to bring camels to take away all this treasure to his home. Now they set out thence on the road leading to Arabia. Avt'handil is a minished moon (by longing) to be united with the sun (T'hinat'hin).

1479 When many days were passed they reached the boundaries of Arabia; they saw villages, castles, frequent, uninterrupted; those dwelling therein had clothed their forms in blue and green, all are bathed in tears for Avt'handil.

1480   Tariel sent a man to the presence of King Rosten to say: "I venture, O king, to approach thee full of desire; I, King of the Indians, come to your royal court; I will show thee the rosebud, unfaded, unplucked.

1481   "Formerly my sight of thy ground made you angry; thou didst ill in attempting to capture me, to urge thy horse against me; I showed thine armies some sign of anger, I massacred many slaves, servants of your palace.

1482   "Now therefore I come before you, I have gone out of my way; you will pardon me that in which I sinned against thee, let thy wrath be sufficient. We have no offerings, as P'hridon and his knights can testify; the only gift I have brought you is your Avt'handil."

1483   Tongue cannot shortly tell how they rejoiced when the messenger of these good tidings came to the king; the brilliancy of three rays was added to T'hinat'hin's cheeks, the shadow of eyebrows and lashes makes fairer the crystal and ruby.

1484   They beat the kettledrums and peals of joyous laughter were heard, the soldiers ran hither and thither, they desired to run to meet them, they began to lead out the horses and to bring out saddles, a multitude of knights, swift-armed, stout-hearted, mounted.

1485   The king mounted, the princes and the armies entire go to meet them; whoever hears, others from divers parts come to his presence; all give thanks to God, they raise their voices, they say: "Evil hath no existence; good things (or, the good) are ever ready for thee!"

1486   When they met and the meeters perceived each other, Avt'handil said with tender words to Tariel: "Behold, seest thou the dust-dyed plains? Therefore a furnace consumes me, my heart is fevered and sad.

1487   "There is my foster-father; he is come to meet you. I cannot go thither, I am ashamed, a furnace consumes my heart; living man hath never been shamed as I am. What you intend to do for me you know, also P'hridon who is beside you."

1488   Tariel said: "Thou dost well to show respect to thy lord. Now stay, come not thither, stay alone without me. I will go; I will tell the king of thy hiding. With God's help I think I shall soon unite thee to that sun with the figure of an aloe."

1489   The lion Avt'handil tarried there; a little tent was put up. Nestan-Daredjan also stayed there, the amazer of beholders; the zephyr of her eyelashes is wafted like a north-east wind. The King of the Indians departed, straight, not secretly.'

1490   P'hridon went with him; of a truth they were a long time crossing the field. The king knew (of their coming). Tariel went forward alone, his figure swayed; he dismounted and did homage to the bold one strong as a lion; he does honour to the King of the Indians as a father.

1491   Tariel also did homage; he goes to kiss, to greet. The king kissed his neck to give pleasure to his lips; in wonder he speaks, in order to embolden him: "Thou art the sun; separation from thee turns day into night."

1492 The king marvelled at his beauty and good looks, he gazes with wonder on his face, he praises the hardihood of his arms. Then P'hridon also greeted him; he did homage to the king, to the king eager for the sight of Avt'handil.

1493 The king shrinks from praising Taria, and is discouraged. Tariel says: "O king, hereby is my heart subjected to thee; I marvel how you can think thus of my worth; since Avt'handil is thine, how can any other please thee!

1494 "Dost thou not wonder at not seeing him, and at his tarrying! Come and let us sit down, O king, pleasant is this meadow of verdure; I will venture to tell you the reason why I could not bring him before you; I have a favour to ask of you, now I must beg leave of you."

1495 The kings sat down; the multitude of the host stood round. A smile brighter than a lamps flits over Tariel's face; the sight maddens the beholders of his bearing and gestures. He began to relate to the king a speech wisely chosen:

1496 "O king, I hold myself unworthy to mention this, but I am come before you to entreat, to beg; he himself beseeches who seems a sun-like shedder of rays, he who is my light and enlightener.

1497 "Now we both venture to approach thee with prayer and entreaty. Avt'handil gave me balm befitting him; he forgot that woes quite equal to ours afflicted him. I will not weary thee; a long story is beyond our powers.

1498 "Your (children) love each other, the maid loves him and he the maid; therefore I think on him pitiful, tearful and wan, on bended knee I entreat thee, let them no longer be consumed by flame, but give your daughter to the strong-armed, stout-hearted one.

1499   "No more than this will I ask of thee, neither short nor long." He drew forth his handkerchief, tied it round his neck, rose up, bent his knee, besought him like a (pupil) before a teacher. It astonished all men who heard this story.

1500   When he saw Tariel on his bended knees, the king was dismayed; he went back a long way, he did homage, he fell down to the earth. He said: "O monarch, all my joy is blown away from me; this abasement of you thus has saddened for me the sight of you.

1501   "How could it be that man should not grant thee whatever thou desirest, or that I should grudge my daughter if thou didst wish (to devote her) to death or slavery even! If you had even ordered it from your home, not even then would my tears flow; none other can she find like him if she fly up even to heaven!

1502   "I could not find a better son-in-law than Avt'handil. Myself I have given the realm to my daughter, she has it and it befits her; the rose blooms anew, my flower is blown. What objection can I make? Only let him be satisfied!

1503   "If thou wert to marry her to some slave, even then I would not grudge her to thee. Who could refuse thee, how could any save a madman quarrel with thee! If I loved not Avt'handil, why did I thus yearn for him? Verily, O God, I am in Thy presence, this is confirmed by me."

1504   When Tariel heard this speech from the king, he bowed himself, humbly did homage, fell on his face. Then the king did homage to him, he came forward, he stood before him. They thanked each other, nor were they at all annoyed.

1505   P'hridon mounted, he galloped as herald of good tidings to Avt'handil--indeed, he also rejoiced at this great joy--he went and took him, led him and accompanied him; but he is abashed before the king, darkly he shed (his) beam.

1506   The king arose, met him; the knight dismounted when (the king) came; in his hands he had a handkerchief, therewith he hid his face. The sun was concealed by a cloud, it grew gloomy, the rose was chilled; but how could anything hide his beauty!

1507   The king would have kissed him, tears no longer flow, Avt'handil embraced his feet, the ray streams down; (the king) said: "Arise, be not ashamed, thou has revealed thy prowess; since thou art loyal to me, be not ashamed; why shouldst thou be ashamed before me?"

1508   He embraced him, he kissed him all over his face; he said: "Thou hast quenched my hot fire, though tardily hast thou appeared to me as water; to her who has herded in the jet and the vicinity (?realm) of the eyelashes to-morrow I shall unite thee, O lion, with the sun, come quickly to her."

1509   The king embraced the neck of that lion and hero-like one, he seats him close, he speaks to him, kisses him, gazes on his face. That sun so met royalty, as he was worthy of it. Then is joy pleasant, when a man hath passed through grief.

1510   The knight says to the king: "I marvel that thou speakest of something else, why thou desirest not to see the sun, or why thou delayest! Meet her gaily, conduct her to your house; be clothed in her rays, set them around as a light."

1511   He told Tariel also; they mounted and went to meet the lady. The cheeks of those three Goliaths were dyed to sun colour (i.e., shone like the sun); they met what they desired, they found what they sought; they had handled their swords, not girded them idly on their loins.

1512   Dismounting afar off, the king greeted the lady, the lightning flashing from her cheeks blinded his eyes; she met him, sitting in the palanquin she kissed him. The king began a eulogy; he was wholly bereft of his wits.

1513   He said: "O sun, how shall I praise thee, O light, and maker of good weather! For thy sake understandings are mad, and not for nought. O sun-like and moon-like, to what planet do they liken thee! No longer do I wish to look on you, O ye roses and violets!"

1514   All they that saw her marvelled at the shedding of her rays. Like a sun she blinded the eyes of the onlookers by the sight of her light; burned by her they found the comfort of their hearts in gazing; wheresoever she appeared crowds came running towards her.

1515   They mounted, they all went homewards, they have the seven planets to compare with that sun; her beauty is incomprehensible, it is beyond their understanding. Soon they came to the place of the king's dwelling-house.

1516   They came in, they saw T'hinat'hin, the bestower of woe on them that look on her; the wearing of the purple? beautified the sceptre and crowns bearer; the radiance of her face rested on the faces of the new-comers. The King of the Indians entered, that hero-like sun.

1517   Tariel and his wife humbly saluted the maid, they met, kissed and held pleasant converse, they illumined that house (hall), they made not the light to fade; they turned crystal and ruby into cheeks, jet into eyelashes.

1518   T'hinat'hin invited them up to the lofty royal throne. Tariel said: "Sit thou; it is desired by the Supreme Judge; this day more than all days thy throne befits thee, I seat the lion of lions beside thee the sun of suns."

1519   Both (? Tariel and Rostevan) took him by the hand and set him on her throne; they placed Avt'handil by the side of her for desire of whom he was slain; she is better than the seen and the unseen, (better) than all sights. Think not any were like them in love, not even Ramin and Vis.

1520   The maiden was bashful and astonished to have Avt'handil seated by her side; her colour paled and her heart shot forth a tremor from within. The king said: "Child, why art thou so bashful before me? the sages say that love in its end will not fail.

1521   "Now, children, God grant you a thousand years' length of life, happiness, prosperity, glory, and, moreover, freedoms from ills; may heaven not make you fickle, may it fall to your lot to be steadfast like it, may my fate be to have the earth heaped over me by your hands."

1522   Then the king commanded the armies to do homage to Avt'handil: "This is your king," quoth he, "such was God's will.

This day he hath my throne, I have old age like an infection. Serve him as well as you have served me, keep my command."

1523   The soldiers and the magnates bent, humbly they did homage; they said: "Let us be as the earth to them that dispose of our lives; them who magnify those of us who are obedient, who liken the disobedient unto corpses, who make the arms of foes to fail (and) encourage our hearts!"

1524   Tariel too spoke with a eulogy the glorification of hope; he said to the maiden: "You are united, no longer the heat of fires burns thee, thy husband is my brother, I desire too that you be my sister, I will bring to nought those who are false and opposed to thee."

HERE IS THE MARRIAGE OF AVT'HANDIL AND T'HINAT'HIN BY THE KING OF THE ARABS

1525 That day Avt'handil sits as lord and is high king; tendernesses beautify Tariel who sits with him. Nestan-Djar, the amazer of onlookers, is with T'hinat'hin; it is as if heaven had bent down to earth, (and) two suns are united.

1526 They began to bring bread to plenish the armies; beeves and sheep are slain more abundant than moss. There was made an offering of presents, fitting to them (i.e., to each after his rank) . The ray of the faces of them all lightens like the sun.

1527 The bowls were of jacinth, the cups were of ruby; moreover, wondrously coloured vessels bear passing wondrous seals. The panegyrist of that wedding would be praised by the sages. O onlooker, thou wouldst have said unto thy heart: "Be not loosed, be bound there!"

1528 The (female) minstrels approached from all sides, there was heard the sound of the cymbal; heaped lies a hillock of gold and cut rubies; for drinkers flows a fountain of wine from a hundred (runlets), like a canal; from twilight to dawn there was noise, the time of morning passed.

1529 None remained without a gift, neither lame nor crippled; pearls rolled to and fro, scattered, thrown about; satin and solid gold were of none account, to be carried away. For three days the King of the Indies was as a groomsman to Avt'handil.

1530 On the morrow the King of the Arabs again entertains; he is not listless. He said to Tariel: "Pleasant it is to gaze on thy sun (Nestan)! Thou art king of all kings, and she queen. It behoves us your footprints (dust of your feet), to pierce our ears for earrings (as slaves) (?).

1531 "Now, O king, it is not fitting that we should sit on a level with you!" The royal throne he (Rostevan) placed for (Tariel), and another couch apart; he placed Avt'handil and his wife lower down, according to their rank First of all they present gifts for Taria; they lie in a heap.

1532 The King of the Arabs plays the host, he does nothing but entertain; sometimes he approaches these, sometimes those, he stands not upon his royal dignity; he gives, and all praise his ungrudging generosity. P'hridon sits near Avt'handil, as one accustomed to kingship.

1533 The king (Rostevan) did honour to the daughter of the Indies and her husband, he gave them love and gifts, as to a son and daughter-in-law; it is impossible to tell even a tenth of what he gave, to each a sceptre, purple and jewelled crowns.

1534 Still he gave to both gifts fitting their fate; a thousand gems born of a Roman hen; then a thousand pearls like a dove's egg; a thousand steeds, in size each like a hill:

1535 To P'hridon he gave nines trays full to the brim with pearls, nine steeds richly saddled. The King of the Indians does homage with dignity; wise, not drunkenly; he gave thanks soberly though he had drunk of the wine.'

1536 Why should I lengthen (speech)? The days of one month passed. They sported, they ceased not at all from drinking. To

Tariel they presented wondrous jewels of ruby stone. Their radiance like the sun's covers them all.

1537 Tariel was like a rose, and was snowing a light snow shower; he sent Avt'handil to Rosten to ask for leave; he gave him this message: "To be near thee is enough for me as full joy, (but) enemies hold my kingdom, I know they are eating up the land.

1538 "The knowledge and art of the learned destroy the unlearned. I think any hurt to me would bring somewhat of sadness into you too. I go that tarrying here may not bring evil upon me, soon again may I see you happy, may God's will grant it!"

1539 Rostevan said: "O king, why art thou so bashful? Whatever is best for you do it, look into it, examine it. Avt'handil will accompany thee, go with a great host; rend in pieces and cut up your enemies and them that are traitors."

1540 Avt'handil said to Tariel those (same) two words (that Rostevan had said). He (Tariel) said: "Speak not thus; guard the crystal mounds. How canst thou, O sun, depart from the newly united moon!" Avt'handil said: "I shall not be seduced by thee with this:

1541 "Of a truth thou wishest not to forsake me while thou goest away slandering me, saying: 'He loveth his wife, forsooth; he hath forsaken me, 'twas like him!' Am I to remain sundered from thee and an object of pity to myself! For a man to forsake his friend! . . . Ugh! Ugh! he will do ill!"

1542 Tariel's smile is like the sprinkling of crystal with roses. He said: "Absent from thee I bewail myself more than thou.

Since thou wishest it, come away with me, accuse me not of flattery." Avt'handil commands troops to be summoned to him from all sides.

1543   He assembled the armies of Arabia, no time is wasted; eighty thousand men were all arrayed, man and horse clad in armour of Khvarazmia. The King of the Arabs eats the gall of bitterness at their separation.

1544   Parting each from other, both maidens, the adopted sisters, sworn with the oath of sisterhood, trusting in each other's word, with breast welded to breast, with neck riveted to neck, wept. The onlookers, too, had their hearts consumed.

1545   When the moon is on a level with the star of dawn, both shine equally; should (one) go away, (the other also) is removed; if it go not away, the sky will make it remove; to look at them the onlooker must become a hill and a mountain (?).

1546   He who created them such, He Himself shall sunder them, though of their own will they desire not parting. They glue together and cleave the rose, they weep and tears flow; all those who parted from them thought their lives of no account.

1547   Nestan-Daredjan said: "Would that I had never come to know thee! Separated from the sun I should not now be thus melted by parting. Thou shalt know tidings of me; let me have news of thee, speak to me in letters. As I am burned up for thy sake, thou shalt melt for mine."

1548   T'hinat'hin said: "O sun, delight of them that gaze on thee! How can I give thee up, or how can I endure parting! Instead of praying for days from God, I shall desire death. Mayst thou have as many days as I shall shed tears!"

1549 Again they kissed each other, those ladies parted; she who was left there could not take her eyes away from her who was gone; she too looks back, therefore flames consumed her. I cannot write down a tenth part of that I could wish!

1550 Rostan at their departure was made more mad than madmen; a thousand times he says, "Woe is me!" not merely once doth he sigh; hot flows the spring of tears, as if a cauldron were being heated. Tariel's face is drawn, the soft snow falls gently, it wastes away.

1551 The king crushed Tariel's rose with embracing and kissing. Quoth he: "Your presence hitherto seems like a dream to me; when thou art gone afar from me I shall remain with my sufferings twentyfold increased. Life was given to us by thee; by thee also shall we be slain."

1552 Tariel mounted and parting from the king gave him a farewell greeting; all the soldiers shed tears moistening the meadows, they said: "The sun hastes to greet thee, haste thou too to meet him." He said: "Weeping for your sake, why should I hasten?"

1553 They set out and departed with many troops and much baggage--Tariel, P'hridon, Avt'handil, (all) well provided; he had eighty thousand men with worthy steeds; the three went on, helpful one to another.

1554 The three went their way--God can never create their like again! They were met; none dared withstand them. In the plain they tarried for dinner when morning was past. As was fitting they feasted; they drank wine, not buttermilk.

1555   What Tariel and his wife had desired fell to their lot, seven royal thrones, (seats) of joy, unassailable; this present solace makes them forget their sufferings. A man unacquainted with sorrow cannot find pleasure in joy.

1556   See the two sitting together; even the sun could not be better! They blow the trumpet and proclaim him king, copper drums make the voices sound sweet; they give him the key of the treasuries, they gave themselves into his hands as subjects. "This is our king!" they cried, and they acclaimed him.

1557   They caused two thrones to be prepared for Avt'handil and P'hridon, they sat royally thereon, they extolled their majesty, what other human beings did God create like them! They related their sorrows; they revealed them to all.

1558   They drank, ate, made merry, they increased the household; as befits a wedding so did they celebrate it; to each of the four they gave presents equally. They gathered together treasure to give to the poor.

1559   All the Indians considered Avt'handil and P'hridon to be helpers (allies). "From you every good happens to us," said they ceaselessly; they looked upon them as lords (suzerains), whatever they willed that they did, they came before them continually to pay court to them.

1560   The King of the Indians said to Asmat'h, the sharer of his sorrows: "What thou hast done, neither upbringer nor upbrought hath done (for each other). Now I enthrone thee over one seventh part of the kingdom of India, thine let it be, serve us, sweet to the sweet!

1561   "Whomsoever thou desirest as husband wed him, rule the kingdom, henceforth serve us, be subject to us." Asmat'h covered his feet with kisses. "From thee is my power," quoth she; "what can I find, what better service can I have than thine!"

1562   The three sworn brothers tarried together a few days. They sported, they received more incomparable gifts; what rare pearls, what excellent horses! But longing (for T'hinat'hin) made Avt'handil to show lines on his face.

1563   Tariel perceived that longing of the knight for his wife. He said: "Of a truth thy heart is angered against me. Now woe is me! thought hath made of thy seven griefs eight. I shall be separated from thee; Fate grudges me my joy."

1564   Then P'hridon begged leave of him. "I will go home," quoth he; "my foot will oft tread this court and land if thou wilt command me as an elder to a younger. I shall desire thee as the deer the fountain."'

1565   As presents for Rostevan, he (Tariel) made him (Avt'handil) take with him beautiful little mantles, also a vessel (full) of cut gems, not spoons(ful), not ladles(ful). "Take them from me, go," quoth he, "disobey me not!" Avt'handil said: "I know not how I shall survive without thee!"

1566   The lady (Nestan) sent to the lady (T'hinat'hin) a little cloak and a veil; who save hers was worthy of such garments! A jewel--he who carried it off could not say: "I have carried it in vain!"--at night it gives light like the sun; it is visible wherever thou lookest.

1567   Avt'handil mounted, he departed, he said farewell to Taria, the flame of the fire of separation burned them both; all the Indians wept, the tear moistened the mead. Avt'handil said: "The poison of this world slays me!"

1568   P'hridon and Avt'handil journeyed together for a few days; the road separated them, each went his way weeping; the things they had planned had turned out well for them; Avt'handil came to Arabia, he had not seen troubles in vain.

1569   The Arabs came forth to meet him, he beautified the realm; he saw his sun, the affliction of his desires fled; he sat with her on the throne, he rejoiced at the joy of the onlookers. The Most High from above endued his crown with sovereignty.

1570   Those three sovereigns loved one another, they visited one another, their desires were fulfilled, they that disputed their rule were put to the sword, they enlarged their kingdoms, they were sovereign, they increased their might.

1571   They poured down mercy like snow on all alike, they enriched orphans and widows and the poor did not beg, they terrified evil-doers; the ewes could not suckle the lambs, within their territories the goat and the wolf fed together.

1572   Their tale is ended like a dream of the night. They are passed away, gone beyond the world. Behold the treachery of time; to him who thinks it long, even for him it is of a moment. I a certain Meskhian bard of the borough of Rust'havi, I write (this).

1573   For the god (goddess--i.e., king, queen, T'hamara) of the Georgians, whom David the sun serves in his course, I have put this story into verse, for her (pl. maj.) entertainment who strikes terror from East to West, consuming those who are traitors to her, strengthening those who are loyal.

1574 How shall I sing to David's harp, attuned and loud-sounding, these wondrous (rare) tales of strange, foreign monarchs! Old-time customs and deeds, praises (eulogies) of those kings, have I found and done into verse. Thus have we chattered!

1575 This is such a world as is not to be trusted by any; it is a moment to the eyes of men, and only long enough for the blinking of the eyelashes. What seek you, what do you? Fate is an insulter. For him whom Fate deceives not it is better to be (happy) in both (worlds).

1576 Mose Khoneli praised Amiran, son of Daredjan; Shavt'heli, whose poem they admired, praised Abdul-Mesia; Sargis T'hmogveli, the unwearying-tongued (praised) Dilarget'h; Rust'haveli (praised) Tariel, for whom his tear unceasing flows.

APPENDICES

AN ENGLISH RENDERING OF THE RUSSIAN TRANSLATION BY PROFESSOR MARR OF THE INTRODUCTORY QUATRAINS OF "THE MAN IN THE PANTHER'S SKIN" ("TEKSTY," T. XII., PP. 7-9).

[The numbers given in round brackets are those of the strophes in the preceding translation.]

GON AND THE KING [1 (1)].--He who by His mighty power created the firmament breathed a celestial spirit from heaven and made what is; to us men He gave the earth: we own its infinite variety. And every king is ordained by Him in the image issuing from Him.

THE GEORGIAN KING DAVID SOSLAN, CONSORT OF QUEEN T'HAMARA [2 (3)].--Behold the lion! (lit., To the lion to whom is fitting . . .). It befitted him to use spear, sword, and shield; (he is the lion of [lit., to the lion of]) Queen T'hamara, the sun, whose cheeks are like rubies, whose hair is like jet: dare I sing of him and extol him in verse? (lit., the singing of the sermon [for doxology] of verses). Of a truth, they that gaze on him cannot but taste sugar and milk. (For khshiri, which breaks the rhythm, read sherisa; Pers. shir = milk.)

THE SUBJECT OF THE POET'S SONGS [3 (25)].--The poet ought not to lavish his labour in frivolity. One (woman) should be the subject of his madness, he must love but one; let him for her alone show his art, laud her alone, embellish her alone (in song). Save her let him need nought: let the music of his discourse sound for her alone. (Cf. Prof. Marr's Odopistsi for another version.)

[4 (26)]--Now you shall know concerning me: I laud her for whom Heaven has already set apart a place in Itself (more literally, whom Heaven has made Its own, or made Its denizen, or adopted for Its own; ikia, second aorist of verb derived from adverb iki = there, is equivalent to "has made its own," etc.). (A song to her) is great praise to me; it is no shame to me. She is my life; she is pitiless as a Circassian (dchiki; cf. Adighe, Ζηκχοὶ). Hereafter I name her name, I bestrew her (with pearls of song), I laud her (lit., her name, bestrewing, I pronounce hereafter, I praise).

THE ODES TO QUEEN T'HAMARA [5 (4)].--Let US sing the Queen T'hamara while shedding tears of blood; in her honour have I indited songs (lit., whose songs I spoke--vst'hkveni, aorist first person singular, with indication of relation to plural [kebani]), not ill-chosen are they: for ink I used a lake of jet (cf. Odes, V. 50, xii. 8), for pen a wavering reed (nai [Pers.]; the terminal i in Rust'haveli is only a mark of the nominative case, and not the Persian semivowel , corresponding to Georgian , which, according to M. E. T'haqaishvili, had not yet come into the mkhedruli [military or civil] alphabet from the khutsuri [ecclesiastical]. For use of na as musical instrument, cf. 178.) A spear, through-piercing, shall rend the heart of him who hears those songs (lit., He who hears, into his heart will pierce a lance, lacerating).

[6 (5)].--She bade me compose in her honour sweet (-sounding) verses, (praise her) eyebrows, eyelashes, and hair, her lips and her teeth, carved (turned) out of crystal and ruby, and firmly set. On an anvil of soft lead even a hard stone can be broken.

NEW BEGINNING [7 (17)].--(My) eyes not enlightened by her rays (or lightless--i.e., blind--on account of her rays) again long to show themselves to her. My heart has gone mad, there remains for it but one thing (lit.. Behold, the heart has gone mad, to it has fallen the lot): to flee to the wilderness. In her power it lies to set the flesh on fire and give joy to the soul; entreat her for me (lit., For me, m[i]-, beg her, iadjet'h, or, For me, m-, intercede, iadjet'h, before her--cf. 816, 819, 1035--who is sufficient to give burning to the flesh, comfort [lkhena, cf. 300] to the soul); I fear verses will fail (me), I am about to laud three forms (or colours--i.e., three types of heroes--Tariel, Avt'handil, and P'hridon).

[8 (16)].--This (is a) Persian tale transferred into the Georgian language: like a rare pearl worthy of fondling (by rolling it) from hand to hand; it came to my hands, and I shall put it into verse (vpove and gardavt'hkvi both in the aorist, despite the future sense), I shall perform a feat, there will be reason for pride. I await the approval of the stately beauty who has robbed me of reason (lit., She has deprived me of reason, the stately and beautiful, let her give me approval! Cf. Odes, xii. 15). REQUEST TO THE BELOVED [9 (6)].--Thus I need for the making of my song tongue, heart and art. Let her give me strength and uphold me. I shall put into (the song all) my mind, which is in her power, and then we shall help Tariel (lit., Now are needful for composition tongue, heart and art. Let her give me power and help. From her I have mind [wit] to put into, etc.; but in the printed texts T'hamara is addressed in the second person singular in this strophe, which perhaps the copyists thought addressed to God. The poet asks T'hamara for mind [wit] because she had robbed him thereof). It is necessary to tell in chosen language of the three stars, giant-heroes, obedient one to another like slaves (lit., It is inherent in them to be slaves one of another).

INVOCATION TO FELLOW-SUFFERERS [10 (7)].--Come, ye to whom from birth the fate of Tariel is appointed (lit., who is born with a birth exactly like his; cf. 852, 4), and whose tears flow undrying for him! (cf. Odes, p. 68). Let us sit down! I, the man of Rust'havi, pierced through the heart by a lance (of sympathy; cf. 5, 4) for him, will sit and expound (both "sit" and "expound" in the past tense in the accepted text; but this is evidently a copyist's error) in verse. That which till now was a tale will henceforth be a threaded pearl.

VARIETY OF VOCATION [11 (18)].--Let everyone be content with that which Fate gives him, and let everyone speak of his own lot. Let the ploughman ceaseless plough, the warrior show his prowess, but let him that is in love cherish mad love, and be compassionate to (lit., acknowledge) the love (of others). Neither have others the right to censure love in him, nor has he that right over others.

LOVE [12 (9)].--Love-madness is a wondrous fair thought, hard to be apprehended; it cannot be compared with carnal passion, it is something different; love is one thing, lust is another; their bounds are separated by a vast space. Confuse them not. Do ye hear my words? (reading gesmist'h for gesmast'h).

[13 (12)].--The highest love is to bury sufferings in oneself: he hides them; when alone, he is always with her in thought (lit., let him always remember at home [alone]), and he loves solitude (lit., he ought to be in solitude). Away (from her) he loses consciousness and dies; absent he burns and flames (lit., Afar to lose consciousness, afar to die, afar to burn, afar to flame). He is ready rather to endure calmly royal wrath, but towards her he feels fear and reverence.

[14 (8)].--The lover must have an exquisitely fair exterior and shine like the sun; he must be sage, rich, open-handed, he must be a knight (lit., have the qualities or attributes of a knight), he must have leisure; he must be a master of speech, a possessor of intelligence and patience, a conqueror of all-powerful adversaries. He who is not endowed with all these things has not the qualities of a lover.

[15 (10)].--He who is possessed by love-madness is constant; he is not an adulterer, no base libertine. Separated from his beloved, his sighs and groans become stronger. His heart is satisfied with one, though she be stern and wrathful. Hateful to me are caresses in which the soul is not felt: huggings, kisses and the smacking of lips.

[16 (11)].--Lovers, you must not call it love if one easily bears the torture (lit., disease or pain, reading lmobasa) of separation, if to-day he want one (woman) and to-morrow another. This reminds me of the frivolous games of youth; (it is) childishness. The true lover is he who checks earthly impulses.

POESY [17 (19)].--Poesy is first of all a branch of wisdom: the divine in it must be hearkened to with reverence; it is very instructive to the hearer. He who is prepared finds satisfaction in this domain. A vast thought may be put into a short phrase: herein is the beauty of poesy.

[18 (20)].--In like manner as the best trial of a horse is a long course and an easy win, as a ball-player is judged in the field by his unerring aim and clever stroke, so with the poet skill to indite lengthy songs and curb (?) (the steed of poesy) if he has exhausted the subject of his discourse and rhyme begins to dry up.

[19 (21)].--Contemplate the poet and his songs when his tongue fails him (lit., when he cannot attain [the perfection] of the

Georgian [speech]; or, when he cannot hit upon [the exact expressions] of Georgian), and his rhymes begin to grow thin! Shortens he not his discourse? Weakens not his speech? (lit., Will he not abridge [diminish] the Georgian language?). Has he heroic hardihood enough to strike cunningly with the chogan (polo-stick)? (lit., Will he strike with the polo-stick with skilful hand? Will he show the high quality of a hero?).

[20 (22)].--He who chances to say two words in verse cannot be called a poet (lit., He is not called a poet if somewhere he says one, two [verses]); in vain he puts himself on a level with singers of renown. He makes one verse, another (lit., of course, to make one [verse], another): they are not like anything; they are incoherent. Yet he asseverates, "Mine is better!" as stubbornly as a mule.

[21 (23)].--Another (form) is fugitive verse; this is the domain of poets powerless to pour out (? mould) heart-piercing thoughts in perfect (forms) (lit., Another versification is small [verse], the domain . . . He is not able in perfection to create words capable of piercing the heart). I liken this to the wretched bow of young hunters: big beasts they cannot bring down; they can kill only small game.

[22 (24)].--A third (kind of) songs is fitting for banquets and merrymakings, for courtship, for amusement and frivolous adventures with friends, and to these songs we gladly have recourse (lit., we like [the making of] them) if the thought in them be clearly expressed. But he who is incapable of creating something great is no poet.

Professor Marr rejects the nine remaining quatrains as spurious. It will be seen that he has rearranged the quatrains, and adopted readings which are not in the printed editions.

BIBLIOGRAPHICAL NOTE

THE following is a list of some books and pamphlets collected by the translator, and now the property of the Bodleian Library, Oxford.

TEXT.

KING VAKHTANG'S edition in quarto, with a commentary. The editio princeps. Tiflis, 1712. A defective copy.

D. CHUBINOV'S edition in octavo. St. Petersburg, 1846. This copy lacks title, and some pages are damaged. Wooden boards covered in velvet, with leather straps. Given as a wedding present to Euphrosyne Cldiashvili, and presented by her to the translator. It was the custom that all Georgian girls learned the poem by heart, and a copy of it was always included among the presents to a bride.

D. CHUBINOV's edition in octavo. St. Petersburg, 1860. References to this are marked "Ch." in the notes.

C. LORTHKIPANIDZE's edition (in unusual type). Kutaïs, 1883.

G. D. KART'HVELISHVILI'S edition de luxe in folio, illustrated, and adorned with borders from old designs. Tiflis, 1888.

T'HAVART'HKILADZE'S edition, with aphorisms in large type, octavo. Ozurget'hi, 1892.

T'HAVART'HKILADZE'S edition, illustrated, octavo. Batum, 1899.

A. S. KHAKHANOV (Professor at Moscow): Gruzinskaya rukopisnaya poema "Barsova Kozha" iz Moskovskago Glavnago Arkhiva Ministerstva Inostrannykh Dyel. (Gives many additional quatrains of doubtful authenticity from the MS. in the Archives of the Ministry for Foreign Affairs at Moscow; extracted from vol. ii. of "Trudy" of Oriental Commission of Moscow Imperial Archæological Society.) Quarto. Moscow, 1895.

VLADIMIR QIPHIANI's edition, illustrated, octavo. Tiflis, 1899.

D. CARIDCHASHVILI'S edition (the nineteenth). With four portraits and twenty-one illustrations. Octavo. Tiflis, 1903.

A handy cheap edition, with preface and glossary and notes. The numbering of the quatrains is that now usually adopted, and agrees with the foregoing English translation. References in the notes are marked "Car."

E. C. (?Bishop Cirion): Vephkhis Tqaosanis shesamotsmebeli masali. (Gives variants, marked in the footnotes "var. E. C.," from a seventeenth-century MS.) Pp. 20-38 in No. v. of "Moambe." Tiflis, 1904.

In December, 1911, Prince George Tseret'heli presented a MS. with illustrations. It seems to be of the seventeenth century.

OTHER WORKS.

PROFESSOR N. MARR: Vstupitelnyya i zakliuchitelnyya strofy Vityazya y Barsovoi Kozhie (the introductory and concluding strophes of "The Man in the Panther's Skin") being t. xii. of "Teksty i Razyskaniya." St. Petersburg, 1910. References to this are marked "M."

PROFESSOR N. MARR: Drevnegruzinskie Odopistsi (ancient Georgian writers of odes, twelfth century), being t. iv. of "Teksty." St. Petersburg, 1902. References to this are marked "M. iv." or "Odes."

J. ABULADZE: Me-xii saucunis Kart'hulis mtserlobis khasiat'hi da Rust'hvelis Vep'hkhis Tqaosani. (Contains a glossary of words derived from Persian, Arabic, etc.) Printed in vol. i. of "Dzveli Sakart'hvelo." Tiflis, 1909. References are marked "Abul."

ARTHUR LEIST: Der Mann im Tigerfelle. (A German verse translation.) Octavo. Preface dated 1889. Dresden and Leipzig.

AL. S(ARADJI)SHVILI: "Vephkhis Tqaosanis" qalbi adgilebi (The spurious passages in "The Man in the Panther's Skin"). Published in "Moambe," beginning in No. xi. of 1895, and ending in No. vi. of 1901, and would make a volume of 590 pages octavo; it gives the results of a critical examination of the whole poem. Tiflis, 1895-1901. Cf. articles in "Iveria," Tiflis, 1899, Nos. 3, 34, 47.

E. C.: An article in "Iveria," No. 93 of 1895.

M. BROSSET: De la littérature romanesque géorgienne (in Mélanges Asiatiques tirés du Bulletin de l'Acad. Imp. des Sciences de St. Pétersbourg, t. viii). St. Pétersbourg, 1877.

FELIX HOLLDACK: Zwei Grundsteine zu einer Grusinischen Staats- und Rechtsgeschichte. Leipzig, 1907.

P. CARBELASHVILI: An article in the Tiflis journal "Iveria" for 1880, pp. 3-54.

ACHAS BORIN: La Peau de Léopard. Tiflis, 1885.

ACHAS BORIN: Contes orientaux. Paris, 1886.

ILIA CHAVCHAVADZE: Ai Istoria! Tiflis, 1887.

ACACI (TSERET'HELI): Ramdenime sitqva bat. Ilia Dchavdchavadzis sapasukhod "Vephkhvis Tqaosanis" gamo. (A reply to his fellow-poet Chavchavadze's pamphlet "Ai Istoria!" on the question whether Tariel, Avt'handil, and P'hridon, are to be taken as types of Karthli, Imerethi, and Guria.) Tiflis, 1887.

ACACI (TSERET'HELI): T'hanamedrove hazrebi Rust'hvelisagan me-12-e saucuneshi natsinastsari. (In the Tiflis paper "Themi," No. 20 of 1911.)

A. S. KHAKHANOV: Ocherki po istorii gruzinskoi slovesnosti. (History of Georgian Literature.) Vol. ii., pp. 243-298. Moscow, 1897. Vol. i., pp. 281, 282. Moscow, 1895. Vol. iii., pp. 73-84, 94. Gruzinskii poet xii. vieka Shota Rustaveli i ego poema "Barsova Kozha," in "Journ. of Russian Min. of Publ. Instr.," part cccii., 1905, No. 12, pp. 200-223.

M. DJANASHVILI: Shot'ha Rust'haveli. Tiflis, 1896.

M. DJANASHVILI: Izrecheniya gruz. poeta Shota Rustaveli. (Aphorisms from the poem translated into Russian.) Tiflis, 1903.

M. DJANASHVILI: Rust'havelis garshemo (criticism of Professor Marr's views), in "Nashromi," part iii. Tiflis, 1910.

N. GULAK: O Barsovoi Kozhe Rustaveli. (Two lectures delivered in Tiflis in 1884. Extracted from part iv. of Sborn. materialov dlya opisaniya myestnostei i plemen Kavkaza.)

U. (? P. UMICASHVILI): O poezii Rustaveli (criticism of N. Gulak's lectures), in No. 248 of the newspaper "Kavkaz." Tiflis, November 6, 1884.

BARON SÜTTNER: Mnyenie inostrantza o "Barsovoi Kozhe."

(Opinion of a foreigner on "The Man in the Panther's Skin.") Russian translation of articles based on Meunargia's prose translation into French, which has not been published. In Nos. 265, 267, 268, of "Kavkaz." Tiflis, 1884.

SH. DAVIDOV: A translation into Russian prose of part (about 300 lines) of the poem, in "Zakavkazie," December 12 and 19, 1910.

E. S. STALINSKII: Barsova Kozha, part ii. (Translations of short passages into Russian, French, German, and Armenian, with an essay in Russian, including notes on versification.) Tiflis, 1888.

G. JOSELIANI: Vephkhis Tqaosani naambobi mozrdilis qmatsvilebisat'hvis. (A prose summary of the poem, for children.) Tiflis, 1892.

G. JOSELIANI: Another edition, illustrated. Tiflis, 1898.

A. P'HURTZELADZE: Shot'ha Rust'haveli da misi tzoli. (A popular legend about the faithlessness of the poet's wife. With a preface of 12 pages.) Batum, 1899.

"R. KINVARI": V Barsovoi Kozhe. Kartiny dlya stseny. (An adaptation for the stage in Russian verse, with preface and illustration.) St. Petersburg, 1901.

Z. MT'HATSMINDELI: Shot'ha Rust'haveli, 1172-1216. Tiflis, 1884 (bound up in volume lettered "Karthuli Mtserloba"). Gives the following rough bibliographical references on pp. i,

(a) Kart'hlis Tzkhovreba. 1852.

(b) Theimuraz Mephe: Sakarthvelos Istoria. 1848.

(c) Brosset's Preface to Chubinov's Dictionary. 1848.

(d) Brosset's Preface to Text of "Man in Panther's Skin." 1840.

(e) Archbishop Timothé's Travels. 1852.

(f) Journal "Tziscari." 1867.

(g) Casimir Lopczynski's Preface (in Polish). 1870.

(h) D. Djanashvili: Sakarthvelos Istoria. 1875.

(i) Newspaper "Droeba." 1881.

(j) D. Djanashvili: Karthveli Kalebi, in journal "Iveria." 1883.

(k) P. Umicashvili: Article in "Iveria." 1884.

(l) Acaci Tseret'heli: Lectures not yet published.

(m) Arsen the Monk (MS.), xvii c.: Leaves from Georgian Ecclesiastical History.

(n) Archimandrite Tarasi: Materials in the Monastery of Kvat'ha Khevi.

(o) King Vakhtang: Preface to Tiflis edition of 1713.

(p) King Theimuraz and others: Poems.

(q) Prince David: MS. information.

(r) Catholicos Anton: Tsqobili Sitqvaoba. 1852.

(s) Platon Joseliani: Notes on Rusthaveli.

(t) Georgian Chrestomathy, part i. 1848.

(u) Khosro T'hurmanidze (xvii c.): Rostomiani (translation of Shah Nameh).

(v) Prince Bagrat's Poems, written in xvii c.

(w) D. Bakradze's Preface to Calmasoba. 1862.

(x) Vakhusht's Geography. 1848.

All the above are in Georgian; the following are in Russian:

(aa) Progress of Science in Georgia, article in "Syevernaya Pchela." 1840.

(ab) Short Sketch of Georgian Literature, in "Tifl. Vyed." 1832.

(ac) Brosset: Georgian Literature in "Syn Otechestva." 1840.

(ad) Monuments of Literature in Georgia, in "Kavkaz." 1849.

(ae) Zakavkazskii Vyestnik. 1850.

(af) "Kavkaz." 1846.

(ag) "Kavkaz." 1870.

(ah) Bakradze: Ancient Meskhia, in "Kavkaz." 1855.

(ai) Pl. Joseliani: Journey from Tiflis to Mtzkhet. 1871.

(aj) Brosset: Review of Georgian Literature, in "Journ. of Education Dept." 1838.

(ak) Golovin: History of Georgia. 1865.

(al) Georgia, published by Alexander Nevsky Academy. 1802.

(am) Prince David: History of Georgia. 1801.

(an) R. Eristov: Rust'haveli, an article in "Kavkaz."

(ao) G. Joseliani: Rust'haveli, an article in "Kavkaz."

(ap) N. Gulak's Lectures on Rust'haveli.

(aq) Bakradze: History and Ethnography of Tiflis. 1873.

(ar) Pl. Joseliani: Shot'ha Rust'haveli.

GROUPS OF REFERENCES

[The references are far from being exhaustive; but with the help of the footnotes to the translation they may be of use.]

(a) Persons. (b) Places. (c) Fauna. (d) Flora. (e) Minerals. (f) Astronomy. (g) Religion. (h) Islam. (i) Superstitions and Customs. (j) Social Relations--Ethics. (k) Numbers. (l) Coins and Weights. (m) Games and Sports. (n) Military and Naval. (o) Public Works, etc. (p) Music.

PERSONS.

Abdul Mesia, 1576

Adam, 182, 192, 229

Asmat'h, 254, 320, 501, 633, 642, 1330-1336, 1365, 1427, 1560

Avt'handil, 40, etc.

Beelzebub, 337; a lexicon of A.D. 1210 gives "she-devil" as the meaning of Belzebeli (v. "T'hemi," No. 46 of 1911).

Boreas, 1432

Caen (Caisi), 1316

Chachnagiri (the), 1183, etc.

Cronos, 1391

Davar, 319, 559, 560, 564-565

David of Israel, 1574

David Soslan, 1573

Dilarget'h, 1576

Dionysius the Areopagite, 176, 1468

Dulardukht, 1199, 1218

Goliath, 1511

Khvarazmsha, 495, 497, 509, 546

Levi the Jew, 797

Mahmad, 1010

Melik Surkhavi, 1043

Mose Khoneli, 1576

Nestan-Daredjan, 316, etc.

Nuradin, v. P'hridon

P'harsadan, 301, 323

P'hatman, 1049, 1054-1056, 1058, 1067, 1074, 1076, 1078, 1275, 1287-1288, 1302, 1403, 1405, 1409, 1419

P'hridon (Nuradin), 583, 605, 1290, 1351, etc.

Plato, 770

Ramaz, 387, 406, 411, 423, 441-442, 453, 457

Ramin, 182, 1058, 1519

Rodia, 1199

Rosan, 1199, 1218

Roshak, 1200-1201, 1207, 1210, 1213

Rosten, 95, 768, 1480

Rostevan, 32, 663, 1240, etc.

Rostom, 192

Rust'haveli, 7, 15, 1576

Salaman, 1316

Samal,? 690

Sargis T'hmogveli, 1576

Saridan, 302

Satan, 2, 768, (786), 854, 1191 (? 690) Shavt'heli, 1576

Shermadin, 70, 148, 655, etc.

Sograt, 44, 57-59, etc.

Taria, 334, 1384, 1387, 1459-60, 1467

Tariel, 6, 7, 254, 279, 1313, 1385, etc.

T'hamara, 3, 4, 1573

T'hinat'hin, 34, 664, etc.

Usam, 1009, 1025, 1032

Usen, 1046, 1054, 1130, 1132-1133, 1139, 1141-1146, 1148, 1150-1151, 1302, 1407

Vis, 182, 1058, 1519

PLACES.

Arabia, 29, 32, 279, 947a, 1250, 1478

Athens, 676

Badakhshan, 3, 176, 1469

Bagdad, 1010

Cathay, 196, 364, 444, 456, 712, 976

China, 834

Eden, 50, 77, 299, 311, 321, 461, 506, 676, 697, 707

Egypt, 947a, 1012

Euphrates, 676

Georgia, 16, 21, 1573

Gibeon, 320

Gihon, 731

Greece, 947a

Gulansharo, 1043, 1205, 1287

India, 301, 406, 521, 548, 550, 947a, 1283, 1559, 1567

Kadjet'hi, 190, 282, 559, 1198, 1220, 1223-1227, 1245-1246, 1263, 1276, 1288, 1327, 1344, 1362-1364, 1403, 1405, 1413, 1419

Khatavet'hi v. Cathay

Khvarazmia, 389, 495, 497, 1543

Kurds, (285)

Mecca, 1144

Meshech, 1572

Mulghazanzar, 583, 952, 957, 1436

Paradise, 132

Persians, 16, 524, 947a

Pison, 701

Rome, 1534

Rust'havi, 15, 1572

Sea Realm (the), 1043, 1403

Turks, 289, 949

FAUNA.

Asp (aspiti), 1209

Ass (viri), 911, 1086, 1144; drove of asses (rema), 54; wild-ass (candjari), 75

Camel (aklemi), 447, 1402

Cat (cata), 317

Chamois (kurtzici), 75

Crocodile (niangi), 947a

Crow (qvavi), 591, 1068, 1231-1232

Deer (iremi), 75, 199, 835, 1564

Dog (dzaghli), 703, 916;? grey-hound, harrier (avaza), 459. Cf. panther, coursing

Dove (tredi), 1162; (mtredi), 1534

Dragon (veshapi), 1136

Dragon-fly, Netonecta glauca (tanadjori), 432

Duck (ikhvi), 606

Eagle (artzivi), 228; (orbi), 959

Ermine (qarqumi), 123

Ewe (tzkhvari), 1571

Falcon (shavardeni), 459, 606 (used as synonym of kori); (kori), 355, 432, 606, 703

Fox (meli), 743, 1184

Goat (t'hkha), 75, 579, 821, 928, 1022, 1571; she-goat (nezvi), 1182; he-goat (vatzi), 223, 1182

Hawk (gavazi), 211. See Falcon

Hen (dedali), 1534

Horse (tzkheni), 54, 630, 918, 959, 1310, 1382, etc.; (taidchi), 55, 96, 201, 1534

Lamb (cravi), 1571

Leopard (djiki), 26

Lion (lomi), 57, 223, 317, 321, 579, 849, 887-890, 1013, 1052, 1306, 1310, etc.

Mule (djori), 22, 447, 999, 1375, 1402

Nightingale (bulbuli), 82, 946, 1064, 1068, 1231, 1232, 1323; (iadoni), 749, 1232, 1331

Owl (bu), 946

Panther (vep'hkhi), 57, 85, 201, 261, 506, 639, 672, 849, 887-889, 891-892, 902, 1020, 1052, 1154, 1243, 1306; coursing panther (vep'hkhi avaza), 1137

Partridge (cacabi), 227-228; wood-partridge (duradji), 330-332, 336, 355; grey partridge (gnoli), 432

Raven (gorani), 591, 1243, 1246, 1284, 1338

Serpent (greli), 881, 1136, 1188, 1208, 1239. See Asp

Sparrow (siri), 310

Wolf (mgeli), 1571

FLORA.

Almond (nushi), 1257

Aloe, or poplar, or plane tree (alva), 77, 223, 275, 319, 357, 506, 537, 676, 693, 697, 1125, 1312, 1334, etc.

Aspen (verkhvi), 139

Bulrush (shambi), 170, 192, 216, 651, 846, 887, 930, 1309

Cucumber (citri), 767

Cypress (saro), 40, 229, 290, 616, 693, 954, 1051, 1157, 1171

Indigo (lila), 385

Lily (sosani), 72

Millet (kvrima), 1197

Narcissus (nargizi, nargisi,), 151, 397, 954, 1432

Orange (narindji), 465

Reed (lertsami), 176

Rose (vardi), 82, 229, 834, 857-85, 899, 1064, 1068, 1144, 1249, etc.

Saffron (zap'hrana), 346, 671, 834, 1135, 1255

Thorn (ecali), 857-858; of rose (katzvi), 671

Violet (ia), 229, 834, 1249, 1255, 1300

Willow (dzetsna), 742

MINERALS, GEMS, ETC.

(Cf. M. Djanashvili's monograph on precious stones in vol. xxiv. of the Tiflis "Sbornik" of the Educational Department.)

Amber (karva), 138, 276

Anvil (grdemli), 5

Bezoar (p'hazari), 318

Copper, bronze (rvali), 157, 547

Coral (dzotsi), 72, 524, 1124, 1313

Carnelian (aqiqi), 1124

Crystal (broli), 204, 260, 404, 676, 693, 1118, 1165

Diamond (almasi), 330, 742

Emerald (zurmukhti), 1345

Enamel (mina),? glass, 292, 320, 404, 671, 679, 798

Gold (okro), 72, 157, 169, 1166, 1174-1175

Iron (rcini), 954

Jacinth (iagundi), 276, 292, 318, 1402

Jasper (amarti), 260 (? amber)

Jet (gisheri, sat'hi), 990, 1124, 1232, 1239, 1257, 1409

Lapis-lazuli (lazhvardi), 1321

Lead (tqvia), 5

Pearl (margaliti), 16, 836, 899, 1142, 1145, 1155, 1160, 1173, 1342; mother-of-pearl (sadap'hi), 836

Pitch (p'hisa), 609, 1407

Ruby (lali), 204, 276, 380, 468, 1118, 1145, 1173, 1402, 1415; ruby of Badakhshan (badakhshi), 5, 72, 176, 380, 404, 676, 1415

Silver (vertzkhli), 157

Steel (cvesi), 192, 262

Turquoise (p'hiruzi), 468

ASTRONOMY.

Bissextile added day (naci), 787

Eclipse (serpent), 122, 125, 277, 1176, 1208, 1396

Ether (et'heri), 283, 404

Firmament (samqaro), 1, 109, 1471

January (ianvari), 1432

Leo (constellation), (lomi), 1179

Moon (mt'hvare): sex of, 811; invocation to, as origin of love, 819; invocation to, 943, 944; phases of, 582; full moon, 106, 1505, 1510

Planets (mnat'hobi), 134, 275, 944, 1349, 1385, 1387, 1515; (etli), 269, 973, 1072, 1188, 1304; Zual, 938, 944, 1397; Mushthar, 939, 944, 1397; Marikh, 940, 944; Aspiroz, 941, 944; Otarid, 942, 944

Pleiads (khomli, khomi), 1117, 1387

Sun (mze): God's image, 816-7; sex of, 811; invocation to, 937, 944; place of the dead, 1281, 1451 Wheel of heaven, 1285, 1391

RELIGION, ETC.

Almsgiving, 157, 784-785, 810, 1558, 1571

Bible: hart and waterbrooks, 835, 1564; charity fails not, 1520; fear makes love (? ironical), 1023; "love exalteth us," say the Apostles, 772 ("tinkling cymbals"); gall of bitterness. 99; through a glass darkly, 110, 656, 707, 1431; regeneration, 184

In list of places, see Eden, Euphrates, Gibeon, Gilson, Pison, Paradise

In list of persons, see Adam, Beelzebub, Levi, Satan, Goliath

Choir of heaven's hosts, 771

Death, 781, 782; better than shameful life, 189a, 781; unites lovers, 862-863; dries up tears, 238

Easter Eve, 536

Eternity, 778, 862, 1431-1432; elements, 864; the sun, 1451

God: the All-Seeing (Seer of beings), 112, 841, 1028, 1119; the One, 816, 1431; the Creator, 1, 341; creates not evil, 1468, 1485; ill is fleeting, good conquers ill, 1337; is generous, though the world be hard, 911, 931; hates cruelty to animals, 77; the sun His image, 816-817

Halo, aureole (bacmi, skhivni), 226, 229, 1110, 1410

Icon (khati), 247

Immortality, 1246; union with the One, 1431

Prayers for the dead, 158

Prayers to God, 342 (Tariel), 790, 845, 897 (Asmat'h), 1228

Prayers to the sun, 816-7, 935, 937

Predestination, 189, 422, 423, 591, 776-777, 883, 1014, 1018, 1151, 1314; freewill, 775

Shrine (luscuma), 1345

Sin and punishment, 242, 1086

ISLAM.

Koran (musap'hi), 339, 1144; oath on, 514 (? "the book"--tsigni, 1189, "the friend foe")

Mahmad, Bagdad merchants, followers of, drink no wine, 1010

Mecca (Maka), 1144

Mosque (? migzitha), heading of Chap. XXII.

Mulimi, 339

Muqri, 339

SUPERSTITIONS--CUSTOMS--SORCERY.

Burial, 297, 853, 862, 979, 1521; grave, 15; mourning garb, etc., 324-325, 977, 1183; mourning colours, 1181, 1479; shroud, 698, 783

Devil, 110; v. Satan

Devis, 98, 637, 672, 977, 1340, 1344

Kadjis, 190, 282, 559, 1198, 1220, 1223-7, 1251, 1263, 1276, 1344, 1362-1364

Life token (?), 156, 691

Merani (Pegasus), 96, 201

Presentiment, 711

Siren (sirino), 329

Sorcery, 1216, 1245-1247; (moly), 1253

Stoning to death, 1080, 1187, 1267

Wizard (prophet), 1456

SOCIAL RELATIONS-ETHICS.

Advice, 644, 830, 863

Avarice, 700, 1174

Cruelty to animals, 77

Equality, 932

Eunuchs, 1167, 1170

Friendship, 296, 684-685, 688, 758, 767, 770, 779, 834, 914, 1464

Grief, 855

Joking, 1352

Love, 8-14, 18, 27-31, 363-264, 695, 709-710, 772, 791, 814, 895, 910, 1158; love to be sacrificed to honour and duty, 292, 685, 688, 1541

Merchants, 1019, 1143; knight as protector of trade, 1013
Munificence, 49, 50, 1532

Negroes, 563, 1107, 1117, 1122

Oaths, 66, 132, 135, 399, 402, 410, 507, 514, 559, 560, 647, 650, 826, 832, 1131-1132, 1148; (momcal), 247, 457, 550, 601, 612, 725, 778, 910, 967, 1142

Philanthropy, 157, 784-5, S10, 1558, 1571

Royalty (god-like), 1; coronation, 45; "great king," 1145, 1166, 1410; "exalted king," 1198, 1240; regicide, 1180, 1344; equals of God, 836-837; born of God, 39; equal of sun, 1150; reverence for, 153, 288, 974, 1523; death for a king, 425, 1431-1434; kings capricious, 283; King of Kadjis, 1198; also 1146, 1452, 1459-1461, 1488, 1530, 1569-1571

Self-renunciation, 860

Slavery, 1023, 1185, 1195, 1503, 1530

Suicide (Satan's deed), 728, 768, 815, 854, 1169, 1278a, 1279

Valour, 580, 780-781, 1182

Vassal and lord, 153, 761, 793, 836-7, 1429, 1488, 1559

Woman, 39, 1059, 1182, 1184, 1561

NUMBERS.

The One, 816, 1431

Seven heavens, 608, 1285

Seven kingdoms, 301, 1555

Seven planets, 275, 944, 1385, 1515 Seven times sin forgiven, 242

"Seven or eight," 622, 633, 689, 1563 Eight, 597, 1312

"Eight upon nine," 1022

Nine, 1167, 1441, 1535

Nine heavens, 399

Sixty slaves, 1149

One hundred and twenty, 1139, 1431

One hundred thousand, 723

COINS AND WEIGHTS.

Dracani, 456, 992

Drama (coin), 668, 1031, 1040, 1195; (weight), 371, 528, 573, 903, 1214

Kkatauri, 456

Litra, 998

Perpera (?), 1413

Tsit'heli, 723, 998

GAMES AND SPORTS.

Acrobats (mushait'hi), 119, 1370

Archery (mshvildosani, archer), 63, 959

Backgammon (nardi) 82, 320

Ball (burt'hi), 20, 63, 317, 322, 804, 1100

Falconry (shavardeni, falcon)

Hawking (kori, hawk); v. Fauna

Hunting (nadiroba), 73-83, 956

Lasso (sagdebeli), 1371

Polo (chogan), 21

MILITARY AND NAVAL.

Armour (abdjari), 426, 430, 998, 1020, 1344-1347, 1375, 1392: Khvarazmian armour, 389, 1543

Army (spa), 956, 1485. 1543; (t'hemi), 536; (eri), 1012, 1053; (djari), 536

Arrow (isari), 322, 458

Arsenal (zardakhana), 1240

Asparezi (lists), 100

Battering-ram (bari?), 1381

Bow (mshvildi), 805

Centre of an army (qolbi), 959

Circle of troops (alqa), 956

Club, bludgeon (veti), 1020

Coat of mail (djadchvi), 426, 1346

Flags (alami), 390, 923; drosha, 1016

Galley (catargha), 596

Greaves (sabarculi), 998, 1345

Gunpowder (?), 420, 429

Helmet (muzaradi), 430, 1375, 1389; (chabalakhi), 597, 1384

Lance (shubi), 3, 430-431; (lakhvari), 4, 506, 566

Quiver (capardchi), 93, 259, 355; (karkashi), 72

Ram for sea-fight (sakhnisi,), 1012, 1016, 1021

Rank (dasi), 536

Saddle (unagiri), 1416

Saddlebag (mandicuri). 433

Scourge (lakhti), 1087

Sea-fight, 596 (Tariel's), 1016 (Avt'handil's)

Sentry (nobat'hi), 908, 1277. 1394

Shield (p'hari), 3, 1372, 1388

Ship (navi), 569, 918, 1016; navi khomaldi. 1423

Spur (dezi), rowel, 211, 611

Squadron (razmi), 301, 389, 432, 1322

Squires (meabdjreni), 200

Sword (khmali), 93, 259, 1142; blades, (tsveri), 1394; (shimsheri), 3; (cota), 594, 1363; (safte), 594

Tent (caravi), 535

Whip (mat'hrakhi), 206, 1390

PUBLIC WORKS, BUILDING, ETC.--FURNITURE.

Bath, 260, 1233

Bridge, 183, 218a, 685, 785

Canal, irrigation (mili), 284, 538, 768, 1297, 1435, 1528; (ru), 926, 1376

Caravanserai, 1052

Carpet (nokhi), 1238

Chair (scami), 742; (selni), 124

Couch (takhti), 1166

Curtain (p'hardagi), 331

Coverlet, 1126

Lock (clite), 1377; key, 1556

Mattress, 1126

Pillow (balishi), 1238; (sasthunali), 514, 1126

Road, 405, 685, etc.

Window (sarcmeli), 259, 261, 1106, 1113

Music.

Clarion--cf. drum (noba), 405, 850, 1170, 1390

Cymbal (tsintsili) 46, 1100, 1528

Drum (dabdabi), 703, 1390, 1436; (? copper drum--kosi), 703, 1436, 1556; kettledrum (? tambourine-tablaci), 435, 1156, 1167, 1170, 1484;? very large kettledrum--noba, cf. clarion

Harp (changi), 101, 120, 178, 472, 704, 1421, 1444; (nachang-dapheni), 1421

Lute (? staff with bells,? castanet--chaghana), 101, 704, 1444

Lyre (? psaltery--barbit'hi), 178, 472

Musicoba, 25

Pipe, reed (na), 4, 178, (1421) Psaltery (knari), 1574

Rattles (ezhvanni), 772

Singing, 165, 946-947, 1055

Singing-girls (mutribi), 356, 470, 704, 1055, 1440, 1523

Tambourine, large tambourine (ebani? = daira), 1100

Trumpet (buci), 46, 168, 405, 435, 1017, 1170, 1390, 1436, 1556

ENDNOTES

[1] Professor Marr (t. xii., p. liv), points out that, while Georgian religious poetry was influenced by Byzantium, the secular poetry was closely akin to Iranic Islam; in the T'hamaran age the currents were distinctly apart, but later the two streams united. (p. 1)

[2] M. Tamarati, L'Église Géorgienne, Rome, 1910 (ch. xiv.-xvi.); and original documents (Latin, French, Italian) in his Istoria Catholicobisca, Tiflis, 1902 (pp. 563-836). (p. 1)

[3] Marr, Ioann Petritzki, St. Petersburg, 1902, p. 61. (p. 3)

[4] ?Athos. (p. 6)

[5] Professor Marr thinks the Odes of the T'hamaran age, of which he recently published a scholarly edition (vide Bibliography), are by Rust'haveli. (p. 6)

[6] Journal of Biblical Literature, Boston, 1894, p. 179; translated from Professor Tsagareli's Svyedeniya. The portrait has been defaced. (p. 7)

[7] Professor Khakhanov, Ocherki, ii. 247, 248; E. T'haqaishvili, Opisanie rukopisei, t. ii. 57, 393, 395, 468, 554-592. (p. 7)

[8] A Sinai manuscript, apparently of the tenth century, contains a hymn for Christmas in honour of the B.V.M., written in rhymed lines of sixteen feet; it is not, however, divided into quatrains (Marr, t. xii., p. liv). (p. 7)

[9] Ioann Petritzki, p. 35. (p. 9)

[10] In the footnotes, words believed to be of Arabic and Persian origin are marked "A." and "P." (p. 10)

[11] Ocherki, ii. 252-255; but Professor Marr thinks the ballads are based on the epic. (p. 10)

[12] 5, 46, 68, 144, 438, 450, 595, 603, 711, 754, 881, 968, 983, 1027, 1073, 1410, 1430, 1435, 1512, 1524, 1574. (p. 10)

[13] Professor Tsagareli has published the Athos text of the "Song of Songs" in his Svyedeniya o pamyatnikakh (St. Petersburg Academy of Sciences). (p. 11)

[14] Cf. E. S. T'haqaishvili's oration at Tiflis on January 24 (O.S.), 1911, reported in T'hemi, No. 4, of January 31 (O.S.), 1911. (p. 13)

[15] black eyes. (p. 37)

[16] Headman, governor, chief of police, arbitrator. (p. 146)

[17] Irrigation canal. (p. 150)

[18] Of purgatory? (p. 153)

[19] ? reference to Gen. xlix. 5-7. (i.e. "cursed for mine anger").(p. 156)

[20] In Georgian folklore the moon is male and the sun female; in [this] English translation the genders are changed. (p. 159)

[21] Invocation to the sun, 816, 817, 935. (p. 182)

[22] Saturn, planet of woe. (p. 182)

[23] Jupiter, planet of justice. (p. 182)

[24] Mars, planet of vengeance. (p. 182)

[25] Hesperus, Venus, planet of healing. (p. 182)

[26] Mercury, planet of learning. (p. 183)

[27] Egypt. (p. 184)

[28] Value seems to be unknown; Ch. gives drakhma as about sixpence. (p. 192)

[29] Gulan Shahr, P., the city of flowers; pl. in an (Abul., 180). (p. 201)

[30] For the Story of the Loves of Vis and Ramin, cf. J.R.A.S., July 1902. There are two other references in Rust'haveli, 182, 1519. (p. 204)

[31] . . . When a Georgian is angry, he puts his hand to his beard as an invitation to his opponent to insult him if he fail to do what he promises. (p. 209)

[32] i.e., when it enters Leo. (p. 227)

[33] For mourning, 1479. (p. 227)

[34] The land of the Kadjis. (p. 235)

[35] The black pupil in his dark eye. (p. 236)

[36] "I, Nestan, thy satellite." (p. 246)

www.ingramcontent.com/pod-product-compliance
Lightning Source LLC
Chambersburg PA
CBHW051605010526
44119CB00056B/783